AF783824

Property Rights in Investment Securities and the Doctrine of Specificity

Erica Johansson

Property Rights in Investment Securities and the Doctrine of Specificity

Springer

Dr. Erica Johansson
Associate - Finance Group
Mayer Brown International LLP
11 Pilgrim Street
London EC4V 6RW
United Kingdom
ejohansson@mayerbrown.com

ISBN: 978-3-540-85903-1 e-ISBN: 978-3-540-85904-8

Library of Congress Control Number: 2008935630

© 2009 Springer-Verlag Berlin Heidelberg

This work is subject to copyright. All rights are reserved, whether the whole or part of the material is concerned, specifically the rights of translation, reprinting, reuse of illustrations, recitation, broadcasting, reproduction on microfilm or in any other way, and storage in data banks. Duplication of this publication or parts thereof is permitted only under the provisions of the German Copyright Law of September 9, 1965, in its current version, and permission for use must always be obtained from Springer. Violations are liable to prosecution under the German Copyright Law.

The use of general descriptive names, registered names, trademarks, etc. in this publication does not imply, even in the absence of a specific statement, that such names are exempt from the relevant protective laws and regulations and therefore free for general use.

Cover design: WMX Design GmbH, Heidelberg

Printed on acid-free paper

springer.com

For Matthias Pannier

Preface

This book is, with some adjustments and additions, largely based on my PhD thesis on Property Rights in Investment Securities and the Doctrine of Specificity, which I defended in London on 15 June 2007 with Professor Lars Gorton and Dr. Kern Alexander as examiners.

The subject matter is the doctrine of specificity and its non-conformity with the developments in the financial markets.

As this book shows, the requirement for specificity in book-entry securities is closely linked to loss allocation. If we decided that the rights that the investor has against its intermediary shall be property rights (as opposed to claims), then, loss allocation is crucial. Should the intermediary become insolvent and there be insufficient securities, the shortfall has to be distributed. Through segregation on designated accounts the level of protection for the investor can be increased. It can also be increased by a requirement that the intermediary should hold a sufficient number of securities corresponding to its customers' securities.

During the course of this work I have received valuable assistance from several persons, for which I am very grateful. First of all, I am indebted to *Tekn. dr. Marcus Wallenbergs Stiftelse för utbildning i internationellt industriellt företagande* and *Företagsjuridik Nord & Co* for the financial support they have provided.

Justice Torgny Håstad initially brought my attention to the issues discussed in Chap. 2 and Professor Sir Roy Goode, QC and Professor Philip Wood kindly met me to discuss the choice of subject. Professor Mads Andenas and Professor Joseph Norton have been of great support and guidance throughout my studies.

Dr. Göran Millqvist and Karin Wallin-Norman provided helpful and thought-provoking comments on earlier versions of the thesis. Their interest in and willingness to discuss Swedish security law and the Nordic Central Securities Depository systems have been of great value. Karin also provided helpful insights in relation to the work of the European Commission's Legal Certainty Group and the work of UNIDROIT on Substantive Rules Regarding Intermediated Securities.

Dr. Staffan Myrdal, from whose work on *Återpantsättning: Om pantsättning av pant och panträtt* (published in 2005) I have benefited greatly, read and provided helpful comments on Chap. 6. He also kindly discussed some of the questions that repledge trigger under Swedish law. Dr. Thomas Keijser read and provided helpful comments on Chaps. 5–7, Professor Hugh Beale, QC FBA, Professor Andrew McKnight and Dr. Rizwaan Mokal provided helpful comments on earlier versions of Chap. 5 and discussed various issues under English law and Dr. Claes Martinson provided helpful comments on the first draft of Chap. 1. Nickos Nassuphis has been of valuable assistance throughout by explaining how the derivatives markets work.

At the earlier stages of the studies, Professor James Penner made himself available to discuss different aspects of property law and legal theory. Dr. Joanna Benjamin kindly met me to discuss the equity of redemption, and Professor Peter Winship answered my ignorant questions on Arts. 8–9 of the UCC.

In the summer of 2005 Professor Jan Kleineman and the Law Department of Stockholm University gave me access to a desk at the Law Department, which I used while working on Chap. 6. During this time I had many interesting discussions with many of my former colleagues, on law and on other subjects.

At the later stages of this work I received helpful inputs from Dr. Laila Zackariasson on the doctrine of specificity. Martin Thomas invited me to Brussels to discuss the European Commission's Legal Certainty project and Geoffrey Davies, who at the time worked on the English Law Commission's project on Property Rights in Intermediated Securities, provided thoughtful and interesting comments on the thesis. Dan Hanqvist provided some thoughtful comments in relation to Swedish law and Iain Walker kindly proofread the text.

During and after the examination, Professor Lars Gorton and Dr. Kern Alexander provided some valuable suggestions on how to improve the text.

I would also like to thank my family, for their love and support.

The aim has been to state the law as of 31 March 2008. The views expressed and the mistakes made are, of course, my own.

London
March 2008

Erica Johansson

Contents

List of Abbreviations

ALI	American Law Institute
BIS	Bank for International Settlements
CCP	Central Counterparty
CDO	Collateralised Debt Obligation
CDS	Credit Default Swap
CESR	Committee of European Securities Regulators
CGFS	Committee on the Global Financial System
CISN	CUSIP International Numbering System
CPDO	Constant Proportion Debt Obligation
CPPI	Constant Proportion Portfolio Insurance
CPSS	Committee on Payment and Settlement Systems
CSD	Central Securities Depository
CUSIP	Committee on Uniform Security Identification Procedures
DTC	Depository Trust Company
DTCC	Depository Trust and Clearing Company
DBV	Delivery by Value
DVP	Delivery versus Payment
EEA	European Economic Area
ECB	European Central Bank
EFMLG	European Financial Markets Lawyers Group
EIB	European Investment Bank
EMA	European Master Agreement for Financial Transactions
ESCB	European System of Central Banks
EU	European Union
FIAA	Financial Instruments Accounts Act
FMLC	Financial Markets Law Committee
FSA	Financial Services Authority
G30	The Group of Thirty
G7	The Group of Seven
GMRA	Global Market Repurchase Agreement
GMSLA	Global Master Securities Lending Agreement

ICMA	International Capital Market Association
ICSD	International Central Securities Depository
IMF	International Monetary Fund
IOSCO	International Organization of Securities Commissions
ISDA	International Swaps and Derivatives Association
ISIN	International Securities Identification Number
LTCM	Long Term Capital Management
MRA	Master Repurchase Agreement
MSLA	Master Securities Loan Agreement
NCCUSL	National Conference of Commissioners on Uniform State Laws
NCSD	Nordic Central Securities Depository
OSLA	Oversees Securities Lending Agreement
OTC	Over-the-Counter
PRIMA	Place of the Relevant Intermediary Approach
RMBS	Residential Mortgage-Backed Securities
RTGS	Real Time Gross Settlement
SEC	Securities and Exchange Commission
SIFMA	Securities Industry and Financial Markets Association
SPV	Special Purpose Vehicle
UNIDROIT	International Institute for the Unification of Private Law

Abstract

This book evaluates the requirement for specificity as a criterion for property rights in securities evidenced by electronic entries made on securities accounts. Three principal questions are examined: (1) reuse of financial collateral and the problems arising from the collateral-taker's right to reuse the collateral; (2) characterisation of repos; and (3) the question of property rights in securities that are unallocated in relation to their entitlement holders. The analysis is made from the perspective of specificity and the requirement that the object of a property right must be identified. English, US and Swedish law are compared with the aim of finding viable solutions to the identified problems.

The main argument is that due to the swift developments within the financial markets over the last 20–30 years, securities as assets have outgrown the traditional property law structure. From the practice of holding bearer or certificated securities in safes or vaults, most securities are today held in dematerialised or immobilised form via intangible electronic records. They are moreover often held on a pooled and unallocated basis through multiple tiers of intermediaries. These developments conflict with traditional property law structures and have caused a great degree of legal uncertainty. As a consequence there is a pressing need to revise related laws.

One of the fundamental problems identified in this study is that securities evidenced in book-entry form are fungible intangibles and as such impossible to separate or otherwise to distinguish. Only through the legal construct that the securities exist on the securities account on which they are recorded can the fiction that these assets can be separated be upheld.

This book identifies different solutions to the problems caused by the lack of identification of securities. It argues that there are certain elements that ought to be included in the analysis of whether the investor has property or personal rights in these assets.

Chapter 1
Introduction

"If one accepts that legal science includes not only the techniques of interpreting the texts, principles, rules, and standards of a national system, but also the discovery of models for preventing or resolving social conflicts, then it is clear that the method of comparative law can provide a much richer range of model solutions than a legal science devoted to a single nation, simply because the different systems of the world can offer a greater variety of solutions than could be thought up in a lifetime by even the most imaginative jurist who was corralled in his own system."[1]

1.1 Subject Matter

The subject of this book is the doctrine of specificity and its non-conformity with the developments in the financial markets; whereas the legal rules are based on dealings involving individualised assets, the trade on the financial markets involves massive volumes of fungible assets incapable of being identified.

Securities evidenced by book-entries on securities accounts do not exist in the physical world and cannot be located on any particular securities account. They are fungible intangibles, i.e. intangible assets with the same characteristics, which cannot be identified in relation to their owners; there is nothing that distinguishes one security from another within the same class of securities.

The property law rules, on the other hand, generally require identification of the relevant asset in order to convey a property right. This means that the investor's claim shall refer to a specific asset for the investor to acquire and maintain its property right in it.

While the financial markets have moved ahead to accommodate the massive volumes of securities that are held, transferred and used as security, the legal rules are based on a property law construct where each asset can be physically located and therefore also identified. As one would expect, the clash between the established practices of holding and transferring securities and the traditional property law structure has lead to a great degree of legal uncertainty.

This Chapter introduces the subject of this book and outlines its disposition. It sets out the book's scope and theme. It also discusses the sources that have been used and the preferred methodology.

[1]K Zweigert and H Kötz, *An Introduction to Comparative Law* (3rd edn OUP 1998) 15.

E. Johansson, *Property Rights in Investment Securities and the Doctrine of Specificity*,

© Springer-Verlag Berlin Heidelberg 2009

1.2 Theme

A number of significant developments have taken place in the securities markets over the past decades. What is generally referred to as dematerialisation and immobilisation have achieved flexibility and efficiency;[2] trade and settlement of investment securities take place electronically via debiting and crediting of book accounts in computer systems. Trading of large volumes is thereby possible, also across national borders. Another equally important development is the move to an indirect holding system; instead of holding investment securities directly in relation to the issuer, securities are today often held through multiple tiers of intermediaries. Together with the custom of holding securities on a pooled and unallocated basis, i.e. unidentified in relation to respective investor, these practices have had significant implications from both a commercial and a legal perspective.

Due to the developments within the securities markets there is a pressing need to clarify the laws relating to property rights in investment securities. The swift developments within the financial markets during the last 20–30 years have led to that securities as assets have outgrown the traditional property law structure.

Recent legislative initiatives demonstrate that there is already a tendency to move away from traditional property law rules in relation to financial assets. In the EC the developments have mainly taken place through the Directive 2002/47/EC of the European Parliament and of the Council of 6 June 2002 on financial collateral arrangements ("Financial Collateral Directive") and the Directive 98/26/EU of the European Parliament and of the Council of 19 May 1998 on settlement finality in payment and securities settlement systems ("Settlement Finality Directive"),[3] but also through the European Commission's work on Clearing and Settlement which seeks to remove identified barriers and improve the environment for cross-border clearing and settlement.[4] On the international level the Convention of 5 July 2006 on the Law Applicable to Certain Rights in respect of Securities held with an Intermediary ("Hague Securities Convention") and the work by the UNIDROIT Study Group on Securities Held with an Intermediary demonstrate these efforts.

One of the main problems identified in this study is that securities evidenced by book-entries on accounts are fungible intangibles and as such impossible to separate

---

[2] Dematerialised securities do not exist in physical form and can only be established via book entries on securities accounts. Immobilised securities are certificated or bearer securities placed in custody; physical movement of them is thereby prevented. Like dematerialised securities, the rights in immobilised securities are established via book entries on securities accounts, see further Sect. 3.2.

[3] Other important EU legal acts are the Directive 2001/24/EC of the European Parliament and of the Council of 4 April 2001 on the reorganisation and winding-up of credit institutions ("Banks Winding-up Directive"); the Directive 2001/17/EC of the European Parliament and of the Council of 19 March 2001 on the reorganisation and winding-up of insurance undertakings; and the Council Regulation (EC) No 1346/2000 of 29 May 2000 on insolvency proceedings.

[4] The project addresses legal issues that have often been cited as barriers to integration of clearing and settlements which were identified in the so-called Giovannini reports 'Cross Border Clearing and Settlement Arrangements in the European Union' (November 2001); and 'Second Report on EU Clearing and Settlement Arrangements' (April 2003).

or otherwise identify. They are indistinguishable in relation to their entitlement holders and therefore bear more resemblance to personal claims than property.

In most jurisdictions the property laws require the object of a property right, regardless of whether it is a tangible or an intangible asset, to be identified for the claimant to have an enforceable and protected interest in it – a right *in rem*.[5] As securities evidenced in book-entry form are fungible intangibles and thereby impossible to separate or otherwise to distinguish, the requirement for identity is, if not impossible, difficult to uphold. In comparison with grain in a silo or oil in a tank they cannot be separated as they do not exist in the physical world.

Similarly, the traditional private international law rule *lex rei sitae* requires that the asset needs to be physically located in order to determine the applicable law for the proprietary law aspects of that asset. Since securities evidenced by book-entries on accounts do not exist in the physical world other than as a record on one or more securities accounts and often are held through complex chains of intermediaries, it is difficult to establish the location of the relevant account on which they are registered.

This book argues that only if the registration of the securities by the intermediary with a direct relationship with the ultimate investor is given constitutive effect or a similar legal effect to possession of a document of title, can the legal construct that these assets can be separated be upheld. If the register merely evidences the securities, then it does not separate the securities as such as fungible intangibles cannot be separated.

A closely related problem is that securities are often held indirectly in relation to the issuer of the securities. The investor's interest is accordingly only shown in the books of the intermediary administering the investor's securities account and cannot be claimed against the issuer, only against the intermediary with whom the investor has a direct relationship.

1.3 Background

The requirement for identity, or the doctrine of specificity as it also is called, means that it is not possible to create property rights in non-identified property; in order to have a protected property right in an asset the asset must be identified.

The requirement for identity is an old rule that can be found in most jurisdictions. Generally it applies to all types of assets: tangibles and intangibles as well as fungible and specific assets and covers both title transfer and security arrangements.

The Financial Collateral Directive, which establishes a new community regime for securities and cash as collateral under both security interest and title transfer structures, provides for an extensive right of use of financial collateral. Under Art. 5 of the Directive, if and to the extent the terms of the collateral arrangement so provide, the collateral-taker shall be entitled to use the collateral as the owner in accordance with the terms of the security financial collateral arrangement.

---

[5] cf J Dalhuisen, *Dalhuisen on International Commercial, Financial and Trade Law* (2nd edn Hart Publishing 2004) 491.

The right of reuse of financial collateral is relevant in relation to the doctrine of specificity as an extensive right for the collateral-taker to use the asset as the owner risks compromising the identity in the collateral and the collateral-provider's property right in the asset. A disposal of the financial collateral by the collateral-taker interrupts the continuing identification of the collateral. At the moment the right of use is exercised, the link between the asset and its owner is broken. By allowing the collateral-taker to return equivalent collateral, the collateral-provider appears to agree on substituting its property right with a contractual claim. It has therefore been questioned whether Art. 5 covers outright transfers and not repledge.[6]

The question of identity is also relevant in relation to the characterisation of repos. The purpose of a repo is often to use the transferred assets as security against a loan (the purchase price). The collateral is transferred outright from the collateral-provider to the collateral-taker together with a right for the collateral-provider to reacquire assets of the same kind. If the bond with the original asset is broken and the repo buyer has the right to dispose of the collateral, i.e. to substitute it, it is difficult to argue that the transaction is a secured transaction. On the other hand, if the collateral-taker is required to return the original collateral, the transaction may be characterised as a security arrangement.[7]

The requirement for identity also causes concern in relation to a whole range of other issues. This is because most legal systems are designed for assets that are identifiable. The rules relating to property rights in securities are based on the notion that these assets until quite recently have been issued and traded in bearer format. Bearer instruments such as bills of exchange and promissory notes do not only evidence the underlying rights against the issuer but also embody these rights. The legal construct that the document is the carrier of the rights against the issuer facilitates the identification of these assets. Problems arise as securities evidenced in book-entry form on securities accounts are held on a fungible basis, i.e. they are unidentifiable in relation to their entitlement holders.

One question that has been debated both on the international and the domestic level is the nature of the investor's rights.[8] Do commingled securities held on an unallocated and intermediated basis convey property rights, personal rights or something in between, i.e. co-property rights? Since one of the fundamental characteristics of property is missing – that the claim shall refer to an identified asset – the rights of investors bear more resemblance with personal claims than property. If the rights are only contractual, the entitlement holders are unsecured in the winding up of the intermediary and have to share *pari passu* with the other unsecured creditors. Under the traditional legal analysis, the lack of identity transforms the property right into a personal claim.

---

[6] cf Sect. 2.3.4.

[7] It should be pointed out that Art. 6(1) of the Financial Collateral Directive requires EU Member States to ensure that title transfer financial collateral arrangements can take effect in accordance with their terms, thus eliminating recharacterisation risk.

[8] Goode vi; Benjamin and Yates 28 and Goode (1996) 167; See also FMLC, 'Issue 3 – Property Interests in Investment Securities' (July 2004) 10.

The requirement for identity is also relevant in relation to the assertion of claims against upper-tier intermediaries. Can the account holder or its attachment creditors look through the account holder's intermediary to reach assets held by intermediaries higher up in the chain of intermediaries or assert claims against the issuer? Without identification of the underlying security it is difficult to trace the security in the indirect holding system. Simply, it is difficult to assert a claim against someone if the entitlement holder cannot identify the asset it is claiming.

Another issue that may arise is how a conflict between competing claims is to be solved. To give one example, how can a bona fide purchaser for value without notice make an acquisition of securities free from adverse claims when it cannot specify what securities it has acquired? Since the investor in the indirect holding system, presumably, holds its interest in common with other investors, it has been argued that the investor cannot achieve bona fide purchaser status unless specific securities are identified. If such status were given to those whose securities are held on an unallocated basis, it would involve a risk of inconsistent claims between two or more entitlement holders in the case of a shortfall in the pool. Similarly, it has been argued that negotiability would involve the risk of inconsistent claims between two or more entitlement holders, thus being contrary to the concepts of co-ownership in a pool of assets and security entitlements as a bundle of rights against the intermediary.

Another problem is that it is difficult to determine whether a security interest is fixed or floating in nature when dealing with a pool of securities which lacks individual characteristics. In many jurisdictions, if the collateral-provider has the right to substitute the collateral and the pool of assets is constantly fluctuating, the security interest is, at the most, a floating charge.

Related issues are how dividends, interest payments, return of capital, voting rights, capital gains taxes, the right to have convertible and exchangeable debt securities exchanged for equity securities and rights to exercise put and call options and pre-emption rights should be allocated.[9]

1.4 Sources and Methodology

1.4.1 Comparative Legal Studies

Comparative legal studies are becoming increasingly important. One reason is the harmonisation efforts that are taking place foremost in Europe but also internationally; another, the increase in transactions across nations' borders. No longer are comparative studies a luxury to which a few academics devote their time; they have become a necessity and are part of legal practice.

It is believed that lawyers of different legal systems can benefit greatly by examining the laws of other jurisdictions. For instance, when comparing the common law

---

9 cf Recital 11 of Directive 2007/36/EC of the European Parliament and of the Council of 11 July 2007 on the exercise of certain rights of shareholders in listed companies.

with civil law it is clear that whereas civil law could benefit from adopting some of the pragmatism, flexibility and creativeness of the common law, the common law could be improved by importing some of the systematic thinking and methodology of the civil law traditions to make the law clearer, more predictable and easily accessible.

'Comparative legal studies' is a great tool in advancing the understanding of the law and can be used both to assess and further develop existing laws.[10]

1.4.2 De Lege Lata *vs* De Lege Ferenda

Jurisprudence can be given a narrower or a broader aim. The narrower and more traditional form concerns the establishment, through abstract analysis, of what the law is – *de lege lata*. The broader form is concerned not only with establishing what the law is but what the law should be –*de lege ferenda.*[11]

Many academics hold the view that research should concern the law in the stricter sense. It is not the academic's role to consider policy issues – that is the role of politicians. The other view is that the role of the jurisprudence is not constrained to analysis of existing laws. To confine academic research to what the law is would lead to a static and less dynamic function of jurisprudence and inhibit developments. Hellner, when elaborating on this issue, concludes that the former view is an inheritance from positivism which cannot be accepted.[12] One can also question whether it is possible to determine what the law is without considering what it ought to be and vice versa.

It should be stated forthright that this book is not a traditional book in the sense that it is not only concerned with *de lege lata*. To a great extent it aims at establishing *de lege ferenda,* i.e. what the law should be. For this reason, it has not been strictly bound by traditional legal methods and sources.

1.4.3 Sources and Methodology

Each legal system should preferably be studied from its own foundations, even when conducting a comparative study. This means that sometimes a comparison is not possible. In other cases a comparison can only be made with an understanding of the variations between the solutions that the legal systems provide and the differences they entail.

The preferred method of this book has been to examine English, Swedish and US law in separate Chapters (Chaps. 5–7) and to use this material as a basis for a

[10] K Zweigert and H Kötz, *An Introduction to Comparative Law* (3rd ed OUP 1998) 15.

[11] J Hellner, *Metodproblem i rättsvetenskapen: Studier i förmögenhetsrätt* (Elanders Gotab 2001) 27.

[12] *ibid.*

comparison, presented in Chap. 9. One important factor in the assessment of existing laws has been to look at the developments and the established practices in the financial markets. The conclusions and recommendations of the study have been made with the aim of finding viable solutions in relation to them.

The sources that have been used are the traditional legal sources such as statutes, preparatory works, cases and legal literature. The significance of different sources depends on the jurisdiction examined and the area of law. Whereas the Swedish legal tradition puts great emphasis on preparatory works, the greatest source in the common law is the cases. For natural reasons, different emphases have been made to different sources depending on the jurisdiction studied.

During the course of this work the legal literature has played an important role. In order to understand foreign legal rules and the context in which they exist, the author has often been forced to approach the legal system through its literature. The importance of the legal literature is also, perhaps, due to the complexities and uncertainties that exist in this area of law.

The area of law covered by this book has been subject to numerous studies made by international organisations such as UNIDROIT, G30, BIS, EFMLG, FMLC and ISDA. Many references are therefore made to reports made by such organisations, which have been used to analyse the issues from a broader perspective.

The aim has been to present the examined issues and the conclusions as straightforwardly as possible. Another aim has been to not duplicate the work of others. The descriptive parts have therefore been limited as much as possible. Notwithstanding this, a description of the law and the various arguments presented has in some cases been necessary in order to provide an accurate picture or to develop the discussion further.

1.4.4 Terminology

For the purposes of this book, the term "reuse" is used as a generic term for repledge, rehypothecation, *pignus irregulare* and the use of sale and repurchase agreements ("repos"). Thus, it is used in the broadest possible sense and covers both traditional security arrangements where the ownership remains with the collateral-provider and title transfer arrangements where the parties use the ownership terminology and structure to secure an underlying transaction.

The term "repledge" is used to denote all types of security where the collateral-taker B uses the collateral extended by A as security in a transaction with a third party C (e.g. all types of sub-security arrangements).[13] Repledge is thus used in a

[13] The prefixes re-, on- and sub- appear to be used interchangeably in the English doctrine to denote the case when B uses collateral extended by A as security in a transaction with C. The three main characters are named "A", "B" and "C". A is the initial collateral-provider and B the initial collateral-taker that reuses the collateral as security in the agreement with the second collateral-taker C, cf Hessler 6 ff and 64 ff.

restricted way and does not include the case where the pledgee has the right to use the collateral as its own.

"Rehypothecation" is a term used by market participants to describe the collateral-taker's use of collateral as security in a separate transaction. ISDA's Collateral Law Reform Group defines rehypothecation as:

> "In its narrow sense this means the use of pledged assets by the pledgee to give as security for the pledgee's own obligations and this will be subject to the original pledgor's rights to return of the property; however it is also sometimes loosely used in a broader sense to mean use of pledged assets by the pledgee as if it owned those assets, for example, sale of the pledged assets by the pledgee to a third party."[14]

Rehypothecation is avoided in this book to prevent misunderstandings and confusions of the different meanings it has obtained.[15]

---

[14] ISDA EU Collateral Report 19.

[15] cf Kettering (1999–2000) 51, who notes that the term rehypothecation increasingly is used to refer to any pre-default use of collateral by the secured party, including outright sales as well as repledges.

Chapter 2
The New Order

The [...] Framework for Action is an aspirational programme for rapid progress towards a single financial market.' All of the initiatives were therefore enveloped in one overarching framework, geared towards a core objective, namely to create a single deep and liquid financial market to serve as a motor for growth, job creation and improved competitiveness in the European economy.[1]

2.1 Introduction

Transfer, holding and settlement of securities and the use of cash and securities as collateral are topics that have received an increasing interest over the last 30 years. This Chapter focuses on the legal changes that have taken place as regards securities and cash as collateral in the EU through the Financial Collateral Directive. It also reviews related initiatives such as the Settlement Finality Directive, the UNIDROIT Draft Convention and the Hague Securities Convention. It argues that a liberalisation of mandatory property and insolvency laws is taking place and that a new order is being established.

2.2 The EU Financial Services Action Plan

During the last decade we have witnessed a substantial flow of legislative measures regarding financial services in the European Union. These measures are part of the Financial Services Action Plan, which has the objective of creating a single financial market in the European Union. It was adopted in 1999 and consists of 42 original measures, including the Financial Collateral Directive.[2]

The single market is expected to boost economic growth, create jobs and improve the competitiveness of the European economy. Through the Financial Services Action Plan measures, financial institutions and market participants authorised in one EU Member State are able to provide the same financial services, raise capital and buy and sell financial instruments throughout the European Union. The cost of capital and intermediation is thereby expected to decrease.

[1] European Commission, 'FSAP Evaluation – Part I: Process and implementation' (October 2005) 5–6.

[2] As of 6 June 2004, 39 out of 42 measures of the Financial Services Action Plan had been finalised, European Commission 'Progress on the Financial Service Action Plan' (Annex to the Tenth Progress Report) (1 June 2004) 1.

E. Johansson, *Property Rights in Investment Securities and the Doctrine of Specificity,*

© Springer-Verlag Berlin Heidelberg 2009

The integration has been credited with resulting in a deeper and more liquid market with a reduction in the credit spread.[3] The most pronounced impact is believed to be in the primary markets. In a report from 2002, the macroeconomic benefits of the European financial integration were estimated to have raised the GDP by 1.1%.[4] However, the real impact is still dependent upon the implementation of the measures in the EU Member States.[5]

2.3 The Financial Collateral Directive

2.3.1 The Successful Lobbying for Law Reform

The need for law reform of collateral arrangements in the European financial markets was recognised early on by organisations such as ISDA and EFMLG.[6] In connection with the European Commission's work on outlining the Financial Services Action Plan, they successfully advocated for law reform in the area of financial collateral. Collateral was included as one of the key areas of high priority in the Financial Services Action Plan.[7] To assist the Commission in its work, ISDA formed its

---

[3] London Economics in association with Pricewaterhouse Coopers and Oxford Economic Forecasting, 'Quantification of the Macro-Economic Impact of Integration of EU Financial Markets: Executive Summary of the Final Report to the European Commission – Directorate-General for the Internal Market' (November 2002) iv.

[4] The report showed that the total business investment was approximately 6,0 per cent higher, private consumption up by 0,8 per cent and total employment 0,5 per cent higher. In terms of changes in the user cost of capital, the study showed a reduction in the cost of equity finance being the most important impact, accounting for 0,5 percentage points (or 45 per cent) of the 1,1 percentage point increase in the EU-wide level of CDP in constant prices, London Economics in association with Pricewaterhouse Coopers and Oxford Economic Forecasting, 'Quantification of the Macro-Economic Impact of Integration of EU Financial Markets: Executive Summary of the Final Report to the European Commission – Directorate-General for the Internal Market' (November 2002) v-vi.

[5] European Commission Tenth Report 'Financial Services: Turning the Corner – Preparing the Challenge of the Next Phase of European Capital Market Integration' (Brussels, 2 June 2004).

[6] ISDA EU Collateral Report; See also EFMLG, 'Proposal for an EU Directive on Collateralisation' (June 2000) and EFMLG, 'Statement on Proposal for a Directive on Financial Collateral Arrangements' (COM(2001) 168). Legal risk was identified as crucial in establishing effective and efficient collateral arrangements by ISDA in 'Credit Risk and Regulatory Capital' (March 1998); 'Guidelines for Collateral Practitioners' (November 1998) and in the ISDA 1999 Collateral Review (March 1999). See also G Morton and R Potok, 'Position Paper on the Taking of Securities as Collateral in the European Union' (13 December 1999), which apparently initiated the Financial Collateral Directive, see Prop 2004/05:30 n 16.

[7] Report by the European Commission, 'Financial Services: Implementing the Framework for Financial Markets: Action Plan' Com(1999)232 (11 May 1999) 8–9.

Collateral Law Reform Group at the beginning of 2000.[8] In March of the same year, a report was prepared in which the legal barriers to an efficient use of collateral were highlighted.[9]

In ISDA's report the legal restrictions on the use of pledge collateral by the holder was acknowledged as impeding an efficient use of collateral. The Collateral Law Reform Group proposed a set of principles that an effective and efficient modern legal regime for collateral arrangements should embody. It was, *inter alia*, recommended that a collateral-taker should be free to deal with the collateral as if it were the outright owner of it and third parties purchasing the collateral from the collateral-taker should be able to obtain a clean title, whether or not they have notice of the original interest of the collateral-provider.[10]

The motivation behind the Collateral Law Reform Group's proposal was based on the argument that financial institutions holding collateral would be able to use it more efficiently, lowering their own costs and therefore the cost of financial services provided to collateral-providers.[11] From a broader perspective, the Collateral Law Reform Group recognised that a clear, practical and robust legal regime for collateral in the Member States of the European Union would strengthen the financial markets, reduce credit risk and minimise systemic risk. Harmonisation was also deemed to promote integration, and deeper, more liquid and competitive European financial markets.[12]

Following the strong lobbying from the securities-trading industry and an increased attention to issues related to financial collateral, the European Commission recognised that the mutual acceptance and enforceability of cross-border collateral is indispensable for the stability of the EU financial system and for a cost-effective and integrated securities settlement structure.[13] It was recognised that there is a high risk of invalidation of the collateral arrangement when trades take place across borders, and a high degree of uncertainty in relation to the enforceability should the collateral-provider become insolvent. If such difficulties were not resolved, cross-border securities transactions would be subject to higher costs and risks.[14] Against this motivation, the Financial Collateral Directive was classified as a priority action in the Financial Services Action Plan that called for immediate attention.[15]

---

[8] The Collateral Law Reform Group was later renamed the Collateral and Financial Law Reform Group, http://www.isda.org (accessed 27 November 2006).

[9] ISDA EU Collateral Report.

[10] ISDA EU Collateral Report 3, 11.

[11] ISDA EU Collateral Report 6–7.

[12] ISDA EU Collateral Report 12.

[13] cf European Commission FSAP Forum Group on the Cross-border Use of Collateral, 'Issues Paper for the First Meeting of the Group' (October 1999).

[14] European Commission, 'Financial Services: Implementing the Framework for Financial Markets: Action Plan' Com (1999)232' (11 May 1999) 8.

[15] European Commission, 'Financial Services: Implementing the Framework for Financial Markets: Action Plan' Com (1999)232' (11 May 1999) 22.

2.3.2 *Objective, Scope and Applicability*

The Financial Collateral Directive is one the most vital initiatives taken in Europe to harmonise substantive laws in order to create a functioning and competitive single financial market. The Directive works not only to reduce systemic risk and to create stability, but also promotes integration and an increased efficiency of the securities markets. It is said to constitute a sound and efficient legal regime for limiting credit risk.[16] The increased possibilities for conducting cross-border business are also deemed to create a more competitive market, which will strengthen economic growth and job creation.[17] Through the Directive, a new Community regime is established for securities and cash as collateral under both security interest and title transfer structures.

The Directive focuses on bilateral financial collateral arrangements. It requires Member States to disapply laws that invalidate the effectiveness of financial collateral arrangements and provisions. Broadly, it aims to limit the administrative burdens in the creation, perfection and enforcement of collateral; to facilitate bilateral close-out netting, set-off, top up, substitution and realisation of collateral; to create legal certainty as regards conflicts of laws in relation to book entry securities; and to ensure that agreements permitting the collateral-taker to reuse collateral for its own purposes are effective.

The Financial Collateral Directive is applicable to financial collateral arrangements engaged in by the following persons: the collateral-taker and the collateral-provider must either be a public authority, a central bank, the ECB, the BIS, a multilateral development bank as defined in Art. 1(19) of Directive 2000/12/EC of the European Parliament and of the Council of 20 March 2000 relating to the taking up and pursuit of the business of credit institutions, the IMF, the EIB, a financial institution subject to prudential supervision, a CCP, settlement agent or clearing house as defined in Art. 2(c)-(e) of Directive 98/26/EC, including similar institutions regulated under national law acting in the futures, options and derivatives markets to the extent not covered by that Directive, and a person, other than a natural person, who acts in a trust or representative capacity on behalf on any one or more persons that includes any bondholders or holders of other forms of securitised debt, or a counter-party to one of these institutions provided it is not a natural person.[18] An opt-out possibility is provided to Member States to exclude persons acting as counter-parties (see Sect. 2.3.3).[19]

Only financial collateral that consists of cash or financial instruments where the collateral has been provided and where that provision is evidenced in writing are

---

16 cf Recital 16 Financial Collateral Directive.

17 European Commission, 'Proposal for a Directive of the European Parliament and of the Council on Financial Collateral Arrangements' (27 March 2001) Com (2001) 168 final 2001/0086 (COD) 27.

18 Art. 1 Financial Collateral Directive.

19 Art. 1(3) Financial Collateral Directive. This provision followed from the extensive discussions in various European jurisdictions, *inter alia* Germany, on whether ordinary companies should be included by the scope of the Directive.

covered.[20] Financial collateral is "provided" when the financial collateral has been delivered, transferred, held, registered or otherwise designated so as to be in the possession or under the control of the collateral-taker or of a person acting on the collateral-taker's behalf.[21] The scope is furthermore limited to collateral arrangements evidenced in writing or in a legally equivalent manner.[22]

Art. 2(1)(e) of the Directive defines "financial instruments" as shares in companies and other securities equivalent to shares in companies and bonds and other forms of debt instruments if these are negotiable on the capital market, and any other securities which are normally dealt in and which give the right to acquire any such shares, bonds or other securities by subscription, purchase or exchange or which give rise to a cash settlement (excluding instruments of payment), including units in collective investment undertakings, money market instruments and claims relating to or rights in or in respect of any of the foregoing. The definition excludes credit claims in the form of bank loans.

2.3.3 Implementation and Opt-Out Possibilities

Although all EU Member States were required to implement the Directive in their national legislations by 27 December 2003, only two Member States met this deadline. The ten countries joining the European Union by accession on 1 May 2004 were required to implement the Directive before joining.[23] In addition to the EU Member States, two EEA countries, Iceland and Norway, have implemented the Directive or parts of it. When the implementation of the Directive into Member States' legislations has been effected, there will be 27 different legal regimes for financial collateral arrangements.

The Financial Collateral Directive allows Member States to opt out from certain of its provisions.[24] These provisions have been criticised and have also caused wide political debate.[25] The opt-out possibility that has the biggest impact can be found in Art. 1(3). Under this provision, Member States may exclude collateral arrangements where one of the parties is an institution covered by the scope of the Directive and the other is a person other than a natural person, for instance an ordinary company, which is not so covered.

As of January 2007, Austria and to some extent Sweden, the Czech Republic, Slovenia and France have used the option to opt out, which narrows the coverage of

[20] Art. 1(4)-(5) Financial Collateral Directive.

[21] Art. 2(2) Financial Collateral Directive.

[22] Art. 1(5) Financial Collateral Directive.

[23] On 1 January 2007 Bulgaria and Romania became members of the EU and were thereby required to implement the Financial Collateral Directive.

[24] See Art. 1(3), Art. 1(4)(b), Art. 4(3) Financial Collateral Directive.

[25] See for instance EFMLG, 'Proposal for a Directive on Financial Collateral Arrangements' (COM(2001) 168) 3.

the Directive drastically.[26] Germany has not opted out, although its new legislation has the equivalent effect.[27] Similarly, not all Member States included the same assets under the definition of financial collateral. To give one example, the new legislation in the United Kingdom excludes book debts and rent payments whereas the French Ordonnance includes receivables and other debt.[28]

Ten Member States, including Denmark, Estonia, the United Kingdom, Spain, Luxembourg, Finland, Italy, France, and Germany have widened the scope of application to cover entities not mentioned by the Financial Collateral Directive.[29]

One consequence of the opt-out possibility and the different implementation approaches is a divergence between the European Member States' laws in the area of financial collateral arrangements. Another effect is that different regimes are established for different groups of creditors. Since the provisions under the Directive are more creditor friendly than the property and insolvency laws of the European Member States generally, certain groups of creditors, among them some corporate entities and natural persons, are discriminated against. Another effect of this development of different regimes for the creation and use of the same kind of collateral but for different types of parties is that it can disrupt collateralised transactions.[30]

---

[26] European Commission, 'Evaluation report on the Financial Collateral Arrangements Directive (2002/47/EC)' (20 December 2006) COM (2006) 833 final, 8; IBA, 'Banking Law Newsletter: Implementation of EU Financial Collateral Directive' (Austria) Vol 12 No 2 (September 2004) 7–8, 'To sum up, due to the limited scope of the FinSG, the revolution with respect to the law applicable to financial collateral has not happened in Austria. This may be regretted from the perspective of a demand for a harmonised legal system for title transfer and security collateral arrangements in one common market. It illustrates, however, the dilemma of putting an artificial system over diverse and complex national legal systems in a growing Europe.' The French regime applies to regulated entities such as clearing houses and settlement systems, credit institutions, investment services providers, insurance companies and governmental authorities, Allen & Overy Bulletin (February 2005); cf IBA, 'Banking Law Newsletter: Implementation of EU Financial Collateral Directive' (France) Vol 12 No 2 (September 2004) 16–17. Malta initially opted out but amended its laws in March 2005 to include persons other than natural persons, including unincorporated firms and partnerships, provided the other party is an entity as defined in the Directive, <http://www.isda.org/c_and_a/eurocoldir.html> (accessed 27 November 2005).

[26]Allen & Overy Bulletin (February 2005).

[27] IBA, 'Banking Law Newsletter: Implementation of EU Financial Collateral Directive' (Germany) Vol 12 No 2 (September 2004) 18–19. This effect is achieved by using a narrow definition of financial collateral in Section 1(17) of the German Financial Institutions Code. The opt-out possibility under Art. 1(3) Financial Collateral Directive caused wide political debate in Germany. The discussions were centred on whether it was justified to favour a 'relatively prosperous financial industry' over other sectors and small and medium-sized businesses.

[28] Allen & Overy Bulletin (February 2005).

[29] European Commission, 'Evaluation report on the Financial Collateral Arrangements Directive (2002/47/EC' (20 December 2006 COM (2006) 833 final, 9. On 9 January 2007 an extension of the Financial Collateral Directive's scope to include certain credit claims that will be eligible as collateral for Eurosystem credit operations was proposed, European Commission 'Securities markets: Commission proposes wider scope for Financial Collateral Directive' (IP/07/22)(9 January 2007).

[30] cf ECB, 'Opinion of the European Central Bank of 26 June 2003 at the request of the Austrian Federal Ministry of Justice on a draft Federal Law implementing Directive 2002/47/EC of the European Parliament and of the Council of 6 June 2002 on financial collateral arrangements'

2.3.4 The Rights of Reuse

Art. 5 of the Financial Collateral Directive regulates the reuse of collateral under security arrangements. If and to the extent the terms of the collateral arrangement so provide, Member States shall ensure that the collateral-taker is entitled to use the collateral as if it were the owner of it in accordance with the terms of the security financial collateral arrangement. Where a collateral-taker exercises a right of use, it thereby incurs an obligation to transfer equivalent collateral, set-off the value of the equivalent collateral against or apply it in discharge of the obligation. The substitute is to be treated as having been provided at the same time as the original financial collateral was first provided. Art. 5 of the Directive on effective use is deemed to enhance liquidity in the market. It aims to reduce volatility and enable investors to buy or sell securities more easily at a fairer price.[31]

Art. 6 covers title transfer arrangements such as repos. Under a repo the ownership terminology and structure is used with the same effect as if a security interest was granted. The legal title of the collateral is transferred from the collateral-provider to the collateral-taker together with an obligation for the collateral-taker to retransfer assets of the same kind. Art. 6 ensures that title transfer agreements can take effect in accordance with their terms, thus excluding recharacterisation risk. Both Arts. 5 and 6 ensure that outstanding obligations are subject to close-out netting if an enforcement event occurs.

The right of use under Art. 5 of the Financial Collateral Directive has been criticised for being incompatible with the property law systems of many, if not all, European jurisdictions.[32] A security interest in an asset is a limited interest, which gives the owner the right to have its asset back upon discharge of the underlying obligation. The owner's interest is a right *in rem*. In the Financial Collateral Directive, a general right of use as the owner is given to the collateral-taker irrespective of whether there is an event of default or not, with an obligation to return the equivalent collateral.[33] The moment the right of use is exercised, the bond between the asset and its owner is broken and the owner is left with a contractual claim – a right *in personam*. By allowing the collateral-taker to return the equivalent collateral, the

(CON/2003/11) 3; ISDA, Letter addressed to the French Ministry of Finance 'ISDA remarks on implementation debate in France of the Directive on Financial Collateral Arrangements' (3 July 2003) and City of London Law Society Report 2.

[31] European Commission, 'Proposal for a Directive of the European Parliament and of the Council on Financial Collateral Arrangements' (27 March 2001) COM(2001) 168 final 2001/0086 (COD) 4–6.

[32] cf UNIDROIT Report on a Right of Use 54, which states that the right of use on the basis of a security interest as set out in the Collateral Directive is incompatible with the property law systems of Denmark, Germany, The Netherlands, Italy and the United Kingdom; E Johansson, 'Transfers and Settlement of Securities; The New Order' (2005) 16 EBLR 1093; and E Johansson,'Property Rights in Securities and the Doctrine of Specificity under Swedish Law (2006) 17 EBLR 1099.

[33] cf Art. 2 (1)(m).

collateral-provider appears to agree to substitute its proprietary right with a contractual claim.[34] It has therefore been questioned whether Art. 5 covers outright transfers and not repledge.[35]

Art. 5(4) provides that Member States shall ensure that the use of collateral by the collateral-taker does not render invalid or unenforceable the rights of the collateral-taker under the security arrangement in relation to the financial collateral transferred by the collateral-taker in discharge of an obligation as described in Art. 5(2). Thus, the security interest of the collateral-taker is ensured even if the right of use is exercised. Art. 5 is silent as to the collateral-provider's rights such as the equity of redemption. The result of the wording and structure of Art. 5 is that the balance of the rights between the collateral-provider and the collateral-taker is disturbed. Whereas the collateral-taker is guaranteed the same rights as under the original security arrangement, after the collateral-taker has exercised the right of use, the collateral-provider is left with a contractual claim, which, at best, can be set-off against the underlying obligation, at least until the equivalent collateral has been acquired or transferred to the collateral-provider.[36]

In a Report prepared for UNIDROIT's Study Group on the Preparation of Harmonised Substantive Law Rules regarding Securities Held with an Intermediary, the imbalance between the interests and rights of the collateral-provider and the collateral-taker is emphasised. The situation where the price of the collateral goes up after the collateral-taker has disposed of the collateral is pointed out as a clear example of how the collateral-provider would, to the extent the value of the collateral exceeds the value of the underlying obligation, bear the credit risk of the collateral-taker. In the case of insolvency, this means that the collateral-provider, to the extent set-off is not possible, would have to share *pari passu* with the other unsecured creditors. As collateral-takers are often powerful banks and collateral-providers can be small and medium sized enterprises, this imbalance is considered unacceptable.[37]

Neither Art. 5 nor Art. 6 states at which point the property rights go over from A to B and, upon sale of the collateral, to C. At least four different alternatives can be identified: (1) before B has reused the collateral (for instance when entering into the collateral agreement); (2) when B reuses the collateral; (3) when B has acquired the equivalent assets; or (4) when B transfers the collateral back to A.[38] Another possibility is when the parties have agreed that the property rights shall go over

---

[34] UNIDROIT Report on a Right of Use 4.

[35] UNIDROIT Report on a Right of Use. See also ECB, 'Opinion of the European Central Bank of 26 June 2003 at the request of the Austrian Federal Ministry of Justice on a draft Federal Law implementing Directive 2002/47/EC of the European Parliament and of the Council of 6 June 2002 on financial collateral arrangements' (CON/2003/11) 4 and T Keijser, *Financial Collateral Arrangements* (Kluwer 2006) 344 ff. It has also been suggested that Art. 5 of the Financial Collateral Directive concerns advances, or more specifically, *pignus irregulare*, and not repledge, cf Sect. 6.3.2; and Prop 2004/05:30 42.

[36] cf Art. 5(3) Financial Collateral Directive.

[37] UNIDROIT Report on a Right of Use 56.

[38] This question is further analysed in Sects. 6.3.2 and 9.2.1.

in the collateral agreement. It has generally been assumed that the ownership of the collateral is transferred when B exercises its right of use and disposes of the collateral.[39] The question as to what moment the ownership goes over is, *inter alia*, important in order to establish who is entitled to exercise voting rights and receive income payments.

Another concern is whether a distinction should be made between different types of use – for instance, repledge, sale and loan – by B. That A's right of redemption is cut off when the collateral is sold to a third party is clear but does A keep an interest in the collateral when it is used by B in a secured transaction with C or when a securities loan is given by B to C? If that is the case, can A still apply its right of redemption to get the collateral back upon discharge of the underlying obligation directly with C? If so, for how many stages does A's right of redemption last? Is there a point when A's right to have the collateral back is extinguished? In the case of a secured transaction, does the same analysis apply to a repledge on more severe conditions, for example for a larger debt or a later maturity, as to a repledge on the same conditions? These questions are closely related to whether Art. 5 of the Financial Collateral Directive concerns outright transfers or repledges. If the right of redemption ceases to exist it is easy to argue that the transaction shall be labelled as an outright transfer as the most fundamental characteristic of a pledge – namely the right to have the property back – is missing.

Another difficulty is that B's right of use deviates from the fundamental maxim in property and security law that it is not possible to create property rights in non-individualised property.[40] That property rights only concern individually specified assets is an old principle that can be found in most jurisdictions.[41] The principle applies to tangible assets as well as to intangible assets and covers both title transfer and security arrangements.[42] Its primary aim has been said to be a practical solution to limiting the number of proprietary claims in insolvency, to distinguish rights *in rem* from rights *in personam*, and to prevent shams and fraudulent transactions where the debtor's assets are withheld from the creditors. Thus, the ultimate objective is to protect the principle of equal distribution (*pari passu*).[43] It is also a practical tool to determine the ownership of a particular asset. Simply, it is difficult to claim the property right over something to which one cannot point.[44]

The preamble to the Financial Collateral Directive declares that the right of reuse should be without prejudice to national legislation about the separation of assets and unfair treatment of creditors.[45] Unfortunately the Directive does not further develop or specify what is intended with this statement.

---

[39] UNIDROIT Report on a Right of Use 56. cf also Art. 5(2)(1) Financial Collateral Directive.

[40] Håstad 152.

[41] It should be pointed out that the discussion concerns property or collateral held by a person other than the owner. As long as the owner keeps the property in its possession there is no need to identify each asset.

[42] Goode (2004), 56.

[43] Håstad 152.

[44] cf Sect. 8.3.

[45] Recital 19 Financial Collateral Directive.

Under Art. 5(3) of the Financial Collateral Directive, the equivalent collateral transferred in discharge of an obligation shall be subject to the same security financial collateral arrangement as the original collateral. Should the collateral be sold or mortgaged to a bona fide acquirer before appropriation by the original collateral arrangement the question arises as to who, upon liquidation of the original security taker, takes priority – the collateral-provider or the bona fide purchaser? It has been pointed out that this may be more of a theoretical problem than real since the collateral-provider can never acquire an interest in the equivalent collateral until it is ascertained, and it would never be ascertained if liquidation supervened before appropriation.[46]

When interpreting the rules on reuse of collateral under the Financial Collateral Directive in light of national legislation, it is clear that they infringe on basic principles in property and insolvency law. Much of this is due to the scope of the right of disposal given to the collateral-taker and also the right to substitute the collateral with equivalent collateral, which involves a deviation from basic principles. It is therefore difficult to see how the right to reuse would be without prejudice to national legislation regarding the separation of assets and the unfair treatment of creditors.[47] As pointed out, the collateral-provider's property rights are neglected and the rules against substitution of collateral and the rule on identification of the collateral violated.[48]

2.3.5 *Substitution and Top-Up of Collateral and the Disapplication of Certain Insolvency Provisions*

Several provisions regulate substitution and top-up of collateral.[49] The overall aim is to ensure that the legislation in the various Member States does not inhibit the validity of collateral arrangements. Unfortunately many of the rules of substantive law character, including the rules on substitution and top-up of collateral, are placed in the preamble, which complicates the reading.

Art. 8 states that Member States shall ensure that top-up of collateral made to take into account changes in the value of the collateral or the underlying obligation, or a right to substitute collateral of substantially the same value, are not treated as invalid or reversed or declared void on the sole basis that such provision was made

[46] City of London Law Society Report 14.

[47] cf Recital 19 of the Directive.

[48] The conclusions in this Chapter should be compared with the conclusions in the evaluation report from the European Commission to the Council and the European Parliament where it is stated that in spite of the fact that the right of re-use for many Member States was a novelty it does not seem to give rise to any problems. The report notes, however, that it remains to be seen what experience the market will have with the use of this right, European Commission, 'Evaluation report on the Financial Collateral Arrangement Directive (2002/47/EC)(20 December 2006) COM (2006) 833 final, 9.

[49] Art. 8(3) and Recitals 5, 9 and 16 Financial Collateral Directive.

on the same day as, but prior to, the commencement of winding-up proceedings or reorganisation measures; or the underlying obligation was incurred prior to the date of the provision of the collateral, additional collateral or substitute or replacement collateral.[50]

Where a collateral arrangement has come into existence or collateral has been provided on the day of, but after the commencement of, winding-up proceedings or reorganisation measures, it shall be legally enforceable and binding on third parties if the collateral-taker can prove that it was not aware, nor should have been aware of the commencement of such proceedings or measures.[51]

A general provision in the preamble declares that the sound market practice whereby market participants substitute collateral of the same value or use top-up collateral to manage and limit their credit risk by mark-to-market calculations should be protected against certain automatic avoidance rules. The intention is, however, not to affect the general rules of national insolvency law in relation to voidance of transactions entered into during so-called suspect periods, Art. 8(4). The intention is merely that the provision of top-up or substitution of financial collateral cannot be questioned on the sole basis that the relevant financial obligations existed before that financial collateral was provided, or that the financial collateral was provided during a prescribed period. This does not prejudice the possibility of questioning the financial collateral arrangement under national law and the provision of financial collateral as part of the initial provision, top-up or substitution of financial collateral, for example where this has been intentionally carried out to the detriment of other creditors. It is stated that this covers, *inter alia*, actions based on fraud or similar avoidance rules which may apply in a prescribed period.[52] It is thereby left to the Member States to determine the scope and applicability of this provision.

The provisions under the Financial Collateral Directive on substitution of collateral contradict the general restriction on proprietary substitutions. In most jurisdictions, proprietary substitutions are only allowed in a limited number of situations such as in the case of perishable goods, insurance payments, damages and appropriation by the government. The purpose of the restriction on substitution is to protect B, whose security interest continues to exist.[53] A general right of substitution transforms – apart from when dealing with exemptions such as the floating charge, trust or fund – the collateral and the proprietary right into an ordinary claim, a personal right.[54] The restriction thereby fills the function of protecting the distinction of property from claims and thus, the *pari passu* principle. As the Financial Collateral Directive protects the provision of substitution of collateral, it generally takes the case of proprietary substitution further than what is otherwise possible.

---

[50] Art. 8(3) Financial Collateral Directive.

[51] Art. 8(2) Financial Collateral Directive.

[52] Recital 16 Financial Collateral Directive.

[53] UNDROIT Report on a Right of Use 57.

[54] cf U Drobnig, 'The Law Governing Credit Security' in the European Parliament Directorate General for Research Working Paper 'The Private Law Systems in the EU: Discrimination on Grounds of Nationality and the Need for a European Civil Code' (June 2000) 73–74.

2.3.6 Perfection

Art. 3(1) of the Financial Collateral Directive states that Member States in implementing the Directive shall not require that the creation, validity, perfection, enforceability or admissibility in evidence of a financial collateral arrangement shall be dependent on the performance of any formal act. The purpose is to prevent unnecessary administrative burdens that hinder an efficient market. Art. 3(2) states that paragraph 1 is without prejudice to the application of the Directive only once it has been provided and if that provision can be evidenced in writing and where the financial collateral arrangement can be evidenced in writing or in a legally equivalent manner.

Art. 3 has been deemed to take effect subject to Art. 1(5). It makes the application of the Directive dependent on the collateral being provided and such provision being evidenced in writing. Goode elaborates on the relations between the provisions in the Directive and concludes that what Art. 3(2) fails to state is that in order for the Directive to apply and the collateral to be considered as "provided" the collateral-taker's interest must be perfected by some form of "dispossession".[55] This view is supported by Art. 2(2), which states that:

> References in this Directive to financial collateral being 'provided' or to the 'provision' of financial collateral, are to the financial collateral being delivered, transferred, held, registered or otherwise designated so as to be in the possession or under the control of the collateral-taker or of a person acting on the collateral-taker's behalf. [...].

Recital 9 provides that in order to limit the administrative burdens for parties using financial collateral, the only perfection requirement which national law may impose should be that the financial collateral is delivered, transferred, held, registered or otherwise designated so as to be in the possession or under the control of the collateral-taker or of a person acting on the collateral-taker's behalf or of a person acting on the collateral-taker's behalf while not excluding collateral techniques where the collateral-provider is allowed to substitute collateral or to withdraw excess collateral. One question that arises in relation to the arrangement where the collateral-provider is allowed to substitute or withdraw excess collateral is: who has the collateral under its control, the collateral-provider or the collateral-taker?[56]

For the same reasons – to limit the administrative burdens – Recital 10 states that the creation, validity, perfection, enforceability or admissibility in evidence of a financial collateral arrangement, or the provision of financial collateral under a financial collateral arrangement, should not be made dependent on the performance of any formal act such as the execution of documents in a specific form or in a particular manner or the making of any filing with an official or public body or registration in a public register, etc. This provision rules out registration of securities in notice filing systems similar to Art. 9 of the US UCC.[57]

---

[55] Goode 229.

[56] cf Ds 2003:38 54.

[57] cf Sect. 7.2.2.

Recital 10 distinguishes between book entry securities and all other types of securities. The latter are exempted from the prohibition of formal acts required under the law of a Member State as conditions for transferring or creating a security interest on financial instruments, such as endorsement in the case of instruments to order, or recording in the issuer's register in the case of registered instruments.

Concerns have been expressed about whether Art. 3 covers the giving of notice of an assignment of the debt to the debtor.[58] This is because the collateral is not in the 'possession' or under the 'control' of the collateral-taker. A related question is whether notice given to a third party that has the collateral in its possession, which in some jurisdictions has the equivalent effect as the taking of possession, is included under the Directive.[59]

It has also been questioned whether floating charges are excluded from the scope of the Directive.[60] As mentioned above, a charge will only fall within the scope of the Directive if the collateral is delivered, transferred, held, registered, or otherwise designated so as to be in the possession or under the control of the collateral-taker or a person acting on its behalf (Art. 2(2)). This requirement is in conflict with the structure and elementary idea behind the floating charge of letting the collateral-provider keep the possession or control of the collateral while continuing to deal with it in its ordinary course of business. The floating charge has therefore been deemed to be outside the scope of the Directive, at least until crystallisation.[61] It is often difficult to determine whether a security interest is fixed or floating in nature and in particular when dealing with a portfolio of securities where the collateral-provider has the right to substitute or withdraw securities. It has therefore been urged that the Directive should be extended to cover floating charges.[62]

2.3.7 Set-Off and Netting

Art. 7 of the Financial Collateral Directive provides that Member States shall ensure that close-out netting provisions can take effect in accordance with their terms notwithstanding the commencement or continuation of winding-up proceedings or reorganisation measures in respect of any one of the parties or any purported assignment, judicial or other attachment or other disposition of or in respect of such rights.

'Close-out netting provision' is defined in Art. 2(1)(n) as a provision of a financial collateral arrangement, or, in the absence of such a provision, any statutory rule by which, on the occurrence of an enforcement event: (1) the obligations of the parties are accelerated so as to be immediately due and expressed as an obligation

---

58 cf City of London Law Society Report 7–8.

59 See for instance Ds 2003:38 53.

60 Goode 230; Benjamin and Yates para 4.45; and HM Treasury Report.

61 *ibid.*

62 City of London Law Society Report 5. An express provision covering floating charges would minimise recharacterisation risk and prevent unnecessary registration under section 395 of the English Companies Act 1985.

to pay an amount representing their estimated current value, or are terminated and replaced by an obligation to pay such an amount; and/or (2) an account is taken of what is due from each party to the other in respect of such obligations, and a net sum equal to the balance of the account is payable by the party from whom the larger amount is due to the other party.

Recital 14 states that the enforceability of bilateral close-out netting should be protected, not only as an enforcement mechanism for title transfer arrangements but more widely, where close-out netting forms part of a financial collateral arrangement. Sound risk management practices commonly used in the financial market should be protected by enabling participants to manage and reduce their credit exposures arising from all kinds of financial transactions on a net basis, where the credit exposure is calculated by combining the estimated current exposures under all outstanding transactions with a counterparty, setting off reciprocal items to produce a single aggregated amount that is compared with the current value of the collateral.

Common qualifications in most jurisdictions for set-off are that the claims should be compatible and reciprocal.[63] The requirement for compatibility means that the claim and the cross-claim should be interchangeable, for example both of them in pounds sterling. The second criterion relates to the mutuality of the parties, i.e. that the claim and the cross-claim must be due from the same parties in the same right.[64]

Recital 15 declares that the Financial Collateral Directive should be without prejudice to any restrictions or requirements under national law on bringing into account claims, on obligations to set-off, or on netting, for example relating to their reciprocity or the fact that they have been concluded prior to when the collateral-taker knew or ought to have known of the commencement of winding-up proceedings or reorganisation measures in respect of the collateral-provider. This means that there is a contradiction in the provisions regarding close-out netting and set-off. Art. 7(1) requires Member States to ensure that close-out netting provisions can take effect in accordance with their terms. Thus, it appears as if it is left to the Member States to determine what restrictions, if any, should apply to close-out netting and set-off.

It has also been questioned whether Art. 7(1)(b) has the effect of restricting the negotiability of financial instruments.[65] This provision states that Member States shall ensure that a close-out netting provision can take effect in accordance with its terms notwithstanding any purported assignment, judicial or other attachment or other disposition of or in respect of such rights. Accordingly, it appears that an assignee of securities does not take them free from adverse claims such as a claim to set-off against the assignor. It has therefore been questioned whether this provision assists in the creation of an efficient and liquid financial market.[66] However, as the article regulates "purported" assignments, it may mean that close-out netting can take place until the assignment has been completed through perfection. Hence, the provision may not target or limit negotiability of financial instruments as such.

---

[63] Goode 239.

[64] Goode 239.

[65] Ds 2003:38 118.

[66] *ibid.*

2.3.8 *Conflict of Laws*

Art. 9 of the Financial Collateral Directive provides that certain proprietary law aspects with respect to book entry securities collateral shall be governed by the law of the country in which the relevant account is maintained. The matters that are covered by the scope of this provision are (1) the legal nature and proprietary effects of book entry securities collateral; (2) the requirements for perfecting a financial collateral arrangement relating to book entry securities collateral; (3) priorities between competing interest, including good faith acquisitions, in relation to book entry securities collateral; and (4) the realisation of book entry securities collateral following the occurrence of an enforcement event. The equivalent rule can be found in Art. 9(2) of the Settlement Finality Directive and in Art. 24 of the Banks Winding-up Directive. In contrast to Art. 9(2) of the Settlement Finality Directive, Art. 9 of the Financial Collateral Directive makes clear that the reference to the law of a country is a reference to its domestic law and excludes *renvoi*.

The rule set out under Art. 9 of the Financial Collateral Directive draws on the so called PRIMA principle (Place of the Relevant Intermediary Approach) and establishes that the governing law is the law in the jurisdiction where the relevant account is maintained. Due to the difficulties of locating electronic accounts, the PRIMA principle has been further developed in the Hague Securities Convention and deviates from the rules set out in the Financial Collateral Directive, Settlement Finality Directive and Banks Winding-up Directive. The EU Member States are currently discussing whether they should sign the Convention (see further Sect. 2.6.1). If the European Community decides to go ahead with the Convention, the three Directives would need to be amended.[67]

2.4 The Settlement Finality Directive

The Settlement Finality Directive is a landmark in the harmonisation of substantive property and insolvency laws in the European Union. It establishes a legal framework for payment and securities settlement systems and was adopted in May 1998. The objective is to limit systemic and legal risk inherent in payment and securities settlement systems. The Directive also aims to contribute to the efficient and cost effective operation of cross-border payments and securities settlement arrangements to reinforce the free movement of capital in the internal markets.

The Directive applies to payment and securities settlement systems in the European Union, to participants in such systems, to collateral provided in connection with the participation in such systems and to operations of the central banks of the EU Member States in their function as central banks.[68] It ensures the finality

[67] European Commission, 'Evaluation report on the Financial Collateral Arrangements Directive (2002/47/EC)' (20 December 2006) COM (2006) 833 final 10–11.

[68] Arts. 1–2 Settlement Finality Directive.

of settlement and the enforceability of collateral and thereby protects collateral and close-out netting arrangements from mandatory rules under national insolvency laws.

Close-out netting and set-off fill an important function in terms of creating efficient, deep and liquid financial markets and in limiting the risks and operational strains involved. Another effect is the lowering of capital requirements for financial institutions. At the same time, close-out netting and set-off involves a major qualification of the underlying principles in insolvency law to the benefit of market participants.[69] A liberalisation of the traditional requirements for set-off inevitably increases the risk of disloyal transactions to the detriment of general creditors. Examples of disloyal transactions are when a cross-claim is acquired close to when the debtor becomes insolvent or when a creditor who finds out about the imminent insolvency makes himself indebted towards the debtor. It is therefore important to strike the right balance between the objectives of protecting the general creditors and the creation of efficient and stable financial markets.

The Settlement Finality Directive allows multilateral netting. Whereas bilateral netting involves two counterparties setting off against each other, multilateral netting involves multiple counterparties. It thereby involves a deviation from the common requirement of mutuality. Under Art. 2(k) netting is defined as "[...] the conversion into one net claim or one net obligation of claims and obligations resulting from transfer orders which a participant or participants either issue to, or receive from, one or more other participants with the result that only a net claim can be demanded or a net obligation be owed". This provision facilitates the operations of CCPs and allows several transactions involving different parties to be set off against the claims of other participants in the clearing and settlement system. Thereby the credit exposures are minimised.

As the Directive ensures settlement finality, unwinding of netting or revocation of transfer orders in the system are not allowed. As a consequence the Directive involves a deviation from rules set up to protect general creditors from fraud such as displacement provisions and voidance rules in national insolvency laws. Recital 13 declares that nothing in the Directive should prevent a participant or a third party from exercising any right or claim resulting from the underlying transaction which they may have in law to recovery or restitution in respect of a transfer order which has entered a system, e.g. in case of fraud or technical error, as long as this leads to neither the unwinding of netting, nor to the revocation of the transfer order in the system.

The conflict of laws rule set out in Art. 9(2) of the Settlement Finality Directive should also be mentioned. Similarly to the Financial Collateral Directive, it draws on the so called PRIMA principle (Place of the Relevant Intermediary Approach) and provides that where securities are provided as collateral security to participants, central banks of the Member States or the ECB, and their right with respect to the securities is legally recorded on a register, account or centralised deposit system located in a Member State, the determination of the right of such entities as holders

[69] Goode 238.

of collateral security in relation to those securities shall be governed by the law of that Member State. As discussed in Sect. 2.6.1, if the EU Member States decides to sign the Hague Securities Convention, a revision of this rule and the equivalent rules in the Financial Collateral Directive and the Banks Winding-up Directive is required.

It can be concluded that the Settlement Finality Directive provides a much more liberal scheme than under the traditional property and insolvency law rules to the benefit of market participants covered by its scope. The general view appears to be that due to the important objectives of minimising legal risks and ensuring stability in the financial systems, the deviation from the traditional rules is legitimate.[70]

2.5 MiFID

A couple of provisions in the Directive 2004/39/EC of the European Parliament and of the Council of 21 April 2004 on markets in financial instruments amending Council Directives 85/611/EEC and 93/6/EEC and Directive 2000/12/EC of the European Parliament and of the Council and repealing Council Directive 93/22/EEC ("MiFID") are relevant for the purposes of this book. In MiFID and the Commission Directive 2006/73/EC of 10 August 2006 implementing Directive 2004/39/EC of the European Parliament and of the Council as regards organisational requirements and operating conditions for investment firms and defined terms for the purposes of that Directive ("MiFID Implementation Directive"), segregation is established as a requirement for investor protection.

MiFID was implemented in England and Wales through the Financial Services and Markets Act 2000 (Markets in Financial Instruments) Regulations 2007 (SI 2007/126)(as amended) on or before 1 November 2007. MiFID was also implemented by other statutory instruments including (but not limited to) the Financial Services and Markets Act 2000 (Regulated Activities)(Amendment No 3) Order 2006 (SI 2006/3384) and by HM Treasury and the Financial Services Authority (FSA) using their powers under the Financial Services and Markets Act 2000. Similarly, in Sweden a new Act (2007:528) on the Securities Markets – which implements MiFID into Swedish law – came into force on 1 November 2007. The MiFID Implementation Directive has been implemented through two regulations issued by the Swedish Financial Supervisory Authority (Sw: *Finansinspektionen*); FFFS 2007:17 and FFFS 2007:16.

Under Art. 13(7) of MiFID, an investment firm shall, when holding financial instruments belonging to clients, make adequate arrangements so as to safeguard clients' ownership rights, especially in the event of the firm's insolvency. Investment firms shall also prevent the use of clients' instruments for their own accounts except with the clients' express consent.[71]

---

70 Goode 238.

71 The equivalent provision for funds is set out in Art. 13(8) of MiFID.

Recital 26 to MiFID confirms that firms shall keep their securities separated from investors' securities to protect investors' ownership rights in these assets. However, the requirement to safeguard clients' ownership rights should not prevent a firm from doing business in its name but on behalf of the investor, where that is required by the very nature of the transaction and this has been agreed with the investor.[72] Moreover, it is not intended to cover transactions where the full ownership of financial instruments or funds is transferred to an investment firm in line with Community legislation, and in particular the Financial Collateral Directive, for the purpose of securing or otherwise covering present or future, actual or contingent or prospective obligations. Such financial instruments or funds should no longer be regarded as belonging to the client.[73]

The requirement to safeguard clients' assets is further developed in Art. 16 of the MiFID Implementation Directive.[74] Investment firms are required to keep such records as are necessary to enable them at any time and without delay to distinguish assets held for one client from assets held for other clients, and from their own assets.[75] They are also required to maintain their records and accounts in a way that ensures their accuracy and must conduct reconciliations on a regular basis between their internal accounts and records and those of any third parties by whom these assets are held.[76]

Art. 16(d) of the MiFID Implementation Directive sets out the main requirements with respect to segregation of financial instruments. Investment firms must take the necessary steps to ensure that any client financial instruments deposited with a third party are identifiable separately from the financial instruments belonging to the investment firm and from financial instruments belonging to that third party, by means of different titled accounts on the books of the third party or other equivalent measures that achieve the same level of protection. They must also introduce adequate organisational arrangements to minimise the risk of the loss or diminution of client assets, or of rights in connection with those assets, as a result of misuse of the assets, fraud, poor administration, inadequate record-keeping or negligence.[77]

Under paragraph 3, if the applicable law of the jurisdiction in which the client funds or financial instruments are held prevents investment firms from complying with the segregation requirement, Member States shall prescribe requirements which have an equivalent effect in terms of safeguarding clients' rights. In other words, if required, other measures than segregation can be taken to protect the clients' ownership rights as long as they have the equivalent effect.

---

[72] Stock lending transactions are given as an example, Recital 26 of MiFID.

[73] Recital 27 of MiFID.

[74] See also Commission Regulation (EC) No 1287/2006 of 10 August 2006 implementing Directive 2004/39/EC of the European Parliament and of the Council as regards recordkeeping obligations for investment firms, transaction reporting, market transparency, admission of financial instruments to trading, and defined terms for the purposes of that Directive.

[75] Art. 16 (a) of the Implementation Directive

[76] Art. 16 (b)-(c) of the Implementation Directive.

[77] Art. 16(f) of the Implementation Directive.

The use of client financial instruments is regulated in Art. 19. In accordance to it, Member States shall not allow investment firms to enter into arrangements for securities financing transactions in respect of financial instruments held by them on behalf of a client, or otherwise use such financial instruments for their own account or the account of another client of the firm, unless the client has given its express consent to the use on specified terms, as evidenced, and this use is restricted to those terms.[78] Investment firm must also have in place systems and controls which ensure that only financial instruments belonging to clients that have given their prior express consent are so used.[79] The records of the investment firm shall also include details of the client on whose instructions the use of the financial instruments has been effected, as well as the number of financial instruments used belonging to each client who has given its consent, so as to enable the correct allocation of any loss.[80]

Under paragraph 2(a), Member States may not allow investment firms to enter into arrangements for securities financing transactions in respect of financial instruments which are held on behalf of a client in an omnibus account maintained by a third party, or otherwise use financial instruments held in such an account for their own account or for the account of another client, unless each client whose financial instruments are held in an omnibus account have given their prior express consent.

The requirement for segregation under MiFID and the MiFID Implementation Directive applies to all securities accounts, regardless of where in the in the chain of intermediaries the relevant securities account is held. This should be compared with the conclusion of the Legal Certainty Group that any segregation requirement must apply to upper tier intermediaries and not at the level of the relevant intermediary.[81] This is contrary to the view of this book which argues that the segregation requirement should be upheld and is relevant at every level in the chain of intermediaries, see Sect. 8.4 and Chap. 9.

As this book shows, the requirement for segregation of book-entry securities is closely linked to loss allocation. Should the intermediary become insolvent and there be insufficient securities, the shortfall has to be distributed. Through segregation on designated accounts the level of protection for the investor can be increased. The level of protection can also be increased by a requirement that the intermediary should hold a sufficient number of securities corresponding to its customers' securities. It should be noted, however, that this may well involve paying a higher price for the intermediary's services.

It can be concluded that the rules discussed above correspond to some of the conclusions in this book in relation to the protection of investors' ownership rights, see Sect. 8.4 and Chap. 9. For instance, this book argues that segregation on separate accounts protects account holders' property rights.[82]

---

[78] In the case of retail clients, the consent has to be evidences by signature or an equivalent alternative mechanism, Art. 19(1)(a) of the Implementation Directive.

[79] Art. 19(2)(b) of the Implementation Directive.

[80] Art. 19(2) of the Implementation Directive.

[81] European Commission, 'Legal Certainty Group: Subject 1 – book-entry securities' (first working draft, 4 September 2007) 37.

[82] See further Sect. 8.3.

2.6 Related Initiatives

The transfer, holding and settlement of cash and securities have also received a high level of attention at the international level.[83] In November 2001, the International Organisation of Securities Commissions (IOSCO) and the BIS issued 19 recommendations for reform. These were endorsed in the G30 report 'Global Clearing and Settlement – A Plan for Action'.

Both the G30 report and the so called Giovannini reports emphasise the importance of clarifying the legal issues involved in clearing and settlement operations.[84] The question of treatment of ownership of securities held through an intermediary has been accentuated in particular, but also issues such as national differences in the legal treatment of netting and conflicts of laws require further clarifications.[85] It has been stressed that without a common framework, cross-border trading and settlement of securities cannot consolidate.[86]

Many projects have been initiated, for instance the European Commission's CESAME, Fiscal Compliance (FISCO) and Legal Certainty Groups, which aim to remove identified barriers and improve the environment for cross-border clearing and settlement.[87] Two other closely related initiatives are the work by UNIDROIT's Study Group on Harmonised Substantive Rules Regarding Indirectly Held Securities and the Hague Conference on International Private Law.

A number of reforms are also taking place at the national level. In the United States Arts. 8–9 of the UCC were revised in 1994 following the market breakdown

---

[83] Recent international reports include CPSS/IOSCO, 'Recommendation for Securities Settlement Systems' (November 2001); G30, 'Global Clearing and Settlement – A Plan of Action' (2003); the reports by the Giovannini Group 'Cross-Border Clearing and Settlement Arrangements in the European Union' (November 2001) and 'Second Report on EU Cross-border Clearing and Settlement Arrangements' (April 2003); the European Securities Forum, 'Call for Action on Integration of Clearing and Settlement in Europe' (May 2003); European Commission, 'Communication on Securities Clearing and Settlements, Communication from the Commission to the Council and the European Parliament - Clearing and Settlement in the European Union - The Way Forward' (COM/2004/0312); the ESCB-CESR, 'Standards for Securities Clearing and Settlement Systems in the European Union' (July 2003), and ESCB-CESR, 'The Scope of Application of the ESCB-CESR in the Field of Safety, Soundness and Efficiency of Securities Clearing and Settlement' (August 2003).

[84] The Giovannini Group, 'Second Report on EU Cross-border Clearing and Settlement Arrangements' (April 2003) 12 ff; 'Cross-border Clearing and Settlement Arrangements in the European Union' (November 2001); and G30, 'Global Clearing and Settlement – A Plan of Action' (2003), see especially Recommendations 11, 15 and 16.

[85] *ibid.*

[86] The Giovannini Group, 'Second Report on EU Cross-border Clearing and Settlement Arrangements' (April 2003) 22 ff.

[87] Closely related initiatives are the work by the European Commission's Fiscal Compliance Experts Working Group and the work on a Directive on shareholders' rights, see European Commission, Proposal for a Directive of the European Parliament and of the Council on the exercise of voting rights by shareholders of companies having their registered office in a Member State and whose shares are admitted to trading on a regulated market and amending Directive 2004/109/EC, (5 January 2006) COM (2005) 685 final 2005/0265 (COD).

and the failure in 1987 of a major participant in the US clearing and settlement system.[88] In the United Kingdom, the Law Commission is undertaking work on Property Interests in Investment Securities with the aim of modernising and clarifying the law in order to keep pace with changes in market practice. The Law Commission's work is also intended to influence and respond to the work of the European Commission.[89] Similar law revisions have taken, or are taking, place in Japan, Canada and Switzerland.

2.6.1 The Hague Securities Convention

The Hague Securities Convention is a significant initiative in the area of private international law. It was adopted on 13 December 2002 at the Diplomatic Session of the Hague Conference on Private International Law by 53 Member States but has not yet entered into force. On 5 July 2006, the United States and Switzerland jointly signed the Hague Securities Convention.[90] On the same date the European Commission released a legal assessment where it concluded that the adoption of the Convention would be in the best interest of the European Community.[91]

The Convention recognises that there is an urgent need to provide legal certainty and predictability as to the law applicable to securities held through intermediaries. Other aims are to reduce legal and systemic risks, to enhance cost efficiency and to facilitate the flow of capital and access to the financial markets across borders.

The Convention applies in all cases involving a choice between the laws of different states. It has no effect on substantive law issues and only concerns securities held with an intermediary. It is not intended to determine the applicable law of purely contractual or otherwise personal issues but covers proprietary aspects of securities held with an intermediary such as the legal nature and effects against the

[88] Since it was not clear what interest securities credited to an account conveyed and due to insufficiencies in the related laws, the netting process that was normally conducted every night could not take place. As a result the US Government had to step in and provide market participants with considerable financial assistance and guaranties in order to permit a closing of the market, UNIDROIT Summary Report 4.

[89] The Law Commission, 'Ninth Programme of Law Reform' (Law Com No 293 HC 353, 2005) 26–27.

[90] Mauritius (a non-member state of the Hague Conference on Private International Law) signed the convention on 28 April 2008.

[91] <http://www.hcchnet> (accessed 9 July 2006). The Commission initially recommended that the Settlement Finality Directive should be amended so that securities settlement systems are governed by one Convention law only, cf European Commission, 'Securities Markets Commission calls upon Member States to sign Hague Securities Conventions' (5 July 2006) (IP/06/930). A proposal for the Hague Securities Convention was initially made by the United Kingdom, the US and Australia during the Special Commission on General Affairs and Policy of the Hague Conference on Private International Law, which met on 8–12 May 2000 in The Hague, Draft Explanatory Report 3.

intermediary and third parties to a securities account; perfection; priority between conflicting interests; and the duties of an intermediary against third parties asserting adverse claims.[92]

Due to developments in the securities markets, market participants have faced vast uncertainties on how to determine the applicable law of proprietary rights in relation to interests in securities. In many jurisdictions it has been alarmingly uncertain what law to apply to cross-border securities transactions, leaving market participants exposed to a substantial amount of legal risk. Such uncertainties can impose large transaction costs and lead to liquidity problems and an increased cost of capital.[93]

The traditional approach under which property law issues are treated and which particularly applies to tangible property is *lex rei sitae.* Accordingly, the governing law is the law of the place where the property is situated. Securities held in book entry form are, however, difficult to locate. This creates great uncertainty in relation to establishing the applicable law, especially where the indirect holding structure involves intermediaries in different jurisdictions.

The main problem is that the traditional approach requires that multiple tiers of intermediaries are looked through to the level of the issuer, register or underlying certificate, depending on the factor that determines the applicable law. In the case of securities held through commingled accounts, there is no record of each individual investor apart from the record of the intermediary with which the investor has a direct relationship. The consequence is that it is not possible to assert the investor's interests against a higher level in the chain since no records exist at those levels. The problems that occur are especially acute in systems of multiple tiers of intermediaries located in different jurisdictions. Usually, there are also great difficulties in obtaining the necessary information required to determine the applicable law.

Art. 4, which is the primary rule under the Convention, states that the law expressed as the governing law in the agreement between the account holder and the intermediary maintaining the securities account shall apply. This rule is beneficial as it avoids the need to locate a securities account, an office that maintains a securities account, the underlying securities or the records of the issuer of the underlying securities.

In accordance with the so-called "reality test", the designated law only applies if the relevant intermediary at the time of the agreement has a "qualified office" in the designated state that regularly maintains securities accounts that provide certain functions.[94] This provision links the possibility to choose the governing law with the PRIMA (Place of the Relevant Intermediary Approach) principle. Under Art. 4(1)(a), an office is a qualified office if it, either alone or with other offices of the relevant intermediary or other persons acting for the intermediary effects or monitors entries to securities accounts; administers payments or corporate actions relating to securities held with the intermediary; or is otherwise engaged in the regular activity

[92] This includes whether so-called upper-tier attachments are permissible, Draft Explanatory Report 11, 23.

[93] Draft Explanatory Report 4.

[94] Art. 4(1) Hague Securities Convention.

of maintaining securities accounts. An office is also a qualified office if it is identified by an account number, bank code, or other specific means of identification as maintaining securities accounts in that state.[95] Art. 4(2) lists a set of functions that disqualify an office from being a qualified office if they, standing alone, were the only functions that office would fulfil in relation to maintaining securities accounts. For instance, offices that serve the mere function of being call centres, keeping computer servers, and providing mailing or filing functions are disqualified.

If the applicable law is not determinable under Art. 4, three fall-back rules in Art. 5 apply. The first fall-back rule provides that if it is expressly and unambiguously stated in a written account agreement that the relevant intermediary entered into the agreement through a particular office, the law applicable is the law in force in the state in which that office is located provided that the office is a qualified office.[96] The second fall-back rule provides that the applicable law is the law in force in the state under which law the relevant intermediary is incorporated or otherwise organised at the time the written account agreement is entered into or, if there is no such agreement, at the time the securities account was opened.[97] Under the third fall-back rule the law in force in the state in which the relevant intermediary has its principal place of business at the time the written account agreement was entered into or, if there is no such agreement, at the time the securities account was opened shall apply.[98]

The major advantage of the Convention is that it enables market participants to identify with certainty the law applicable to securities held with an intermediary *ex ante* to entering into a specific transaction. Another advantage is that it subjects all of an investor's interests in respect of one portfolio to the law of one single jurisdiction even when the portfolio consists of securities of issuers from different jurisdictions. In comparison with the traditional approach, which often results in many different laws being applicable to the same portfolio, this is a clear advantage.

The Convention has, however, not been without criticism.[99] The concerns have foremost been that the Convention opens up competition between the mandatory property and insolvency law rules of different jurisdictions, as it allows the parties to a securities account agreement to select the applicable law. In civil law jurisdictions critics also argue that the Convention favours US practices with indirect holding systems at the expense of direct holding systems. An ancillary argument is that,

---

[95] Art. 4(1)(b) Hague Securities Convention.

[96] Art. 5(1) Hague Securities Convention.

[97] Art. 5(2) Hague Securities Convention.

[98] Art. 5(3) Hague Securities Convention.

[99] See for instance European Banking Federation, 'Letter addressed to the European Council Committee on Civil Law and the European Commission' (29 June 2004); and European Banking Federation, 'Letter addressed to the European Commission' (18 November 2004). See also ECB, 'Opinion of the European Central Bank of 17 March 2005 at the request of the Council of the European Union on a proposal for a Council decision concerning the signing of the Hague Convention on the law applicable to certain rights in respect of securities held with an intermediary' (CON/2005/7).

through the possibility of choosing the applicable law, market participants can easily circumvent the rules of jurisdictions protecting investors through so-called forum shopping.[100]

The Convention has also been criticised for a lack of transparency. Since it is the account agreement between the account holder and the intermediary that determines the applicable law, it may not always be clear to third parties, including entitlement holders. On the other hand, as Goode points out, the rule set out in the Convention has been in place in the US over a decade and has worked successfully.[101]

As previously mentioned, governing law under Art. 9 of the Financial Collateral Directive, Art. 9(2) of the Settlement Finality Directive and Art. 24 of the Banks Winding-up Directive is the law in the jurisdiction where the relevant account is maintained. This rule reflects the initial thinking of the Convention at the time that the Financial Collateral Directive came into effect and draws on the so called PRIMA principle. However, as the principle has developed over time, due to the difficulties of locating electronic accounts, the Convention was developed further and gives the parties to the account agreement the choice of selecting the applicable law, thereby departing from *lex rei sitae* and the traditional approach of letting the location of the asset determine the applicable law.

The EU Member States are currently discussing the conditions under which the European Community could sign the Convention. Since the Convention is incompatible with the existing conflict of law rules in the Financial Collateral Directive, Settlement Finality Directive and Banks Winding-up Directive, a revision of either the Convention or these Directives is required if the Member States decide to go ahead with the Convention.[102]

2.6.2 The UNIDROIT Draft Convention on Substantive Rules regarding Intermediated Securities

Following the increased recognition of the legal issues and difficulties relating to the holding and transfer of securities, UNIDROIT decided in the second half of 2002 to constitute a Study Group on the Harmonisation of Substantive Rules regarding Intermediated Securities.[103] Although a substantial amount of work has already been

---

[100] cf Recital 4 of Council Regulation (EC) No 1346/2000 of 29 May 2000 on insolvency proceedings: 'It is necessary for the proper functioning of the internal market to avoid incentives for the partics to transfer assets or judicial proceedings from one Member State to another, seeking to obtain a more favourable legal position (forum shopping)'.

[101] R Goode, 'Rule, Practice, and Pragmatism in Transnational Commercial Law' (2005) 54 ICLQ 539.

[102] cf European Commission, 'Legal assessment of certain aspects of the Hague Securities Convention' (3 July 2006).

[103] UNIDROIT, 'Transactions on Transnational and Connected Capital Markets' (June 2002). "Intermediated securities" usually refers to the practice where book-entry securities are credited to a securities account by an intermediary, cf Art. 1(b) UNIDROIT Draft Convention (CONF 11 – Doc 3).

undertaken through the Financial Collateral Directive and the Settlement Finality Directive to harmonise the laws of EU Member States and through the Hague Securities Convention, it was recognised that these initiatives are limited in their scope and do not fully address all the issues.[104]

The objective of the Study Group is to draft an international instrument capable of improving the worldwide legal framework for securities holding and transfer, with special emphasis on cross-border situations.[105] The instrument is intended to increase legal certainty and economic efficiency in the holding and transfer systems in the global financial markets.[106] The project covers all forms of intermediation regardless of whether the investor holds its rights directly or indirectly and regardless of the type of the relationship between the issuer of the securities and the intermediary directly below it in the chain.[107] Only substantive law issues are covered.[108]

Harmonisation has been deemed appropriate only if it is clearly required for the reduction of legal or systemic risk or the promotion of market efficiency.[109] Uniform rules have, *inter alia*, been conceived desirable in relation to the following issues: (1) the effects of the credit of securities to a securities account; (2) formalities regarding creation and realisation of collateral; (3) the role of non-book-entry dispositions of securities; (4) the possibility of a provisional credit that does not correspond to the total number of securities credited to the account; (5) the prohibition of upper-tier attachments; (6) good faith acquisitions; (7) the net settlement confirming that book entries made by an intermediary may reflect the net overall change in the aggregate balance of its account holders taken together; (8) the finality of transfers of book entry securities; (9) priority issues of competing interests; and (10) loss allocation and the effects of a shortfall.[110] Issues such as the protection of the client's assets against claims of general creditors of the insolvent intermediary may also be included, either in the instrument or in the form of benchmark criteria.[111] Other issues that may be covered are the right of use, top-up and substitution of collateral, netting, set-off, novation and legal problems related to depository receipts, nominees and voting rights.[112]

---

[104] UNIDROIT Recommendations on Legal Certainty; UNIDROIT Position Paper 5; the UNIDROIT Preliminary Draft Convention on Harmonised Substantive Rules Regarding Securities Held with an Intermediary, Doc 18 (November 2004); and the UNIDROIT Explanatory Notes.

[105] UNIDROIT Position Paper 2.

[106] UNIDROIT Final Report, Doc 23 (August 2005) 2.

[107] UNIDROIT Summary Report 2.

[108] UNIDROIT Position Paper 5.

[109] UNIDROIT Recommendations on Legal Certainty; UNIDROIT Position Paper 6.

[110] *ibid.*

[111] cf UNIDROIT Position Paper 16–17, 6.

[112] UNIDROIT Summary Report 3. It should be noted that the scope has been altered since the UNIDROIT Summary Report was published, cf Preliminary Draft Convention.

The first version of the Draft UNIDROIT Convention on Substantive Rules regarding Intermediated Securities was published in April 2004.[113] It has been succeeded by several versions of which the latest was published in February 2008.[114] Without going into the Convention in any detail, it is clear that many of the rules, as with the provisions under the Financial Collateral and Settlement Finality Directives, alter basic property and insolvency law rules and structures.[115]

2.6.3 The Legal Certainty Group

The European Commission's Legal Certainty Group held its first meeting in Brussels on 31 January 2005. The issues that the Group addresses include the legal effects of book entries made to securities accounts, recognition of indirect holdings, corporate actions and voting rights, transfer of interest in securities and priority issues (including bona fide acquisitions).[116] The aim is to develop proposals for legislation and remove the legal issues that have been identified as impeding an efficient, safe and cost-effective cross-border clearing and settlement in the European Union.[117]

On 28 July 2006 the Legal Certainty Group submitted its advice to the European Commission. The advice identifies a set of principles for new legislation in relation to the legal effects of book entries made on securities accounts. Three identified problems of legal uncertainty are included in the Group's mandate: (1) the absence of an EU-wide framework for the treatment of interests in securities held with an intermediary; (2) differences in national legal provisions affecting corporate action processing; and (3) restrictions relating to the issuer's ability to choose the location of its securities.[118] The Group's advice is, however, only conclusive in relation to the first issue.

New legislation is deemed to be needed in relation to the legal effects of book entries made on securities accounts. The legislation should aim at minimum harmonisation of EU Member States' laws.[119] It is suggested that the new legislation should be based on the fact that book entries on securities accounts are a source

---

[113] UNIDROIT Draft Convention, Doc 13 (April 2004).

[114] UNIDROIT Draft Convention, Conf 11 – Doc 3. The diplomatic Conference to adopt the Convention will be held in Geneva on 1–13 September 2008.

[115] UNIDROIT Draft Convention, Conf 11 – Doc 3.

[116] cf European Commission, 'EU Clearing and Settlement Legal Certainty Group Summary of Action Points' (13 September 2005) 1–2; and Legal Certainty Group Comparative Survey; Legal Certainty Group Advice 3.

[117] European Commission, 'Financial services: Commission sets up expert group on legal certainty issues in clearing and settlement' (IP/05/123) (1 February 2005).

[118] Legal Certainty Group Advice 1.

[119] *ibid.*

of rights for account holders. A credit on a securities account should accordingly constitute evidence of the book-entry rights of the account holder.[120]

The legal effect of a book entry in favour of an account holder arises upon a credit entry to the account, provided that the entry is valid. The account holder becomes entitled to the rights at the moment the credit entry is made by the account provider and ceases to be entitled upon a debit entry being made.[121]

The book entry rights of the account holder include, *inter alia*, to instruct the account provider to make a book entry on the account for such purpose as to dispose of the rights, pledge or otherwise charge the rights; to retrieve the securities to which the rights relate by delivery of a certificate or any other means to the extent provided for under the terms of the issue and applicable law; to instruct the account provider to facilitate the exercise of such rights as the account holder has in respect of the securities to which the book entries relate such as the right to vote, receive dividends, interest, income capital, subscribe for further securities, etc.; and to receive from the account provider corporate information relevant for the exercise of voting rights or other corporate rights.[122]

The Group further recommends that an option for Member States to prohibit conditional settlement should be provided. In other words, it should be possible for Member States to require that account providers, before making a book entry in respect of particular securities in favour of an account holder, have aggregate holdings designated as holdings for the account holder that are at least equal to the aggregate book entries in respect of such securities, or, where individual accounts are used, have sufficient coverage at the upper tier for the specific account holder. To the extent that this is not required, it must be made clear to account holders.[123]

Certain duties are also set out which shall be imposed on account providers, including to maintain holdings matching the balance of credits on its account holder's accounts; to pass down to the account holder corporate information that is communicated to it in that capacity and relevant for the exercise of voting rights or other corporate rights; to follow the account holder's instructions in relation to the account; to segregate its own securities from that of its account holders; and, if there are insufficient assets at the upper tier, to cover the rights of its account holders and, subject to contractual agreement and applicable rules on limitation and exclusion of liability, to replace the missing assets, failing which to reimburse the value of the assets.[124]

It is pointed out that nothing in the new legislation shall prohibit or impede any market practice for holding securities, such as direct holding by the account holder with the issuer, holding securities in a pool, or holding through individually segregated accounts.[125] It is also emphasised that the new legislation does not aim to

[120] Legal Certainty Group Advice 6.

[121] Legal Certainty Group Advice 8.

[122] Legal Certainty Group Advice 6.

[123] Legal Certainty Group Advice 7.

[124] *ibid.*

[125] Legal Certainty Group Advice 5.

restructure national ownership concepts or property rules concerning securities. It does not seek to change the rights contained in securities but rather the way in which these rights are administered, exercised and enforced. Notwithstanding this, in the event of a conflict, existing laws will have to conform.[126]

The pragmatic and groundbreaking approach adopted by the Legal Certainty Group should be welcomed. It can be questioned, however, whether the principle that the credit to the account is the establishing factor of the rights of the account holder does not contradict the fact that a credit on a securities account only evidences the book-entry rights. In other words, if the legal effects of a book entry arise upon a credit to the account, does this not mean that the registration creates the rights and not merely evidences them?[127] If this is correct, the effect is that the risk of error in relation to registration of the account holder's rights, including omissions, is placed on the account holder.[128]

2.7 Summary and Conclusions

During the last decade we have witnessed a substantial flow of legislative measures relating to transfer, holding and settlement of securities and the use of securities and cash as collateral. This Chapter focuses on the legal changes that have taken place in the European Union through the Financial Collateral Directive. It also briefly examines the Settlement Finality Directive, MiFID and the MiFID Implementation Directive, the Hague Securities Convention, the work by the European Commission's Legal Certainty Group and the UNIDROIT Draft Convention on Substantive Rules regarding Intermediated Securities. It argues that a new legal order is currently being established with a liberalisation of mandatory property and insolvency law rules.

The Financial Collateral Directive establishes a new Community regime for securities and cash as collateral under both security interest and title transfer structures. As shown, many of the provisions under the Financial Collateral Directive deviate from basic property and insolvency law rules. One example is Art. 5, which gives the collateral-taker an extensive right of use of the collateral. As the collateral-taker does not have to return the same asset, i.e. the equivalent asset is sufficient, it has been questioned whether Art. 5 covers outright transfers and not repledge. Another concern is that the collateral-taker's right of use for its own purposes involves an exemption from the requirement of identity. Through these deviations, the Directive distorts the distinction between property and contractual claims, i.e. rights *in rem* and rights *in personam*.

---

[126] Legal Certainty Group Advice 5–8.

[127] cf Sects. 8.4 and 9.3 and the discussion on book-entries made on securities accounts having constitutive versus evidentiary effect.

[128] That is, unless the intermediary is obliged to remedy any potential loss. However, also in this case the question arises as to whether the account holder bears the ultimate loss should the intermediary become insolvent.

Many of the provisions under the Financial Collateral Directive are also ambiguous and contradictory. Some of the substantive rules are placed in the preamble (see for instance Recitals 14 and 15) whereas others are very general. The rules on close-out netting, use of collateral, enforcement of financial collateral arrangements and the disapplication of certain insolvency provisions leave room for the Member States to determine the applicability and the scope of the provisions in the implementation of the Directive. This is an unfortunate effect of legislating through Directives, which, by setting only minimum standards, thus permit different approaches in the implementation by the Member States. The result is uncertainty, which follows from the implementation of unclear and contradictory rules in the 27 different legal regimes of the EU Member States.

Another effect is that a more liberal regime is created for creditors covered by the Financial Collateral Directive. It is clear that the new regime infringes on the pari passu principle on which most legal systems rest. By allowing certain institutions to be covered by a more preferential scheme an imbalance is created.

Like the Financial Collateral Directive, the Settlement Finality Directive involves major disqualifications from the principle of equality amongst creditors. As the Directive ensures settlement finality, the unwinding of netting or revocation of transfer orders in the system is not allowed. As a result, the Directive entails a deviation from rules set up to protect general creditors from fraud, such as displacement provisions and voidance rules under national insolvency laws. The Directive also involves a liberalisation of the traditional requirements for set-off, such as the requirement for reciprocity. The general understanding of the importance of close-out netting and set-off to limit legal and systemic risks appears, however, to have gained ground. The creation of a separate regime for payment and clearing and settlement systems therefore seems to be justified.[129]

The UNIDROIT Draft Convention and the Hague Securities Convention also establish more liberal regimes in their respective areas. Whereas the Hague Securities Convention applies in all cases involving a choice between the laws of different states and concerns securities held with an intermediary, the work of the UNIDROIT Study Group covers substantive law issues relating to securities holdings and transfers. Neither of the two Conventions are limited to collateralised transactions.

As with the Financial Collateral Directive and Settlement Finality Directive, many of the proposed rules in the UNIDROIT Draft Convention would alter current property and insolvency law mechanisms and structures. Similarly, the Hague Securities Convention deviates from the traditional international private law principle – *lex rei sitae* – which determines that the governing law of proprietary rights is the law where the asset is situated. Under the Hague Securities Convention, the law expressed as the governing law in the agreement between the account holder and the intermediary maintaining the securities account shall apply. Under the so-called "reality test", the designated law only applies if the relevant intermediary at the time of the agreement has an office in the designated State that regularly maintains

[129] cf Goode 238; Prop 1994/95:130 p 14.

securities accounts. The Hague Securities Convention has therefore been deemed to be compatible with the PRIMA principle.

Because the Hague Securities Convention allows the parties to a securities account agreement to select the governing law, concerns have been raised that it opens up the possibility of competition of mandatory property and insolvency law rules of different jurisdictions and thereby allows market participants to engage in forum shopping. Another concern is that the Hague Securities Convention is not fully compatible with the Financial Collateral Directive and Settlement Finality Directive. A revision of the latter two instruments is therefore necessary if and when the Convention enters into force.

Another concern is that many of the legal instruments reviewed vary in their scope, with overlaps and gaps as a result. For example, cash used as collateral is covered by the Financial Collateral Directive but excluded from the scope of the Hague Securities Convention. Without a revision of the Financial Collateral Directive, the establishment of the applicable law for transactions containing both securities and cash as collateral may have unintended consequences.

Chapter 3
Developments of the Securities Markets

"We strongly suspect, though we do not know for sure, that the accelerating expansion of global finance may be indispensable to the continued rapid growth in world trade in goods and services. It appears increasingly evident that many forms and layers of financial intermediation will be required if we are to capture the full benefit of our advances in technology and trade. Indeed, the potential for a far larger world financial system than currently exists is suggested by the seemingly outsized implicit compensation for risk associated with many investments worldwide."[1]

3.1 Introduction

This Chapter examines the practices in the wholesale financial markets with particular emphasis on the developments of the securities holding systems. The aim is to examine market practices in relation to the principal question analysed in this book: the requirement for identification of the collateral as a criterion for property rights in securities evidenced in book-entry form on securities accounts.

3.2 Developments of the Securities Markets

3.2.1 Background

A number of significant developments can be identified in the securities markets over the past 30 years. Together they support the argument that investment securities should be treated separately when designing a security law system.

Between 1980 and 2001 the value of shares traded yearly increased nearly 63 times.[2] Today the turnover on the securities markets involves trillions of dollars.[3] Electronic trading has transformed the market structure and gives participants more

---

[1] Remarks by Chairman Alan Greenspan, Federal Reserve Board, at Lancaster House, London, United Kingdom (September 25, 2002).

[2] G30, 'Global Clearing and Settlement: A Plan of Action' (2003) 1.

[3] The turnover of securities is estimated to be roughly 50 trillion Euros over at peak times every two or three days. The securities held in the indirect holding system is estimated to have a value of approximately 50 trillion Euros, G Morton, 'Legal Risk and its Impact on Market Efficiency' in 'Legal Risk and Market Efficiency' UNIDROIT Seminar on Harmonised Substantive Rules regarding Securities Held with an Intermediary (February 2004) 4.

© Springer-Verlag Berlin Heidelberg 2009

choices. It enables the handling of bigger volumes and a widening participation.[4] Other improvements are the move to real-time settlement and increased netting, which have been identified as crucial in dealing with the increased volume of securities trade.[5] On an institutional level, banks, exchanges, money brokers and clearing and settlement systems are merging. Links and alliances are increasingly being established between institutions, especially in Europe.

The traditional legal analysis regarding investment securities refers to a time when securities were held in paper format and trade mostly took place on a domestic basis. As late as in the 1980s, custody services consisted of safekeeping of securities in strong boxes. The legal rules depended on the concept that the paper instruments constituted the underlying rights, which could be transferred by delivery of them.[6]

In the late 1960s and early 1970s, the so-called paper crunch threatened the operations of the US markets as the settlement systems could not keep up with the pace of the trades. A similar paper crunch took place in the UK in the 1980s.[7] The turnovers in the securities markets were so large and paper intensive that the industry could not cope with all the paperwork involved in the settlement of the trades.[8] In the market crash of 1987, the failure of timely settlement increased the losses of investors desperate to sell their securities as the markets fell.[9] In Sweden, the Swedish Central Securities Depository, VPC AB, was established in 1971 as a result of the problems that occurred with paper-based securities.[10]

In answer to these crises the securities markets reorganised themselves. Increasingly certificated and bearer securities were immobilised and held in custody. Instead of shipping vast quantities of bearer documents, securities were held, transferred and pledged by credits and debits made to securities accounts maintained by intermediaries without any change of possession of the underlying securities. Trades were thus effected on the records of intermediaries who organised themselves in indirect holding structures. It was discovered that the holding of securities in multi-tiered systems with CSDs as intermediaries substantially reduced losses, theft, illiquidity costs and risks.[11]

---

[4] H Allen, J Hawkins and S Sato, Research Paper No 7 'Electronic Trading and its Implications for Financial Systems' (November 2001).

[5] European Securities Forum, 'Submission on the New Basel Capital Accord' (2001).

[6] Benjamin and Yates 5.

[7] Benjamin 20.

[8] In 1968, these practices in the US were so out of hand that the Stock Exchange in New York had to close two hours early, followed by being closed every Wednesday so that market participants could catch up with the paper works of the trades.

[9] Benjamin 20. The market collapse, which took place on 19 October 1987 led to a fall in the Dow Jones Industrial Average of 508 points, or, approximately 23 per cent of its value. The turnover on the same day was 604 million shares, J Seligman, 'The Internationalization of the Securities Markets: Preface to a Symposium' Michigan Yearbook of International Legal Studies Volume IX (1988). 1.

[10] Afrell Klahr and Samuelsson 52.

[11] R D Guynn, 'Modernizing Securities Ownership Transfer and Pledging Laws: A Discussion Paper on the Need for International Harmonization' (Capital Markets Forum, International Bar Association 1996) 21.

In 1989 the G30 published its well-recognised report on Clearance and Settlement in the World's Securities Markets. In the report, the Group encouraged the holding of both physical and dematerialised securities in CSDs.[12] Two models that facilitate electronic settlement were identified; immobilisation and dematerialisation.[13] By 1992, most markets had organised one or more CSDs and centralised local settlement through them.[14]

Dematerialised securities do not exist in physical form and can only be established via book entries on a register. In other words, the securities exist only as computer records. Immobilised securities are certificated or bearer securities placed in custody, often together with other investors' securities. The majority of immobilised securities are issued in jumbo or global format. This means that one single instrument is issued which represents the whole issue of securities.[15] Through immobilisation, the physical movements of underlying documents are eliminated.[16]

Like dematerialised securities, the rights in immobilised securities are established via book entries.[17] Immobilised securities are held indirectly through multiple tiers of intermediaries whereas dematerialised securities can be held either directly or indirectly.

One important difference between dematerialisation and immobilisation is that dematerialisation requires enabling legislation to be effective. Immobilisation, on the other hand, is effected through the custody arrangement, i.e. through placing the securities in custody and regulating the effects of the arrangement in the custody agreement.[18]

What is generally referred to as computerisation (i.e. dematerialisation and immobilisation) of the securities markets has achieved flexibility and efficiency. Transactions take place electronically via debiting and crediting of book accounts. As a result, larger volumes of securities are traded faster and more easily, whether domestically or across national borders.

Another equally important development is the move to indirect holding systems with multiple tiers of intermediaries (see Fig. 3.1). As indirect holding reduces costs and complexities of record-keeping and lowers the risk of losses caused by the physical transfer of securities, it is widely used in international securities trade and settlement.[19]

The creation of indirect holding structures involves an increased intermediation in the securities markets. Since participation in clearing and settlement systems is

---

[12] G30, 'Clearance and Settlement in the World's Securities Markets' (1989) Recommendation 3.

[13] Benjamin and Yates 14.

[14] R D Guynn, 'Modernizing Securities Ownership Transfer and Pledging Laws: A Discussion Paper on the Need for International Harmonization' (Capital Markets Forum, International Bar Association 1996) 21.

[15] Benjamin and Yates 14–15.

[16] *ibid.* G30, 'Report on Clearance and Settlement in the World's Securities Markets' (1989).

[17] Benjamin and Yates 14–15.

[18] Ooi 96.

[19] SL Schwarcz, 'Indirectly Held Securities and Intermediary Risk' (2002–01) Uniform L Rev (*Revue de droit uniforme*).

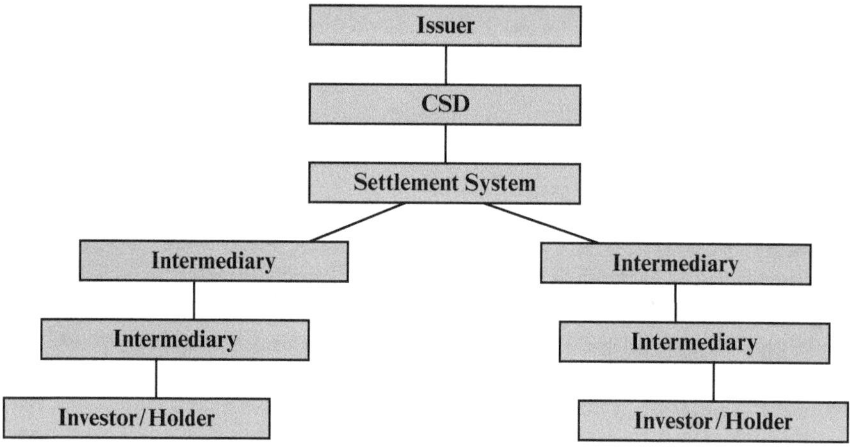

Fig. 3.1 Illustration A: Indirect holding system

not always available or practical for investors some investors gain access to these systems through an intermediary. In many cases this means that title to the securities can only be claimed through the intermediary.[20] In 2004 it was estimated that securities worth 50 trillion euros were held through intermediaries world-wide.[21]

3.2.2 Risks

The developments of the financial markets and the technical improvements have reduced some of the risks involved. For instance, the move to Delivery versus Payment settlement ("DVP") in the UK in 2001 meant that the exchange of securities in CREST between the seller and the buyer and the transfer of funds from the buyer's bank to the seller's bank took place simultaneously. DVP is essential in minimising principal risk, or "Herstatt risk" as it also is called.[22]

The increased use of close-out netting, involving elements such as early termination, acceleration and valuation of claims with the calculation of outstanding amounts into one single net amount, is also an important feature in terms of reducing risk. Set-off and close-out netting effectively reduce credit[23] and systemic risks.[24]

---

[20] Benjamin and Yates 21.

[21] UNIDROIT Explanatory Notes 11.

[22] The risk a party faces when it has delivered its part of a trade, but the counterparty defaults before its delivery. The failure in 1974 of Bank Herstatt gave rise to the term Herstatt risk.

[23] Credit risk exists whenever a counterparty has an obligation to make a payment in the future and is the probability that the counterparty defaults on the obligation, cf ISDA, 'Guidelines for Collateral Practitioners' (1998) 3–4.

[24] The risk that the failure of one institution spreads and affects other institutions and the financial system as a whole.

The use of Central Counterparties ("CCPs"), which facilitate multilateral netting, also reduces credit and systemic risks. Together with the move to real-time settlement, this has been identified as crucial in dealing with the increased volumes of securities trades.[25]

The technical developments however, do not only reduce risk, they also increase and create new risks. For instance, the involvement of several actors and trade, clearing and settlement across borders increase settlement,[26] operational[27] and legal risks.[28] The indirect holding structures also involve intermediary risk. The longer the chain of intermediaries, the bigger the risk that an error occurs or that the legal title or benefits from an investment are misappropriated when passed down the chain of intermediaries.[29] The holding of securities indirectly through chains of intermediaries also entails systemic risk, and consolidation inevitably involves a concentration of risks. [30]

3.2.3 Indirectly Held Securities

Securities are held 'directly' when the investor can exercise its rights in the securities directly against the issuer. 'Indirectly held securities' refers to the system where one or more intermediaries are interpositioned between the issuer and the investor and the investor can only exercise its property rights against the issuer through its intermediary (cf Fig. 3.1).[31] 'Intermediary' is usually used to mean an institution that maintains securities accounts for others and includes not only banks and custodians in the indirect holding structure but also the operator of the clearing and settlement system and the CSD, which stands between the issuer and the ultimate investor.[32] The investor's interests are shown only on the books of the account administered by the intermediary. The investor's interest is therefore indirect and cannot be claimed against the issuer, only against the intermediary with whom the investor has a direct relationship.[33]

---

[25] cf European Securities Forum, 'Submission on the New Basel Capital Accord' (2001).

[26] The risk that cash or securities are not delivered within the agreed deadline, PC Harding and CA Johnson, 'Mastering Collateral Management and Documentation: A Practical Guide for Negotiators' (Financial Times Prentice Hall/Pearson Education 2002) 71.

[27] The risk of loss due to inadequate support and control systems, management failure and human error.

[28] The risk that a contract cannot be legally enforced.

[29] AO Austen-Peters, *Custody of Investments: Law and Practice* (OUP 2000) 71.

[30] When too great an investment of the same security is made or taken as collateral, PC Harding and CA Johnson, 'Mastering Collateral Management and Documentation: A Practical Guide for Negotiators' (Financial Times Prentice Hall/Pearson Education 2002) 73.

[31] Benjamin 36 f; Ooi xxx.

[32] cf UNIDROIT Draft Convention Doc 42, Art. 1(c).

[33] Benjamin 26–27.

In this book the term 'securities' means any shares, bonds or other transferable financial instruments or financial assets or any interest therein other than cash. For ease of reference 'securities' is used rather than 'interests in securities' to denote rights in securities held on an indirect basis.[34]

Investments made across borders can involve numerous intermediaries located in different jurisdictions. Usually the international holding patterns consist of a large number of national and international holding systems, with the multi-tiered holding structure being replicated over and over again.[35] It should therefore be stressed that the illustration above is a vast simplification.

It should also be pointed out that the classification of holding systems as direct or indirect is often misleading as different legal systems treat the rights of investors differently. In a sense, all securities evidenced in book-entry form are intermediated and in that way held indirectly. However, in some legal systems, even though one or more intermediaries stand between an account holder and the issuer, the account holder is considered to be the direct owner. The intermediary has no interest in the securities but merely acts on behalf of the investor.[36] In other legal systems, the account holder's rights are considered to be enforceable only against the intermediary with whom the account holder has a direct relationship.[37]

3.2.4 Unallocated and Intermediated Securities

Another important development of the securities markets is that securities are often held by intermediaries on a fungible and unallocated basis; the securities are mixed with other investors' securities and unidentifiable in relation to respective investor.

Since fungible units normally lack specific characterisation they can only be identified through segregation. By segregating a certain number of units fungible assets can normally be distinguished. Illustrating examples are grain in a silo, or oil in an oil tank. By separating the grain or the oil in a compartment, a specific quantity can be marked. The fungible units are thereby converted into a specific asset.

Generally there are two ways in which an intermediary can hold book-entry securities for its customers:(1) through omnibus accounts where all investors' interest in the same securities are pooled without individual designation, or (2) on non-fungible designated accounts where the intermediary is recorded as holding a block of shares specifically for each investor.[38]

---

[34] cf Sect. 3.2.5.

[35] RD Guynn and NJ Marchand, 'Transfer or Pledge of Securities Held through Depositories' in HV Houtte (ed), *The Law of Cross-border Securities Transactions* (Sweet & Maxwell London 1998 1999) 51.

[36] cf Appendix 2 UNIDROIT, 'Seminar on Intermediated Securities – Bern, Switzerland' Sem 1 (15–17 September 2005) 2.

[37] cf 'UNIDROIT Seminar on Intermediated Securities – Bern, Switzerland' (15–17 September 2005); and Draft Explanatory Report 10.

[38] Goode (2002) 104.

The reason for holding securities on a fungible, unallocated and intermediated basis is that it reduces administrative costs and is more efficient. It enables transfers of securities from one customer to another through the books of the intermediary without involving upper-tier intermediaries or the issuer.[39] It also enables the intermediary to use the securities it is holding for overnight lending. This way credit and liquidity exposures are limited.[40]

The indirect holding system has, together with the fact that securities do not exist in a physical format, been pointed out as the main reason for the legal issues that arise.[41] This book argues that the root of the problem is not the development of the indirect holding system as such, but rather that the computerisation of the securities markets makes it impossible to identify these assets in relation to respective entitlement holder.[42] As securities evidenced by book-entries on accounts are fungible intangibles they are impossible to identify regardless of whether they are registered on an omnibus account or on a designated account.[43] In contrast with oil in an oil tank or grain in a silo, it is not possible to separate or otherwise to locate them as they do not exist on the account. The idiom 'pooling' is therefore a misconception, or rather, a construct. As securities registered on accounts do not exist in the physical world they cannot be 'pooled'. Only if the registration which evidences the financial instrument and the relationship between the ultimate investor and the intermediary is given constitutive effect or a similar effect to possession of bearer securities, would these assets be possible to separate and thus to identify.[44]

A comparison with intellectual property rights illustrates this point further. Intellectual property rights, such as patents and trademarks, are intangible assets that account as property.[45] Similarly to securities evidenced in book-entry form they do not exist in physical format. However, in contrast to securities evidenced in book-entry form, intellectual property rights are not fungible. Rather they are highly specific and in most cases easy to identify. Usually the requirement for identity does not cause any problems in relation to these assets.

3.2.5 *Interest in Securities*

The increased practice of holding securities on an unallocated and intermediated basis raises several issues in relation to the acquisition and retention of property

39 Goode 207.

40 RD Guynn, 'Modernizing Securities Ownership Transfer and Pledging Laws: A Discussion Paper on the Need for International Harmonization' (Capital Markets Forum, International Bar Association 1996) 24–25.

41 UNIDROIT Explanatory Notes 17 and JS Rogers, 'Negotiability, Property, and Identity' 12 Cardozo L Rev (1990–1991) 471.

42 It is the lack of identity that prohibits tracing and also requires losses to be shared *pro rata*.

43 cf Austen-Peters 15.

44 cf analysis in Sect. 8.3.

45 Penner 109.

rights. In the intermediary's insolvency, the commingling of different investors' assets means that a shortfall may have to be shared amongst investors.[46] Should the securities not be separated from the intermediary's securities, the commingling of the securities moreover means that the investor takes the credit risk of the intermediary.

Another disadvantage of the indirect holding system is that investors in many jurisdictions are dependent on the intermediary with whom they have a direct relationship to enforce their rights against the issuer.[47] Whereas bearer or certificated securities entitle investors to income and administrative rights through possession of the relevant document and, in relation to shares, by being registered in the share register, the increased intermediation and the practices of holding securities on an unallocated basis, often mean that the interests of the investor is only shown in the books of the intermediary.

In many jurisdictions it is unlikely that the issuer or the CSD would recognise the interest of an investor who is unable to assert a claim against any intermediary other than the one with whom it has an established account arrangement. Thus, the investor lacks a direct right in the underlying securities. As a consequence it is sometimes argued that what is traded in the indirect holding system is the investor's claim against its own intermediary.[48] This claim – which by Benjamin has been dubbed 'interests in securities'[49] – and its legal effects, has caused wide debate and is subject to legislative work by the European Commission,[50] the English Law Commission,[51] and UNIDROIT.[52]

The requirement for identity also causes concern in relation to a whole range of other issues, including the characterisation of the investor's rights, assertions of claims against higher tier intermediaries, priority between competing claims, perfection, transfer of investors' rights, the protection of bonafide purchasers and negotiability. This is because the legal systems are designed for assets that are identifiable. The rules relating to property rights in securities are based on the notion that these assets until quite recently have been issued and traded in bearer format. The legal construct that the bearer document is the carrier of the rights against the issuer facilitates the identification of these assets. Problems arise as securities registered on accounts are held on a fungible basis; they are unidentifiable in relation to their entitlement holders.

---

[46] A shortfall occurs when the investors' entitlements with respect to securities on a securities account exceed the intermediary's entitlement (which that intermediary is holding on behalf of the investors) with the intermediary immediately above it in the chain.

[47] cf Ooi 95 ff; Austen-Peters 10 ff.

[48] cf Austen-Peters 74.

[49] Benjamin 5.

[50] <http://europa.eu.int/comm/internal_market/financial-markets/clearing/certainty_en.htm> (accessed 20 January 2006).

[51] <http://www.lawcom.gov.uk/investment_securities.htm> (accessed 20 January 2006).

[52] <http://www.unidroit.org/english/workprogramme/study078/item1/main.htm> (accessed 20 January 2006).

3.3 Clearing and Settlement

Although the same commercial developments have more or less taken place in all securities markets, the different legal systems vary significantly as to the classification of the account holders' rights. This section examines the structure of the holding and settlement systems in Sweden, the United Kingdom and the United States and the degree of identification of securities held in the holding and settlement systems in each jurisdiction.

3.3.1 Sweden

As from September 2004, the Swedish and Finnish CSDs, VPC and APK, are operating under the brand NCSD. APK, which manages the securities register and settlement system in Finland, is a subsidiary of VPC.

VPC provides registration and account holding services for most types of financial instruments. It also handles the share register and corporate actions for registered companies. The services include notification of transfers, and the handling of payments, redemptions and annual statements of accounts. VPC is also responsible for the administration of withholding taxes. In addition, VPC acts as a clearing house for shares and other financial securities.[53]

In Sweden securities are generally issued in either registered or bearer format. All Swedish securities registered in the VPC system are dematerialised.[54] VPC offers two alternative legal methods of holding securities: through owner; or nominee accounts.[55] Owner accounts, which are designated accounts, are operated in the owner's own name by an account operator authorised by VPC.[56] Any changes to the account are registered directly in the VPC system. In the case of nominee accounts, which resembles omnibus accounts, a custodian holds the securities on behalf of the owner. The custodian must be authorised by VPC to act as a nominee.[57]

The VPC system encompasses both direct and indirect holdings. Securities registered on owner accounts are directly held, whereas securities registered on nominee accounts are indirectly held. Registrations on owner accounts give the account holders the 'legitimate capacity' as the owner of the securities on the account, even though the registrations lack constitutive effect and only evidence title to the securities.[58] A person registered as the owner has the right to dispose of the securities as

---

[53] <http://www.vpc.se> (accessed 20 April 2005).

[54] Some foreign securities registered in VPC are, however, immobilised, cf Chap. 4 Sects. 4–5 FIAA; and VPC Disclosure Framework (Dec. 2004) 5.

[55] <http://www.vpc.se> (accessed 9 June 2005).

[56] Ch. 3 FIAA.

[57] Ch. 3 §7 FIAA.

[58] cf Ch. 6 §1 FIAA. The same applies to security interests, Ch. 6 §7 FIAA. See also Afrell and Wallin-Norman 279.

long as the disposal does not interfere with the limitations set forth in the account. As for nominee accounts, the owner's holdings are registered in the books of the custodian, who keeps an account with VPC (cf above).[59] In other words, it is the custodian who is registered as the holder on the account with VPC and who is presumed to have the right to dispose of the securities.[60] The custodian is required to keep its own holdings separated from its customers' holdings but can commingle the customers' securities in the nominee account.[61] It should also be pointed out that the owner of securities has a right to have the securities registered on an owner account in its own name.[62]

Securities held on nominee accounts can belong to different owners. Thus, it is possible for the account holder to mix the securities and hold them on an unallocated basis. However, also in relation to securities held on owner accounts, the securities are held on a fungible basis. The International Securities Identification Number (ISIN) assigned by VPC that identifies securities does so only in relation to name, type and series of the securities. Even if the securities are registered on an owner account they do not exist on the account and as such cannot be located or otherwise identified. The conclusion can therefore be made that securities held in the Swedish VPC system are held on a fungible basis although the structure of the system allows securities to be registered on different accounts.[63]

Since registrations of securities in the VPC system lack constitutive effect and securities are held on a fungible basis the question of the nature of investors' rights is uncertain. The main problem is, however, that the Financial Instruments Accounts Act (1998:1479)(FIAA) only covers holdings of securities in the VPC system. This means that the legal effect of securities held on custody accounts outside the VPC system is unregulated.[64]

3.3.2 United Kingdom

The settlement operations in the United Kingdom have been centralised in recent years. In 1999, the responsibility for the settlement of UK government debt securities, gilts, and money market instruments were transferred from the Central Gilts Office and the Central Moneymarkets Office of the Bank of England, to

[59] Registration of the ultimate owner (or collateral-taker) is thus only made in the books of the custodian. cf Prop 1997/98:160 118. In Prop 1997/98:160 it is pointed out that the system with nominee registration is of great practical importance as it implies that double registrations are avoided, the number of registrations in the VPC system is reduced and custody arrangements are made simpler.

[60] cf Ch. 3 §10 FIAA; Prop. 1997/98:160 118; Afrell and Wallin-Norman 279.

[61] cf Afrell and Wallin-Norman 279.

[62] cf Afrell and Wallin-Norman 278 f.

[63] VPC, 'Disclosure Framework' (December. 2004) 5.

[64] Afrell and Wallin-Norman 280; cf Prop 2004/05:30 89, 93.

CRESTCo.[65] CRESTCo (or Euroclear UK & Ireland as it is called today) is the CSD for United Kingdom and Ireland and operates the CREST system. It settles UK, Irish and international securities and money market instruments.[66] In September 2002, CRESTCo Ltd was acquired by Euroclear.[67] As of 1 July 2007, CRESTCo Ltd has changed its legal and operating name to Euroclear UK & Ireland Ltd.

Euroclear UK & Ireland provides settlement services and a variety of other services, including collateral, stock lending, tax and stamp duty services and transaction reporting to the UK and Irish regulators. It also offers corporate actions such as proxy voting, income and redemptions, issuer and new issues services. Generally, Euroclear UK & Ireland does not act as a custodian or holder for UK and Irish securities but rather facilitates the holding and transfer of securities through the CREST system.[68]

Participants can be direct members of CREST, act through a sponsored member, or through a nominee or custodian.[69] A direct member has one or several accounts registered in its name which records the number of securities held by the member.[70] Likewise, a sponsored member has the securities registered in its name.[71] Where the participant acts through a nominee or a custodian, it is normally the latter that is registered on the CREST register.[72]

Custodians can register the securities in CREST (1) without client designation in a commingled account; (2) with a particular client designation on a designated accounts; or (3) in the client's name through a sponsored membership. An investor who is a sponsored member has its name on the CREST register but it is the custodian who manages the account. On a designated account, the name of the client is not revealed. It is, however, common to hold securities through a custodian in a commingled client account, i.e. where securities of different investors are mixed. The different alternatives of holding securities in CREST facilitates both direct and indirect holding.[73]

Securities held by Euroclear UK & Ireland are dematerialised and thus recorded in electronic form. Legal title is conferred by book entry on the relevant register of securities. The account is thus the client's root of title.[74] Even though CREST

---

[65] M Evans, 'Opportunities for Collateralisation: Recent and Prospective Developments in Settlement' (1999) 9 JIBFL 365.

[66] <http://www.euroclear.com> (accessed 14 April 2005).

[67] The Euroclear settlement system is operated by the parent company of the Euroclear group, Euroclear Bank SA/NV, which is based in Brussels, Belgium. The Euroclear group offers settlement services for domestic and international securities transactions in more than 80 countries, <http://www.euroclear.com> (accessed 14 April 2005).

[68] CREST White Book 'The International Legal Framework' (July 2001) 1.

[69] CREST White Book 'The Domestic Legal Framework' (March 2002) 5; see also Euroclear, 'Delivering Low-cost Cross-border Settlement' (January 2003) 4.

[70] CREST White Book 'The Domestic Legal Framework' (March 2002) 5.

[71] Benjamin and Yates 175.

[72] CREST White Book 'The Domestic Legal Framework' (March 2002) 5.

[73] Benjamin 207 f.

[74] Legal Certainty Group Comparative Survey 4.25.

facilitates the delivery of collateral, for instance through so-called escrow accounts, security interests are not created in the CREST system but take place outside the system.[75]

As mentioned, several of CREST's members act as nominees or custodians on behalf of investors. It is therefore their name and not the name of the investor that appear on the register. The investor is, accordingly, not the legal but the beneficial owner.[76] The title of the account must however make it clear that the assets belong to a client. Moreover, the nominee or custodian must make sure to segregate the client's assets from its own assets.[77]

The root of title in unallocated and intermediated securities is the book entry on the intermediary's accounts. As for securities held in CREST and in relation to CREST members, the Uncertificated Securities Regulations 2001 (SI No 3755) (as amended) establishes the CREST records as the register of title for UK uncertificated securities.[78] The register does not have constitutive effect but only evidences title.[79]

Securities held by an intermediary are generally held on trust for its clients provided that a valid trust is established. In the absence of an effective trust arrangement, the beneficial title of the clients may be at risk.[80]

In the 1990s the question whether fungible securities held on an unallocated basis could constitute a trust was widely discussed.[81] The uncertainty, which was referred to as the allocation question, concerned whether the requirement of certainty of subject matter to establish a valid trust was met. This question is of particular importance since if the trust is not valid, the client only has a contractual right in the custodian's insolvency. Following recent case law,[82] the general view appears to be that securities held in a fungible bulk constitutes co-ownership rights, or in the case of security a co-security interest, under a trust relationship and therefore can be ascertained against other creditors as long as they are separated from the intermediary's assets.[83] The requirement for certainty of subject matter is upheld on the basis that the custodian holds all clients' securities together on a global trust.

---

75 Benjamin and Yates 186.

76 CREST White Book, 'The Domestic Legal Framework' (March 2002) 4–5; cf Sect. 5.2.2.

77 cf FSA's Handbook, CASS 2.2.5 and CASS 6.

78 The Uncertificated Securities Regulations 2001 (SI 2001/3755) have been amended by the Uncertificated Securities (Amendment) (Eligible Debt Securities) Regulations 2003. The Uncertificated Securities Regulations 2001 (SI 2001/3755) replaced the Uncertificated Securities 1995, (SI 1995/3272), as amended by the Uncertificated Securities (Amendment) Regulations 2000 (SI 2000/1682).

79 Legal Certainty Group Comparative Survey 4.25.

80 J Benjamin and M Yates, *The Law of Global Custody* (2nd edn Butterworths 2002) 174.

81 *ibid*, 25 ff.

82 Hunter v Moss [1993] 1 WLR 934; [1994] 1 WLR 452.

83 J Benjamin and M Yates, *The Law of Global Custody* (2nd edn Butterworths 2002) 27 ff; R Goode 'Property Rights in Commercial Assets: Rethinking Concepts and Policies' in R Goode, *Commercial Law in the New Millennium* (Sweet & Maxwell London 1998) 78; J Benjamin, *Interest in Securities* 58–59.

The classification of the custodian-client relationship as a trust affects the client's rights against the custodian. As the assets only take effect in equity, it is not possible to acquire legal interests in them. This is because equitable interests only are recognized by equity and not by common law.[84] The classification also affects the rights of the client against third parties, since equitable interests have to yield for legal interests when competing.[85] Accordingly, computerisation has the effect of minimising the protection of the client.

Another consequence of the re-classification of the client-custodian relationship is that a trustee is subject to a higher level of fiduciary duties towards the client. Custodians who do not want to undertake these obligations need to be very careful when drafting the documentation.[86]

Where the relationship between the custodian and its client is set up as a trust, CREST will not recognise the trust in relation to the client.[87] Furthermore, CREST does not assist any clients in a dispute or claim against its custodian.[88]

Similarly to the Swedish VPC system, securities held in CREST are given an ISIN number, which assists in the identification of the transferred securities. As in Sweden, the ISIN number identifies the type of securities, not the individual securities as such.[89] The CREST system thus operates on the basis that the securities settled in the system are fungible.[90]

3.3.3 United States

In the United States clearing, custody and settlement services are mainly provided by the subsidiaries of the US ICSD – the Depository Trust and Clearing Company (DTCC) . The subsidiary, Depository Trust Company (DTC) , is the largest CSD in the world and provides custody and asset management for over two million securities issues.[91] Most securities held in DTC's custody service, which include most

---

[84] J Benjamin and M Yates, *The Law of Global Custody* (2nd edn Butterworths 2002) 42–43.

[85] *ibid*, 250.

[86] *ibid*, 26–27.

[87] *ibid*, 174–175.

[88] *ibid*.

[89] cf s 182(2) of the Companies Act 1985 which provides that each share certificate shall be numbered unless all the issued shares in a company or all the issued shares in it of a particular class are fully paid up and rank *pari passu* for all purposes. Certificates of shares quoted on the London Stock Exchange and settled through CREST are, however, unnumbered as the system operates on the basis that shares are fungible, Ooi 47 n 20.

[90] Ooi 47 n 20.

[91] <http://www.dtcc.com> (accessed 23 April 2005).

corporate securities and commercial paper, are immobilised.[92] DTC is, however, increasingly moving towards a completely paperless environment. The services provided by DTC include tax and corporate action services such as income distribution and proxy voting.

Transfers and holdings of securities in the DTC system are regulated by Art. 8 of the New York Uniform Commercial Code (NY UCC). Investors who hold their securities through DTC can choose to hold them either directly or indirectly.[93] The question of the nature of the investor's rights has been elegantly solved through the concept of securities entitlements. Art. 8–5 NY UCC, which regulates indirectly held securities, is based on the notion of security entitlements as a *sui generis* interest representing both personal and property rights in the underlying pool of assets.

A person acquires a security entitlement if a securities intermediary indicates by book entry that a financial asset has been credited to that person's securities account. A person can also acquire a security entitlement if the securities intermediary receives a financial asset from the person or acquires a financial asset for the person and, in either case, accepts it for credit to the person's securities account.[94] Moreover, a person is entitled to a security entitlement if the intermediary becomes obligated under other law, regulation or rule to credit a financial asset to the person's securities account.[95] This means that the registration merely evidences the entitlement.[96]

Under NY UCC 8–501(d), if a financial asset is registered in the name of an investor and has not been indorsed to the securities intermediary or in blank, the investor is treated as holding the financial asset directly rather than as having a securities entitlement with respect to the underlying asset through the intermediary. A securities entitlement is protected in the insolvency of the intermediary and is only enforceable in relation to the intermediary with whom the investor has a direct relationship.[97]

US securities are commonly identified by a CUSIP number, CUSIP International Numbering System (CISN) or an ISIN number. As in the United Kingdom and Sweden, these numbering standards do not identify the individual securities as such.[98] Immobilised and dematerialised securities are thus held on a fungible basis.

---

[92] CPSS, 'Payment and Settlement Systems in Selected Countries: International Payment Arrangements' (April 2003) 449. The Federal Reserve Banks act as CSD for all marketable US Treasury securities, federal agency securities and some mortgage-backed securities.

[93] See further Sect. 7.2.3.

[94] NYUCC 8–501(b)(2).

[95] NYUCC 8–501(b)(3).

[96] cf NY UCC 8–501.

[97] cf NY UCC 8–503; See further Chap. 7. See also R D Guynn, 'Modernizing Securities Ownership Transfer and Pledging Laws: A Discussion Paper on the Need for International Harmonization' (Capital Markets Forum, International Bar Association 1996) 46.

[98] <http://www.cusip.com> (accessed 23 April, 2005).

3.4 Summary and Conclusions

This Chapter has shown that a vast number of changes have taken place in the securities markets over the past 30 years. It has examined the transformation of the securities holding and settlement systems with dematerialisation and immobilisation, the indirect holding structures with increased intermediation, the practices of holding securities on a fungible and unallocated basis in relation to their entitlement holders and the structures of the holding and settlement systems in Sweden, the United Kingdom and the United States.

Even though the holding and settlement structures vary, the examination shows that in all three jurisdictions, common practice is to hold book-entry securities in fungible form, i.e. unidentifiable in relation to their entitlement holders. Even if different degrees of separation can be created through segregation on designated accounts, the securities identification numbers (ISIN or CUSIP) provided to different types and series of securities do not identify individual securities as such. Thus, even if the securities are registered on a designated account they do not exist on the account and cannot be located or otherwise identified. It should also be noted that all in three jurisdictions it is possible to hold securities on both a direct and indirect basis.

The reason for the changes in the securities markets that have taken place, including computerisation and the holding of securities on an unallocated and intermediated basis, is foremost increased efficiency in terms of costs and time. Thus, ultimately, the underlying motive has been to enhance returns.

Chapter 4
The Use of Collateral in the Securities Markets

"Concerns about an increasing scarcity of low-risk, liquid collateral have been based on the expectation that demands for collateral would continue to expand faster than the stock of preferred forms of collateral. [...] At present, however, market participants interviewed for this study found little evidence of scarcity, although they noted the rapid current and prospective growth of collateral needed to support payment and settlement activities, including access to intraday credit and new clearance and settlement mechanisms in some markets."[1]

4.1 Introduction

During the last decade we have seen a significant growth in the use of collateral in the wholesale financial markets. Collateral is increasingly used in lending, securities and OTC derivatives trading and in payment and settlement systems to mitigate credit risk.[2] At the end of 2006, the amount of collateral used in privately negotiated derivatives transactions and related margin activities alone was estimated to be approximately USD1.335 trillions.[3] Similarly, the repo market has been growing rapidly over last couple of years. To give one example, in December 2005 the EU repo market had a total value of EUR5.883 billion, compared to a total value of EUR1,863 billion in June 2001.[4] Another trend is the increasing use of complex and innovative products for the transfer of credit risk such as credit default swaps (CDS) and collateralised debt obligations (CDO). This Chapter examines the use of financial collateral in the securities markets, with particular emphasis on reuse of financial collateral. Other risk management techniques are also discussed.

4.2 The Use of Collateral

The use of collateral has become one of the most widespread risk mitigation techniques in the wholesale financial markets. Collateral is most common in the derivatives markets, securities and payment clearing and settlement, and in repo and

[1] CGFS Report 2.

[2] CGFS Report; and CPSS and the Euro-currency Standing Committee of the Central Banks of the Group of Ten Countries, 'OTC Derivatives: Settlement Procedures and Counter Party Risk Management' (CPSS Publications No 27) (September 1998).

[3] ISDA Margin Survey 2007 4.

[4] European Commission, 'Evaluation report on the Financial Collateral Arrangements Directive (2002/47/EC)' (20 December 2006) COM (2006) 833 final 4.

E. Johansson, *Property Rights in Investment Securities and the Doctrine of Specificity,*

© Springer-Verlag Berlin Heidelberg 2009

securities lending transactions.[5] Generally, central banks also require collateral in their lending practices.[6]

There are different theories as to why market participants choose to take security. Besides the reduction of credit risk, collateral is deemed to give the creditor control over the debtor, which prohibits the debtor from taking excessive risk or misusing its assets. Security also functions as a substitute for an assessment of the creditworthiness and the monitoring of the collateral-provider. Another theory is that security leads to an increase in lending as some creditors would not lend at all if collateral was not provided.[7]

Four main reasons have been identified as the source of increased collateralisation in the wholesale financial markets. Firstly, the growth of trading has lead to increased exposure to risk, which has prompted risk mitigation in the cash and derivatives markets. The growth of trading has also lead to an expansion of payment and securities settlement. Secondly, this growth has lead to a broader range of participants in the markets. Thirdly, new techniques have been introduced to manage payment and settlement risks, and, finally, following the Asian financial crises in the 1990s and especially the turbulence in 1998 with the default of Russia and the failure of the hedge fund Long Term Capital Management (LTCM), market participants have become increasingly sensitive to risk.[8]

The ISDA Margin Survey 2004 confirms that as to the privately negotiated derivatives market, credit risk reduction is the most important reason for using collateral. The second most important reason is to free up credit lines. Large firms place importance on the regulatory capital reduction involved in the taking of collateral.[9] Other reasons for using collateral are access to more complex or higher risk trades, that it is a requirement by the counterparty and increased competitiveness, i.e. the possibility to reduce the price of credit by taking collateral.[10]

Collateral, however, does not only reduce credit risk but also creates new risks such as legal, liquidity, custody and operational risk.[11] Collateral should therefore not be used as a substitute but rather as a complement to credit analysis.[12]

---

[5] cf Harding and Johnson 67, who notes that collateral is used in Euroclear and in the Target Euro Payment systems.

[6] CGFS Report 2.

[7] CGFS Report 18. The question whether collateral should be promoted is very complex and involves different theories and arguments for and against, cf HW Flesig, 'Economic Functions of Security in a Market Economy' in JJ Norton and M Andenas (eds.), *Emerging Financial Markets and Secured Transactions* (Kluwer Law International 1998) 15. For the purpose of this study it is deemed sufficient to recognise that the use of collateral is an established practice in most economies of the world.

[8] CGFS Report 6.

[9] Benjamin and Yates 37.

[10] ISDA Margin Survey 2004 2 and 13.

[11] 2005 ISDA Collateral Guidelines iv.

[12] Benjamin and Yates 37–38, who argues that this is the most important lesson to be drawn from the near collapse of LTCM in 1998.

Usually cash, G7 government securities or sovereign debt is used as collateral.[13] Due to the increased use of collateral, some market participants have started to diversify their portfolios to include cash in currencies where they make markets (i.e. other than US dollar, euro or sterling), government securities other than those from the G7 countries, US government agency securities, mortgage-backed securities, corporate bonds, commercial papers, letters of credit, financial guarantees, and equities.[14]

There are two principal legal methods to set up a collateral arrangement: either through the extension of a security interest or through the transfer of title. Both techniques achieve the economic effect of security. In relation to reuse of financial collateral, they are represented by repledges and the use of repos, respectively.

4.2.1 Repos and Securities Lending

The repo and securities lending markets have grown significantly since the 1980s.[15] Repo transactions are often used as a means of raising finance. They are also often used as an instrument of monetary policy by central banks to supply or absorb liquidity and to adjust volatility. Other motives for using repos and securities loans are to cover short positions, facilitate settlement and for hedging and arbitrage purposes.[16] Both repos and securities loans are, typically, privately negotiated agreements, i.e. traded outside trading systems.[17]

Even though repos and securities lending on the surface appear to be different, they have many similarities. Both types of transactions can be used as, and have the economic effect of, security.[18] In this respect, the term securities lending is somewhat misleading as the transaction, similarly to a repo transaction, normally does not involve a loan but an outright transfer with an obligation to retransfer securities of the same type at a specified date and price in the future.[19] Thus, the obligation to retransfer securities does not concern the same securities but rather the equivalent securities. Another transaction similar to repos and securities loans is the sale and

---

[13] 2005 ISDA Collateral Guidelines 53. cf ISDA Margin Survey 2006 2 where it is noted that cash is the most commonly used type of collateral making up over 75 per cent of collateral. The only other assets that come close to cash are US and eurozone government securities.

[14] Harding and Johnson 67. See also 2005 ISDA Collateral Guidelines 53.

[15] CGFS Report 7. In the US, outstanding repos and reverse repos of securities dealers grew by an average of 13.5 per cent per year during the second half of the 1990s, amounting to USD2,500 billion by mid-2000. This should be compared with the survey conducted by ISMA, which shows that the repo market has grown by 16 per cent since June 2001 amounting to EUR 3,305 billion in September 2002.

[16] Giovannini Repo Report 3; CGFS Report 14; and Benjamin 139.

[17] CPSS/IOSCO, 'Securities Lending Transactions: Market Developments and Implications' (CPSS Publication No 32) (July 1999).

[18] cf Benjamin 141, who notes that traditionally, repos served as a source to raise finance whereas securities loans often were used to cover a short position in securities.

[19] CRESTCo, 'A Guide to Stock Lending and Collateral Transfers in CREST' (October 2000) 2.

buy back transaction.[20] Broadly, the three types of transactions resemble a temporary exchange of cash for securities.[21]

Intermediaries benefit from the use of repos by being able to borrow or lend securities or by charging fees for arranging repo transactions between its customers and other parties. Investors benefit by being able to use their assets more efficiently and to increase returns.[22]

Although the price, i.e. the interest, is structured differently under a repo and a sell and buy back arrangement, the commercial objective of the two transactions is more or less the same. They are driven by the need of the collateral-provider to raise funds and the need of the collateral-taker to effectively use its assets to be more profitable. The securities are provided against a purchase price and an additional price, which represent the interest for the loan. In the case of sell and buy backs, the purchase and additional price are usually included in one single forward price.

In a stock lending arrangement, the collateral-taker usually borrow the securities to cover a short position, whereas the collateral-provider makes effective use of its securities by lending them against a fee. The ownership of the securities is transferred with an obligation to retransfer the equivalent securities. The only money consideration involved is the fee that the securities are borrowed against.[23]

Title transfer structures are also often used in margin lending transactions. 'Margin lending' usually denotes the practice where an investor borrows against existing securities, managed funds or cash as collateral.

4.2.2 OTC Derivatives Markets

Between 1998 and 2004, the privately negotiated derivatives markets grew from approximately USD50 trillion to USD164 trillion.[24] At the end of June 2007, the notional amount of OTC derivatives stood at USD 516 trillion and their gross market value, which measures the cost of replacing all existing contracts, amounted to USD 11 trillion.[25] This speedy growth makes them the most flourishing and dynamic markets of our time. However, at the time of writing, the derivatives markets are suffering from breakdown in confidence. Due to the credit crisis, the spreads of credit default swaps (i.e. the price) has widened considerably and trading has become thin and volatile.[26] The turbulence in the credit derivatives markets is also having a significant impact on the wider financial system.[27]

---

[20] CRESTCo, 'A Guide to Stock Lending and Collateral Transfers in CREST' (October 2000) 4.

[21] CGFS Report 6 n 3.

[22] Austen-Peters 18.

[23] Goode 218–219.

[24] 2005 ISDA Collateral Guidelines 21.

[25] BIS, 'Triennial Central Bank Survey: Foreign exchange and derivatives market activity in 2007' (December 2007) 21–22.

[26] Financial Times (12 March 2008).

[27] cf Sects. 3.1-2.

The main technique for managing credit exposures in the OTC derivatives market is close-out netting, even though the use of collateral has increased vastly in recent years.[28] At the end of 2006, about 59% of the derivatives transactions were estimated to be secured by collateral arrangements. In comparison with other products, credit derivatives have the highest coverage.[29]

The use of collateral is especially relevant in derivatives transactions as the parties' obligations are set out to take place at some point in the future. The parties are therefore exposed to a greater degree of credit risk than what is normally the case.

Most collateral arrangements in the OTC derivatives markets are two-way, i.e. both parties extend security. This is because both parties are exposed to a certain degree of risk. In the case of a swap, the cashflows that will be exchanged at different stages of the transaction are unclear to both parties at the commencement of it. The parties may therefore choose to collateralise their exposures.

4.2.3 Clearing and Settlement

Collateral is also widely used in payment, clearing and settlement systems. It is mainly used to mitigate settlement risk, i.e. the risk that the cash or the securities are not fully delivered, but also to enhance liquidity.[30] In many clearing and settlement systems collateral is provided against intraday credit.[31]

Clearing is the process that precedes settlement. It involves the establishment of the parties' obligations, often into one single net amount, and the process of checking that securities, cash or both are available.[32] Settlement is the process whereby a transaction in securities is completed, often by delivery of securities against payment but also in terms of a free-of-payment delivery of securities or delivery of cash only.[33] Settlement takes place in a settlement system whereas payment of funds in most cases is effected in a payment system.[34] When settlement is made of securities evidenced in book-entry form, the transferor's and the transferee's accounts are debited and credited respectively.

---

[28] CPSS and the Euro-Currency Standing Committee of the Central Banks of the Group of Ten Countries, 'OTC Derivatives: Settlement Procedures and Counterparty Risk Management' ((CPSS Publications No 32) September 1998) 21–22.

[29] 2005 ISDA Collateral Guidelines 9; and ISDA Margin Survey2007 4.

[30] CGFS Report 34.

[31] CGFS Report 8.

[32] cf J Benjamin, 'Overview of Post-trade Infrastructure, Part 1' (2003) 4 JIBFL 128; and European Commission, 'EU Clearing and Settlement CESAME Group: Report on Definitions' (24 October 2005) 7.

[33] European Commission, 'EU Clearing and Settlement CESAME Group: Report on Definitions' (24 October 2005) 10.

[34] Giovanni Group, 'Cross-Border Clearing and Settlement Arrangements in the European Union (November 2001) 5–6.

'Matching' is the process which involves finding instructions where the key transaction and settlement details, including the identities of the parties, type of securities, quantity of the securities, payment, and settlement date, are met. After the instructions have been matched, they are locked until settlement takes place.[35]

One of the most important elements in limiting the credit risks is the use of well capitalised clearing houses, or Central Counterparties (CCP) as they also are called. A CCP interposes itself between every buyer and seller in order to assume their rights and obligations, i.e. it takes over all parties' credit risks and reduces them through netting to a single amount. The CCP thus facilitates netting on a multilateral basis.[36] To cover the exposure that the CCP takes on, participants are often required to extend collateral. They post collateral as margin against the positions held with the CCP to protect it from market movements and credit risk. Usually an initial margin is deposited with an additional intraday variation margin, which reflects movements in the prices over the day.

Another technique which limits credit risk is Delivery versus Payment (DVP). DVP is the simultaneous exchange of securities and cash to settle a transaction.[37] By minimising the time between the trade and the delivery of the securities against cash, the settlement risk, i.e. the risk that the party that has delivered its undertaking takes in relation to the counterparty's failure to discharge its deliveries, is curbed. Many settlement systems have today reached the aim of executing DVP three business days following the trade date (T + 3).[38]

There are also other techniques to mitigate risk in relation to clearing and settlement, for instance Real Time Gross Settlement (RTGS). RTGS settles inter-bank funds transfers throughout the processing day on a continuous, transaction-by-transaction basis.[39] Collateral is widely used in relation to intraday credit in RTGS systems, which require a high level of liquidity.[40]

Another risk mitigating technique is loss sharing rules, which allocate credit losses among surviving members upon default by one member.[41]

4.3 Risk Management Practices

Collateral is foremost used to manage credit risk. The credit risk is reduced through the right of recourse to the collateral. Collateral does, however, increase other risks such as liquidity, market price, operational and legal risks. It therefore requires

[35] CREST White Book, 'The Domestic Legal Framework' (March 2002) 8.

[36] Giovannini Repo Report 16.

[37] G30, 'Clearance and Settlement Systems in the World's Securities Markets' (1989), Ch. 1; and BIS, 'Delivery Versus Payment in Securities Settlement Systems' (1992).

[38] cf Benjamin and Yates 149.

[39] CPSS, 'Real-Time Gross Settlement Systems' (March 1997) 3.

[40] CGFS Report 6.

[41] cf Remarks by Governor Edward W Kelley Jr, Clearinghouses and Risk Management at the 1996 Payments System Risk Conference, Washington, DC (3 December 1996).

continuous risk management by the collateral-taker. Together with other methods such as traditional credit analysis, set-off and close-out netting, securitisation, selective termination and credit derivatives, the use of collateral is one of the tools available to credit risk managers.[42]

4.3.1 Collateral Management

Management of collateral through collateral programmes is increasingly becoming more complex and includes elements such as monitoring and mark-to-market valuation of the collateral and the counterparty's exposures, calculation of initial margin, variation margin and haircuts and thresholds. It also involves determination of what types of assets are eligible as collateral, verification that the collateral has been received, payment of income on the collateral to the collateral-provider, substitution of collateral, margin calls and return of surplus collateral. Market participants may also need to deal with defaults and disputes.[43]

The terms 'collateral' and 'margin' are used interchangeably and denotes the assets posted by the collateral-provider to the collateral-taker as security. They are normally used both when the transaction is structured as a security interest and a title transfer arrangement.[44] Initial margin is posted at the commencement of the transaction or relationship. Due to the fact that the value of the exposure of the collateral fluctuates, top-up or variation margin (i.e. additional collateral), may be required. 'Margin calls' is the process by which the collateral-taker requires initial or additional collateral,[45] and 'mark-to-market' the process by which the book or collateral value of a financial instrument is adjusted to reflect current market value. Usually the parties agree on a certain credit threshold that has to be met before the collateral-provider is obliged to extend security.

Haircuts are designed to cover losses in a decline of the value of the collateral as well as costs likely to be incurred in liquidating the assets, for instance taxes and commissions.[46] Usually market participants assign less than the market value to the collateral to account for any possible decline and to provide a cushion. The discount, typically calculated in terms of per cent, is the haircut.[47]

Collateral management involves the valuation of the collateralised position, which can include small changes such as accrual of interests to big fluctuations

---

[42] 2005 ISDA Collateral Guidelines iv.

[43] Harding and Johnson 12–13.

[44] ISDA Margin Survey2004, Appendix 3, 18.

[45] ISDA Margin Survey 2004, Appendix 3, 19.

[46] 2005 ISDA Collateral Guidelines 21.

[47] ISDA Margin Survey 2004, Appendix 3, 19.

of the collateralised positions, and the valuation of the collateral.[48] The collateral, including the margin and the haircut, is intended to cover the potential exposure, and is especially required in markets where the positions change rapidly, for instance in the derivatives markets.[49]

Price volatility of the collateral can, depending on the type of collateral posted, be severe, especially in periods of market stress. Should the value of the collateral go down the collateral-provider is usually required to post additional margin. The exposure is affected by the value of the collateral and the underlying position but can also be affected by correlations of price movements in the collateralised position and the collateral as well as correlations between the creditworthiness of the collateral-provider and the value of the collateral.[50] The exposure can moreover be affected by the exposure period, i.e. the time it takes from the change of the value in the underlying position to the corresponding verification of the posting of margin or liquidation of the collateralised position.[51]

Collateral managers often seek to use collateral that increases in value or that moves in line with the underlying position. Assets like government bonds and cash are deemed to be suitable as the value of these assets is often uncorrelated with the movement of the underlying position and the creditworthiness of the collateral-provider. Cash and government securities from G7 countries are moreover preferred during stress periods as they entail less risk and are highly liquid. A broadening in the range of assets used as collateral to include assets such as corporate bonds and equity often means that it is more difficult to assess the exposure due to the price volatility and the low liquidity that may be involved.[52]

The risks involved in collateral management were revealed in the financial markets events that followed the default by Russia and the large losses of the hedge fund LTCM in the autumn of 1998. The Committee on the Global Financial System (CGFS) has described the outcome as a global flight to liquidity, spurred by a global "margin call":[53]

> "Some of the positions affected were leveraged through collateralised financing arrangements, including securities lending, repurchase agreements and margin accounts at future exchanges, which required positions to be marked to market daily. Many financial market participants incurred losses, reduced the scale of their operations and trimmed their risk exposures, in response to pressures from increasingly cautious counterparties and their own need to preserve capital in an environment of heightened uncertainty and reduced tolerance for bearing risk. At the same time, collateral requirements were increased in many parts of the markets because of heightened concerns about counterparty credit risks.

---

48 As indicated, the collateral is often specified in relation to a certain value. As this book shows this may cause severe problems in relation to the requirement for identification of the collateral under the traditional property law analysis, cf Sect. 6.4.4 and Chap. 9.

49 CGFS Report 21–22.

50 CGFS Report 21.

51 CGFS Report 22.

52 CGFS Report 23.

53 CGFS Report 27; and CGFS, 'A Review of Financial Market Events in Autumn 1998' (October 1999).

> As a result of these and other factors, liquidity in many markets declined sharply, with bid-ask spreads widening and large transactions becoming more difficult to complete. Demand for the most liquid benchmark securities was further increased by the need for certain market participants to provide top-quality collateral as well as by investors stepping in to benefit from an expected further decline in bond yields in the light of ongoing concern about global deflation."[54]

CGFS points out three shortcomings in relation to collateralisation that added to the severity of the 1998 crisis. First of all, collateralisation facilitated the leveraging of positions in the run-up to the crisis. Secondly, market participants relied too heavily on collateral and risk mitigation techniques and overlooked the possibilities of swift volatility in market prices, which eventually led to a tightening in collateral standards and a drain of liquidity. Thirdly, concentrations of the activities in the markets accentuated the spread of the crisis across the markets.[55]

In the current credit crisis, market participants have seen a move from unsecured lending to an increase in collateralisation of positions. Closer attention is also being paid to the type of collateral delivered and received.[56] Over the course of the crisis, the value of highly-rated assets has fallen which has lead to a dramatic widening of haircuts and an increase of margin calls. Due to market participants' unwillingness to lend to each other, many have been forced to sell assets with prices falling even further.

As a response to the lack of liquidity in the market, the Federal Reserve Board is lending primary dealers treasury securities against other securities, including federal agency debt, federal agency residential-mortgage-backed securities (RMBS), and non-agency AAA/Aaa-rated private-label RMBS as collateral for a term of 28 days.[57] The ECB has taken similar measures. The intention is to promote liquidity in the financial markets. Whether it will have the desired effect remains, however, to be seen. Many expect the turmoil in the markets to go on for much longer than the crisis in 1998.

4.3.2 Other Methods of Mitigating Credit Risk

Other methods that are available for managing credit risk include set-off and close-out netting, the use of creditworthy and well capitalised custodians and counterparties, traditional credit analysis including sound due diligence and selective termination, and close management of existing collateral programmes to minimise the risk of under- or over-collateralisation. Over-collateralisation can arise as a result from posting too much collateral, but also if the value of the collateral increases. It

---

54 CGFS Report 27.

55 CGFS Report 27–28.

56 www.thetradenews.com/1571 (accessed 25 February 2008).

57 http://www.federalreserve.gov/newsevents/press/monetary/20080311a.htm (as of 13 March 2008).

can also be caused by the payment of coupons or principals, which can lead to an increase in the value of a position.[58]

Another technique to mitigate credit risk is to transfer it to third parties. Through the use of securitisations, repackagings, credit derivatives, insurances, financial guarantees and letters of credit, the credit risk is passed on to or shared with, a third party.[59]

Collateralised Debt Obligations (CDO) has experienced a tremendous growth in recent years and was, until the sub-prime crisis hit the financial markets in the late summer of 2007, a fashionable method of transferring credit risk. A CDO typically involves the transfer of the credit risk related to a portfolio of reference entities and references obligations to a Special Purpose Vehicle (SPV), which issues notes bearing the credit risks of the underlying portfolio. The transferred credit risk of the underlying portfolio in a CDO is often "tranched", i.e. divided into different segments. Whereas equity tranches, or first-loss tranches as they also are called, are the first to absorb losses, senior and super-senior tranches involve less credit risk. The segments in between are referred to as mezzanine tranches.[60] A monoline insurer often guarantees the super-senior tranche.

The trend of using techniques involving third parties has led to an increased sharing of risk and a more efficient pricing of that risk.[61] However, as is clear from the current sub-prime crisis, while the use of insurers, credit derivatives, CDOs and financial guarantees not only make credit risk more manageable it also introduces new risks.[62]

Due to the sub-prime crisis, the CDO market has to a large degree derailed. The future use of CDOs and other similar securitisation techniques is therefore uncertain. Financial innovations such as CDOs, Constant Proportion Portfolio Insurances (CPPI)[63] and Constant Proportion Debt Obligations (CPDO) [64] have distributed the

[58] 2005 ISDA Collateral Guidelines 15.

[59] 2005 ISDA Collateral Guidelines 8. The credit derivatives industry has expanded tremendously over the last couple of years. ISDA notes that in 2004 the outstanding amount totalled USD5,440 billion. In 2006 the notional value of the CDS market increased by 46 per cent, BIS, 'Monetary and Economic Department: OTC Derivatives Market Activity in the First Half of 2006' (November 2006) 1.

[60] Joint Forum, 'Credit Risk Transfer' (October 2004).

[61] cf Remarks by Vice Chairman Roger W Ferguson Jr, The Federal Reserve Board, at the Bond Market Association's 1st Annual Credit and Risk Management Conference, New York, New York (16 October 2001).

[62] cf 2005 ISDA Collateral Guidelines 8; and Joint Forum, 'Credit Risk Transfer' (October 2004).

[63] A dynamic asset allocation strategy designed to protect the principal of the investment. The strategy rebalances the exposure to high-risk and low-risk assets in a synthetic or cash portfolio ("lev/de-lev strategy"), depending on its performance.

[64] A dynamic asset allocation strategy designed to generate a high return by taking leveraged exposures on credit indices such as CDX and iTraxx. By periodically rolling the indices the weakest credit in the portfolio is supposed to be disposed off. In contrast to a CPPI, a CPDO is not structured to protect the investor's income. When the net asset value of the portfolio decreases, the CPDO increases the risk until it either has a profit or has lost all of its money. If the CPDO is performing well, a "cash-in event" is usually triggered and all funds are invested in risk-free assets. Conversely, a "cash-out event" is triggered with the net asset value of the portfolio falls below a minimum

risks inherent in the underlying assets broadly without investors always appreciating the complexities and risks involved. As a result, the rating agencies have come under increased scrutiny for the high ratings given to these instruments and the monoline insurers have suffered significant losses due to the financial guarantees provided. Another effect is the current credit crunch, with the reduction of liquidity in the financial markets and a substantial increase in the cost of borrowing.

4.4 Reuse of Financial Collateral

The rapid growth of the use of collateral is deemed to have the potential of creating considerable liquidity pressures due to the practice of using high credit-rated assets such as G7 government securities and cash.[65] The growth has lead to concerns whether the practices have the potential of creating a shortage of low-risk liquid collateral, and, if such shortage materialises, how the markets would react, especially during stress periods.[66] Volatility in market prices can also produce requirements for additional collateral when the value of existing assets declines. With an increasing demand for new collateral, there follows an increasing demand to reuse current stocks of collateral in order to increase the liquidity of the markets and, ultimately, to increase returns.[67]

Increased liquidity and a more efficient use of collateral are two of the main arguments for introducing reuse of financial collateral under Art. 5 of the Financial Collateral Directive.[68] Art. 5 is also assumed to reduce volatility and enables investors to buy or sell securities more easily at a fairer price.[69]

As of March 2001, no signs of scarcities of collateral had emerged in the financial markets although it was noted that the growth of collateral and the use of collateral in payment and settlement systems did bear the potential for demand pressures in some markets.[70] In relation to the reuse of financial collateral, it should be noted that other studies claim that it is perfectly possible to reach the goal of liquid markets on the basis of outright transfer arrangements.[71] Moreover, it should be noted that due to the scarcity of highly liquid collateral such as cash and G7 government securities,

percentage of its initial value, cf E Parker, *Credit Derivatives: Documenting and Understanding Credit Derivative Products* (Globe Law and Business 2007) 137–140.

65 Cash is the most common type of collateral with approximately 72 per cent of the market share, whereas government securities, mostly US, are the second most common type of asset with approximately 16 per cent of the market share, ISDA Margin Survey 2003.

66 CGFS Report 2.

67 CGFS Report 12–13.

68 European Commission, 'Proposal for a Directive of the European Parliament and of the Council on Financial Collateral Arrangements' (27 March 2001) COM(2001) 168 final 2001/0086 (COD) 4–6.

69 ISDA EU Collateral Report 3.

70 CGFS Report 12–13; and UNIDROIT Report on a Right of Use.

71 UNIDROIT Report on a Right of Use 60.

some of the larger banks have expanded their eligible collateral to include cash in currencies where they make markets, government securities (often direct obligations of G10 countries), US government agency securities such as Fannie Mae or Freddie Mac debt securities, mortgage backed securities, corporate bonds and commercial papers, bank letters of credit, guarantees and equities.[72]

The underlying rationale behind a reuse of financial collateral is that it is an inexpensive source of financing.[73] The collateral is usually used to meet incoming collateral calls or is reinvested.[74]

ISDA reports that from 2003 to 2005 the reuse of financial collateral increased from 54 to 68%.[75] Whether this is due to the increased demand for collateral or the liberalisation of the legal rules introduced through the new EU regime is not clear.

4.4.1 Repledge

The term rehypothecation is used by market participants for the arrangement where A delivers assets as security to B who uses the same assets as security in a transaction with C. As the term has obtained different connotations – sometimes referring to repledge and sometimes including both repledge and outright transfer arrangements – it is avoided in this book.[76] Instead the term repledge is used to describe the case where the pledgee B uses the collateral as security for its own obligations in a separate transaction with a third party C subject to A's right to return of the property.

From a legal perspective, repledge differs from outright transfer in that the collateral-provider normally keeps the ownership rights in the asset. The equity of redemption gives the collateral-provider a right to redeem the collateral upon discharge of the underlying obligation.[77]

Under English law the collateral-provider's property rights include the equitable rules against 'clogs on the equity of redemption', 'collateral benefits', and the equitable maxim 'once a mortgage, always a mortgage'.[78] The equivalent rules in civil law jurisdictions have been said to be the duty of care, the non-allowance

[72] Harding and Johnson 67.

[73] Johnson (1997), 969.

[74] Harding and Johnson 23.

[75] ISDA Margin Survey 2004, 2. cf Harding and Johnson 11 who state that over 70 per cent of the financial institutions that participated in ISDA's Margin Survey 2001 reused the collateral they received, mostly to meet outgoing collateral requirements. About 60 per cent repoed securities collateral. See also ISDA Margin Survey 2005, 2, 6, where it is reported that 77 per cent of medium and large programs reuse collateral as a matter of policy. Among large programs, 18 out of 19 reuse collateral.

[76] ISDA EU Collateral Report 19; cf Johnson 1997), 951, who notes that rehypothecation is often used to denote the right to sell, pledge, rehypothecate, assign, invest, use, commingle, or otherwise dispose of posted collateral; and ISDA Margin Survey 2004, Appendix 3, 20.

[77] cf Sect. 5.3.1.

[78] Benjamin, 111–113. See also HM Treasury, 'Implementation of the Directive on Financial Collateral Arrangements' (July 2003).

of appropriation and the prohibition of repledging assets on more stringent conditions than under the original security agreement. These rules protect the ownership of the collateral-provider and guarantee that the interests of the parties are well-balanced.[79]

A repledge involves, as in the case of security interests generally, that the requirements in relation to the creation, perfection and enforcement of the security interest have to be complied with. These requirements often differ between different jurisdictions and can involve both time-consuming and cumbersome processes. In fast moving markets the requirements often impede an efficient use of the collateral. The parties may therefore choose to use an outright transfer structure. It should be pointed out, however, that many of these restrictions have been removed through the Financial Collateral Directive.[80]

In relation to accounting practices, the collateral-provider usually keeps the collateral repledged as an asset on its balance sheet and the secured obligation, for instance a margin loan, is recorded as a liability. The opposite applies to the collateral-taker; the collateral is normally booked as a liability whereas the loan is booked as an asset.

4.4.2 Repos

Sale and repurchase agreements, or so-called repos, are often treated as secured loans as they have the same economic effect as traditional security arrangements.[81] In contrast to a repledge where the ownership remains with the collateral-provider, repos and other title transfer agreements are structured so that the parties use the ownership terminology to secure the underlying obligation. The title to the collateral is transferred outright from A to B together with an option for A to re-acquire assets of the same kind. There is no obligation to return the same assets as were used as security and there are no limitations on B's ability to freely deal with the collateral since B is the owner of it. In other words, B has an unlimited right of disposal.

Although repledge and reuse through a title transfer arrangement are different types of transactions where the legal characteristic differs, they often fill the same function. The economic rational is to give assets to secure a loan. In a repo transaction the element of security is the transfer of ownership of the assets to the collateral-taker. In reality, the security for the collateral-taker consists of the possibilities to set off the value of the collateral against the underlying obligation upon default by the collateral-provider. The collateral-provider has an option to reacquire the equivalent assets, which shall be compared with the collateral-provider's equity of redemption in a security arrangement. The redelivery obligation is a personal right and not of proprietary character. Therefore, the collateral-provider's rights under a repo are weaker than under a traditional security structure.

---

[79] UNIDORIT Report on a Right of Use 51.

[80] See further Sect. 2.3.

[81] cf Goode 11 at n 64.

Even if repos involve the transfer of title of the collateral from the repo seller to the repo buyer, the repo seller usually retains the securities as assets on its balance sheet and includes the obligation to repay the underlying obligation as a liability. The opposite applies to the repo buyer; the secured claim is booked as an asset and the repos received as a liability.[82] These accounting practices reflect the fact that repos are used as security, i.e. that the intention of the parties is that the title should pass only temporarily. In certain jurisdiction, however, for tax purposes, repos are considered to involve a disposal, incurring capital gains or other tax liabilities.[83]

As previously mentioned, outright transfer structures are often preferred to repledge arrangements as they give market participants an increased freedom to deal freely with the collateral. In addition, mandatory rules on creation, perfection and enforcement of the security do not have to be complied with. The negative aspect of repos is that they may involve recharacterisation risk.[84] However, as the Financial Collateral Directive eliminates this risk, it has, as to those collateral arrangement covered by its scope, been removed.[85]

As mentioned, the element of security in a title transfer structure is embodied in the possibilities to net and set off the value of the collateral against the underlying obligation. Upon default by either party, a close out provision often converts the obligation to retransfer securities of the same kind into a money obligation, which is set off against the loan or purchase price.[86]

The different standard agreements used by market participants in relation to collateral arrangements and repos are drafted to facilitate close-out netting and set-off to the broadest extent. If default occurs, the agreements and their annexes and supplements are structured so that the obligations of the two parties are consolidated into one single net amount.[87] Different standard master agreements may also be tied together under one "master master" or "umbrella" agreement in order to facilitate cross-product netting between the net close-out positions under one or more master agreements.[88]

Close-out netting and set-off fill an important function in terms of creating efficient, deep and liquid financial markets and in limiting the risks and operational strains involved. Another effect of close-out netting is that the capital requirement for financial institutions is lowered.

---

[82] Giovannini Repo Report 16.

[83] K Tyson-Quah, 'Overview of International Securities Finance Markets' in K Tyson-Quah (ed.), *Special Report on Cross-Border Securities: Repo, Lending and Collateralisation* (Sweet & Maxwell 1997) 9.

[84] Recharacterisation risk is the risk that the courts look beyond the classification of the transaction made by the parties, Benjamin 130.

[85] cf Art. 6 Financial Collateral Directive.

[86] Goode 220.

[87] 2005 ISDA Collateral Guidelines 7.

[88] 2005 ISDA Collateral Guidelines 50.

4.5 Examples of Market Documentation

4.5.1 ISDA Credit Support Documentation

The most common market standard agreement for derivatives transactions is the ISDA Master Agreement. There are two main versions; the 1992 ISDA Master Agreement (Multicurrency – Cross Border) and the ISDA 2002 Master Agreement. There are also other market standard agreements under which derivatives transactions can be documented, for instance the German Rahmenvertrag, but these are not as widely used.

The most important aspect of the ISDA Master Agreement is probably that it, together with the Schedule and all Confirmations entered into under it, forms one single agreement. The Master Agreement is a pre-printed form and the parties make their elections in a Schedule attached to the Agreement. Each transaction entered into is documented in a Confirmation, which supplements, forms a part of, and is subject to, the ISDA Master Agreement. In the event of any inconsistency between the Master Agreement and a Confirmation, the Confirmation usually prevails.

Section 1(c) of the Master Agreement states that the parties intend that the Master Agreement and all Confirmations form a single agreement. This provision forms the basis for close-out netting under Section 6(e) of the ISDA Master Agreement. Upon the occurrence of an early termination date following an event of default or termination event, the value of all the terminated transactions is determined under the applicable method and together with any unpaid amounts reduced to a single net amount payable by one party to the other.

ISDA has produced a number of documents that can be used in collateral transactions. The ISDA Credit Support Annex, which is subject to English law, is based on a title transfer arrangement whereas the ISDA Credit Support Annex, which is subject to New York law, is based on a security interest created in the financial assets. All ISDA credit support documentation, apart from the English Credit Support Deed, takes the form of an annex or supplement to the ISDA Master Agreement.[89] Both ISDA Credit Support Annexes facilitate a reuse of collateral by the collateral-taker B as if it were the owner. This means that B can repledge or transfer the collateral outright.

The ISDA Credit Support Deed is structured so that the collateral-provider grants a security interest subject to English law. Paragraph 6(d) of the Deed explicitly prohibits reuse of collateral. It states that the collateral-taker is forbidden to sell, pledge, rehypothecate, assign, use, commingle or dispose of, or otherwise use in its business any collateral that it holds under the Deed.

Paragraph 6 of the Deed also provides that the collateral-taker shall exercise reasonable care to assure the safe custody of the posted collateral to the extent required by applicable law. The collateral-taker shall hold and at all times keep the collateral (other than cash) on a segregated account. There is no equivalent provision under

[89] 2005 ISDA Collateral Guidelines 34.

the English law Credit Support Annex. The collateral is transferred outright to the collateral-taker who becomes the owner of it.

Regardless of the choice of documentation, income distributions (i.e. dividends, interests, etc.) are usually passed on to the collateral-provider. This is due to the fact that, for economic purposes, the collateral-provider is considered to be the owner regardless of the structure of the transaction. In relation to notes and bonds, the value of the collateral may be reduced upon payment of income, which may lead to a collateral call, i.e. a demand for the collateral-provider to extend further collateral.[90]

Paragraph 5 of the English law Credit Support Annex provides that each party agrees that all rights, title and interests in and to any collateral are transferred outright free of any liens, claims, charges or encumbrances or any other interest of the transferring party or third party. Moreover, it provides that no security interest is created over the collateral transferred under the agreement. As the collateral is often registered in the name of the collateral-taker B, interests on notes and bonds and dividends on shares will be paid to it. However, as mentioned, usually such payments are passed on to the collateral-provider.[91] If the collateral-taker is reluctant to enter into such arrangement, for instance for tax reasons, the parties sometimes arrange for a substitution of collateral prior to the coupon payment date or payment of dividends.[92]

The most important provision in the English law Credit Support Annex is paragraph 6 which provides that if an early termination date is designated or deemed to occur as a result of an event of default in relation to a party, an amount equal to the value of the collateral that has been provided to the collateral-taker will be deemed to be an unpaid amount due to the collateral-provider for the purposes of Section 6(e) of the ISDA Master Agreement and included in the single net amount owed by one party to the other.

Under paragraph 2 of the New York law Credit Support Annex, the collateral-provider grants a security interest in, a lien on, and a right to set-off against all the collateral posted to the collateral-taker. Provided that the security interest is perfected, the collateral-taker has a valid security interest in the collateral.

Due to the vast statutory powers given under UCC Art. 9–207(c)(3) to repledge collateral (see Sect. 7.3.1), the differences between the English law and the New York law Credit Support Annexes are minimised. Under US law, the risk that the collateral-provider's claim after agreeing on a repledge right as the owner (or rather, not limiting the collateral-taker's statutory right to repledge) is transformed into a contractual claim if the collateral is no longer in the collateral-provider's possession, has been recognised.[93] The consequence is deemed to be that where the collateral-provider A has not yet paid the underlying obligation, the protection that is left

[90] Harding and Johnson 25.

[91] cf Harding and Johnson 99.

[92] *ibid.* At least in relation to English law, it is important that the substitution is subject to the collateral-taker's consent as the arrangement otherwise risks being recharacterised as a floating charge and as such rank after fixed charges.

[93] Harding and Johnson 56.

is the right to set-off a claim in relation to the value of the collateral against the underlying obligation.[94] In effect, both Annexes, in the event of default, rely on close-out netting and set-off. In the case of over-collateralisation, the collateral-provider is left with an unsecured claim to the extent that the collateral exceeds the value of the underlying obligation.

The 2001 ISDA Margin Provisions, incorporated through the 2001 Supplement, can be described as a modernised version of the Credit Support Annexes. Through a single document the contracting parties can select jurisdiction-specific provisions to apply to their margin arrangements, including New York law, English law and Japanese law. The Margin Provisions are not as widely used among market participants as the Credit Support Annexes.[95]

4.5.2 Repo Documentation

Market participants usually use one of the established market standard agreements in repo transactions, for instance the Master Repurchase Agreement (MRA) published by the Securities Industry and Financial Markets Association (SIFMA) or the Global Master Repurchase Agreement (GMRA), published jointly by SIFMA and the International Capital Market Association (ICMA).[96] The former agreement is used in the US markets whereas the latter is the standard repo agreement in the London markets.[97] Securities lending transactions are also often documented using market standard documentation such as the Master Securities Loan Agreement (MSLA), the Global Master Securities Lending Agreement (GMSLA) or the Overseas Securities Lending Agreement (OSLA). In Europe, the European Banking Federation's European Master Agreement for Financial Transactions (EMA) is often used. In addition, most jurisdictions have one or more domestic standard forms of master agreements for different types of financial transactions.[98]

As noted, the collateral arrangements involved in a repo or in a securities lending transaction are similar and generally involve an outright transfer of the underlying securities. Upon default the obligations are terminated, valued and netted against each other resulting in one single outstanding amount owed by one party to the other. Some securities lending agreements such as the Master Securities Loan Agreement, however, use a security interest approach.[99]

---

[94] Harding and Johnson 56.

[95] cf ISDA Margin Survey 2004 9; and 2005 ISDA Collateral Guidelines 37.

[96] 2005 ISDA Collateral Guidelines 35.

[97] Benjamin 139.

[98] 2005 ISDA Collateral Guidelines 35–36.

[99] *ibid.*

4.6 Summary and Conclusions

The use of collateral has become one of the most widespread risk mitigation techniques in the wholesale financial markets. This Chapter has examined the increased use of collateral and other risk management techniques. It has also looked into the practices of reusing financial collateral, both in relation to security interest and title transfer arrangements. The examination shows that the underlying reason for the increased reuse of financial collateral is that it increases liquidity, provides a more efficient use of the collateral and is an inexpensive source of financing.

The impact that the increased use of collateral could have on the financial markets is not yet certain. That the use of collateral can lead to increased liquidity, operational and a legal risk is clear. It is also clear that an increased use makes market participants more vulnerable to volatility.

Chapter 5
Property Rights in Securities and the Doctrine of Specificity under English Law

"Everybody knows that the story of the trust is the story of how an obligation was turned into a right of property"[1]

5.1 Introduction

Common practice in the financial markets is to allow the collateral-taker to reuse financial collateral as the owner in order to take advantage of market opportunities. This Chapter examines the reuse of financial collateral under English law, before and after the implementation of the Financial Collateral Directive. It also discusses substitutions, mixtures and the doctrine of specificity with particular emphasis on unallocated and intermediated securities.

5.2 Interests in Securities

5.2.1 Introduction to English Security Law

In English law, there are four general types of security: mortgage, charge, lien and pledge. A mortgage may be legal or equitable and involves a security transfer of bare title. Upon discharge of the secured obligation, the title is retransferred to the mortgagor. Except in the case of land, a charge is always equitable.

A charge differs from a mortgage in that it does not involve the transfer of title. Goode describes the incumbrance that constitutes the charge as '[..] a weight hanging on the asset which travels with it into the hands of third parties other than a bona fide purchaser of the legal title for value and without notice.'[2] A mortgage on the other hand involves a conveyance of either legal or equitable title, which is subject to the mortgagor's equity of redemption. Since a charge does not involve any transfer of title, the chargor is still the owner of the property and therefore does not have an

---

[1] L Smith, 'Property Transferred in Breach' in P Birks and A Pretto (eds.), *Breach of Trust* (Hart Publishing 2002) 134.

[2] Goode 36.

© Springer-Verlag Berlin Heidelberg 2009

equity of redemption in the asset.[3] Instead the chargor has a right to extinguish the encumbrance that is the charge.[4] Another important difference is that the mortgage gives the mortgagee a right of foreclosure, depending on court approval. Foreclosure vests the collateral in the mortgagee free from the equity of redemption. As the mortgagee takes the property in satisfaction, the mortgagor's debt is extinguished. In contrast to Swedish law, the mortgagee is not obligated to return any surplus that remains after the foreclosure. For this reason English courts are generally reluctant to make foreclosure orders.[5]

The mortgage, which involves a transfer by way of security, should also be distinguished from an outright transfer. In the case of a mortgage, the title is transferred but the collateral-provider keeps the equity of redemption, i.e. the right to redeem the collateral upon discharge of the underlying obligation. In contrast, an outright transfer is a transfer of the whole bundle of rights that the property consists of.

The significant difference between legal and equitable security interests is that, as a general rule, a legal interest takes priority even if it was created subsequent to the equitable interest, provided that the collateral-taker acquires the legal interest for value and without notice of the equitable interest.[6] Thus, a legal interest is stronger than an equitable interest. An equitable interest cannot exist independently from a legal interest. Hence, there will always be legal interest in the underlying asset.

Whereas common law cannot extend to security over future assets, this is in some cases possible in equity. Moreover, whereas several legal interests cannot exist in the same asset, this is possible for equitable interests.[7] The most significant development in equity is probably the development of the trust. Another important development is the floating charge.

The pledge is a common law form of security over chattels that is dependent on possession by the pledgee.[8] It is therefore only possible to create a pledge over tangibles and documents of title. Another effect is that it is a type of bailment.[9] Two different legal interests are said to exist in the case of pledge: the ownership vested in the pledgor, and the "special" property vested in the pledgee.[10] Usually the pledgee takes actual possession over the collateral but it is also possible for the collateral-taker to only have constructive possession over the collateral.

---

[3] cf *BCCI (No 8)* [1998] AC 214 (HL), 226; and *Re Cosslett (Contractors) Ltd* [1998] Ch 495 (CA) 508.

[4] RJ Mokal, 'Liquidation Expenses and Floating Charges–the Separate Funds Fallacy' [2004] LMCLQ 396.

[5] Goode (2004) 641; *Palk v Mortgage Services Funding Plc* [1993] Ch 330.

[6] Goode 8–9. There are however exceptions, for instance the rule in *Dearle v Hall* (1828) 3 Russ 1.

[7] A McKnight, 'Seminar Sheet 1' LLM Course: The Law of Credit and Security, Queen Mary, University of London 16–7.

[8] cf Palmer and Hudson 624.

[9] *Coggs v Bernard* [1703] 2 Ld Raym 909.

[10] A McKnight, 'Seminar Sheet 1' LLM Course: The Law of Credit and Security, Queen Mary, University of London 6.

As the pledgee is considered to acquire a special property in the pledge, the pledgee's interest is capable of being transferred.[11] The pledgee is also invested with a common law power of sale in the event of default by the pledgor in relation to repaying the underlying debt.[12] Any surplus must however account to the pledgor.[13]

Similarly to the pledge, the lien is a limited legal interest delivered by possession. It differs from the pledge in that the collateral is deposited for some other purpose than to serve as security, for instance for repair.[14] Since most securities are in immobilised or dematerialised form, the pledge and the lien are of subordinate importance in relation to these assets. In contrast, a mortgage or a charge does not depend upon possession. Such security can therefore be taken over any kind of asset.

In general no formalities are required under English law to create a charge, which usually takes effect in equity.[15] A fixed charge is generally taken over particular assets,[16] whereas a floating charge is taken over a shifting class of assets, present and future. The floating charge allows the chargor to continue to deal with the assets in its business.[17] It attaches to specific assets upon crystallisation, when it is turned into a fixed charge.[18] The main distinction between a fixed and a floating charge is that in the case of a fixed charge, the chargor cannot deal with the asset without the consent of the chargee. In other words, the chargee must have control of the asset.[19]

Floating charges, and some fixed charges, are registrable under Section 395 of the Companies Act 1985 and therefore subject to the formalities and the administrative burden of registration. For this reason, the parties to a secured transaction usually try to avoid forming it as a floating charge. Another reason for avoiding taking a floating charge is that it ranks after both fixed charges and preferential creditors in the bankruptcy of the debtor.[20]

---

[11] *Donald v Suckling* (1865–66) LR 1 QB 585.

[12] *Ex p Hubbard* (1886) 17 QBD 699.

[13] cf *Halliday v Holgate* (1868) LR 3 Ex 299; for pawn see s121(3) Consumer Credit Act 1974 (as amended).

[14] Goode 5, 34.

[15] Benjamin 101. It should be noted however that s53(1)(c) Law of Property Act 1925 requires that a disposition of an equitable interest, including some charges, must be in writing.

[16] The term fixed charge is sometimes used interchangeably with the term equitable mortgage, Benjamin 102.

[17] Benjamin 103 and *Re Yorkshire Woolcombers Association Ltd* [1903] 2 Ch 284 at 295.

[18] Benjamin 102.

[19] *Agnew v Commissioner of Inland Revenue* [2001] 2 AC 710 (PC(NZ)); Re *Spectrum Plus Ltd (In Liquidation)* [2005] 2AC 680 (HL); *Re Cosslett (Contractors) Ltd* [1998] 2 WLR 131 per Millet LJ at 143.

[20] ss 40, 175 Insolvency Act 1986; see also s176A.

5.2.2 *The Concept of Trust*

The trust is a special vehicle in the common law that has come to play a crucial role in banking and finance.[21] As FMLC puts it 'The use of trusts in the financial world is not only widespread, but there is a trust relationship behind most situations of ownership which are found in this area.'[22] Although the trust is not an independent type of security its significance in relation to security and insolvency law should be recognised.

Under a trust structure, the trustee is the legal owner of the trust assets whereas the beneficiary is the real owner. This means that the trustee is entitled to the legal ownership whereas the beneficiary is entitled to an equitable ownership. The trustee has the right of management and control over the trust assets while the benefits are preserved for the beneficiary. In the trustee's insolvency, the beneficiary's interest is protected from the trustee's creditors as long as the trust assets are separated from the trustee's own assets and the three certainties – intention, object and subject matter – are met.[23] Hence, the beneficiary has a proprietary interest in the trustee's estate.[24] The simplest form of trust is an express trust but a trust can also be imposed as a resulting or constructive trust.

5.2.3 *Security over Investment Securities*

Securities can generally be issued in either registered, certificated or bearer format. Securities held in CREST, which is part of the Euroclear group, are dematerialised and thus recorded in electronic form.

The traditional legal analysis of bearer securities held in custody is that they are held on bailment. The custodian's function as a bailee is based on the premise that the securities are physically possessed. Following computerisation and the move from tangible to intangible securities, bailment is no longer available. Instead the relationship between the custodian and its client is deemed to constitute a trust, provided the qualifications for establishing a trust are met.[25]

---

[21] D Hayton, H Pigott and J Benjamin, 'The Use of Trusts in International Financial Transactions' (2002) 1 JIBFL 23 ff.

[22] FMLC, 'Issue 62 – Trustee Exemption Clauses: Analysis of the role of the trustee in the wholesale financial markets and of the proposals contained in the Law Commission's Consultation Paper No 117 "Trustee Exemption Clauses"' (May 2004) 1 ff.

[23] JE Penner, *The Law of Trusts* (3rd edn Lexis Nexis Butterworths 2002) 177 ff; see *also Knight v Knight* (1840) 3 Beav 148. The certainty of intention concerns the settlor's declaration to create a trust; the certainty of subject matter whether the trust assets meet the requirement of identity and the certainty of object whether the beneficiaries are identifiable.

[24] Wood 75 ff.

[25] Benjamin and Yates 25 ff; cf Sect. 2.2.

Even though CREST facilitates the delivery of collateral, for instance through so called escrow accounts, security interests are not created in the CREST system but take place outside.[26]

Security over registered securities is evidenced and transferred by registration and can be created either via transfer of title by way of security, which involves re-registration of the owner (so called book-entry transfer), or via the establishment of an escrow account. Another method commonly used is outright transfer where the ownership of the asset is transferred, for instance in a repo or securities loan transaction. Transfer of title and pledge of bearer securities is made via transfer of possession of the instrument.

A transfer of title by way of security of intermediated securities involves re-registration of the securities in the name of the collateral-taker. Through registration a legal mortgage is created with the collateral-provider retaining the equity of redemption, i.e. the right to have the securities back upon the discharge of the secured obligation. The equity of redemption means that the collateral-taker cannot deal freely with the collateral. The security the collateral-taker acquires is therefore less than an outright ownership.

The establishment of an escrow account can be compared with the creation of an equitable mortgage or charge. The establishment involves the transfer of securities to a sub-account of the collateral-provider and blocking them for the benefit of the collateral-taker.[27] The securities are thereby subject to the collateral-taker's control. Presumably an equitable mortgage is created to the benefit of the collateral-taker without having the securities re-registered on the issuer's or operator's register. This is because equity regards as done that which ought to be done.[28]

An outright title transfer involves the transfer of ownership of the collateral from the collateral-provider to the collateral-taker. The latter commits to retransfer the equivalent number of securities as was transferred to it as security for the secured obligation. Sections 136 and 53(1)(c) of the Law of Property Act 1925 impose certain formalities in relation to the transfer of intangible assets. The general view appears to be, however, that these requirements do not apply to unallocated and intermediated securities.[29] In relation to book-entry transfers made through CREST, Regulation 38(5) of the Uncertificated Securities Regulations 2001 expressly disapplies Sections 136 and 53(1).[30]

A method that involves outright transfer is the arrangement called Delivery by Value (DBV). Benjamin notes that in a DBV it is the value of the securities and not the individual securities as such that are specified. The securities are transferred outright at the end of the business day from one member's account to another member's account. The next day the value is retransferred. The securities redelivered are

---

[26] Benjamin and Yates 186.

[27] The establishment of an escrow account resembles the creation of a pledge in the Swedish VPC system (cf Sect. 6.2.2).

[28] Benjamin and Yates 186–187.

[29] Benjamin Ch. 3; Benjamin and Yates 19–20, 168, 200; Legal Certainty Group Comparative Security, Q No 3 UK.

[30] cf Benjamin and Yates 20.

chosen by the CREST system and are not the same securities that are transferred, only the equivalent securities.[31] As DBV's are registered on the issuer's register or on the account of the relevant CREST participant, they are perceived to confer legal interests.[32]

5.2.3.1 Attachment and Perfection

In order to take security over securities, the interest must attach to the securities. Attachment is when the security interest becomes effective between the collateral-provider and the collateral-taker. Under English law there are no formal requirements for attachment other than that the secured obligation must be current and the collateral be identified and consist of present assets.[33]

The security interest must also be perfected in order to be valid against third parties. A security interest can for example be perfected by the collateral-taker taking control over the collateral. Control can be established in different ways, for instance through a transfer of the securities into the name of the collateral-taker or through an undertaking by the intermediary to act on the instructions of the collateral-taker.[34] Bearer securities need to be taken into possession by the collateral-taker whereas for securities held by an intermediary, the intermediary needs to be notified.[35] The relevant intermediary is the intermediary on whose accounts the interests are recorded.[36] In accordance with the rule in *Dearle v Hall*,[37] such notification establishes the priority order between competing interests (cf Sect. 2.3.2).

Fixed charges over shares may in certain cases be automatically perfected through attachment.[38] Floating charges are perfected through registration under Section 395 of the Companies Act 1985. Book debts also need to be registered. The prudent collateral-taker may therefore want to make sure dividends, interests and proceeds are registered to prevent the charge from being ineffective.[39]

The Financial Collateral Directive provides, however, that no registration requirements shall apply to security financial collateral arrangements covered by its scope. The implementation of the Financial Collateral Directive through the Financial

---

[31] Benjamin and Yates 188–189.

[32] Benjamin 208.

[33] Benjamin 86.

[34] FMLC, 'Issue 3 – Property Interests in Investment Securities' (July 2004) 12.

[35] Benjamin 87.

[36] *ibid.*

[37] *Dearle v Hall* (1828) 3 Russ 1; [1824–34] All ER Rep 28.

[38] Goode 74–75.

[39] cf s396 Companies Act 1985; Goode 77 n 1. A charge on a bank deposit is generally not considered a book debt, see *Re Brightlife Ltd* [1987] 1 Ch 200 (Ch D); *Re Permanent Houses (Holdings) Ltd* [1988] BCLC 563 (Ch D); and *Northern Bank Ltd v Ross* [1991] BCLC 504 (CA).

Collateral Arrangements (No 2) Regulations 2003 (SI 2003 No. 3226) thus disapplies registration of investment securities under the Companies Act 1985.[40]

5.2.3.2 Priorities

The question of priority is determined against a complex set of principles whose applicability is dependent on the circumstance in each specific case.[41] Similarly to US law, the main rule is that 'first in time' prevails. There are however numerous exceptions, for instance 'equity's darling', i.e. that an equitable interest is overridden by a subsequent legal interest if the subsequent claimant is a bona fide purchaser who takes the legal interest for value without notice of the equitable interest.[42] Another exception is that a good faith purchaser of a negotiable instrument takes the instrument free from any prior defects in title and thus, has priority over earlier claims.[43]

Where there are successive assignments of intangible choses in action, priority is determined by the order in which notice is given to the debtor, provided the creditor does not have notice of the competing claim.[44] In practice this rule is interpreted to mean that where a security interest is extended over intermediated securities, it is the intermediary on whose account the collateral is recorded that shall be notified.[45]

5.3 Reuse of Financial Collateral

In the United Kingdom, the Financial Collateral Directive was implemented through the Financial Collateral Arrangements (No 2) Regulations 2003 (SI 2003 No. 3226) (Financial Collateral Arrangements Regulations), which came into force on 26 December 2003.[46] It was previously uncertain whether a right to repledge investment securities existed under English law, although authorities showed that there was some room for this type of security.[47] Thus, repledge is an undiscovered area of law. Through the implementation of the Financial Collateral Arrangements the

---

40 cf HM Treasury, 'Implementation of the Directive on Financial Collateral Arrangements' (July 2003).

41 Benjamin and Yates 47 f.

42 cf Austen-Peters 100 ff; Benjamin and Yates 47 f.

43 It is uncertain whether intangible securities are negotiable instruments under English law as they do not exist in physical format, cf Benjamin and Yates 16 ff, 47 f. See also s24 Bills of Exchange Act 1882 which provides an exception from this rule.

44 *Dearle v Hall* (1828) 3 Russ 1, [1824–34] All ER Rep 28.

45 Legal Certainty Group Comparative Survey Q 23 UK.

46 The Regulations where first issued in a No 1 version which was revoked due to a drafting error before they came into effect.

47 *Donald v Suckling* (1865–66) LR 1 QB 585; Goode 31, 225–226; Benjamin 5.46 ff; Palmer and Hudson 622.

right to reuse financial collateral has, for the transaction covered by its scope, been put beyond doubt.

Sect. 5.3.1 below analyses repledge under English law as it stood before the implementation of the Financial Collateral Arrangements Regulations. As the Regulations are limited in their application, the analysis applies to transactions falling outside their scope. Sect. 5.3.2 examines the implementation of Art. 5 under the Financial Collateral Directive and Sect. 5.3.3 the use of Repos.

Unless otherwise indicated, the term repledge is here used to denote all types of security under English law where the collateral-taker B uses the collateral extended by A as security in a transaction with a third party C (e.g. re-, on- or sub-pledge, sub-charge and sub-mortgage, etc.).[48]

5.3.1 Repledge

B has, as long as there are no contractual restrictions, a general right to repledge the collateral as a means of dealing with its own security interest.[49] The consent of A is not required and C takes the collateral subject to A's equity of redemption.[50] As long as the parties have not expressly agreed that B shall not have a right to repledge, B can transmit its interest to C without terminating its rights or A's right to have the collateral back upon discharge of the underlying obligation.[51]

One of the authorities often referred to in relation to repledge is the case *Donald v Suckling*.[52] The question in this case was whether the pledgee of debentures, B, by repledging them to C as security for a larger amount before any default in payment by the pledgor A, made void the contract upon which the debentures were deposited with B. Did A have an immediate right to possession of the debentures notwithstanding that his debt remained unpaid? It was held that the repledge by B to C did not put an end to the contract of pledge between A and B and B's interest and right of detainer under it; and that A therefore could not maintain detinue without having paid or tendered the amount of the bill. The discussion concerned, *inter alia*, whether B had a proprietary right in the pledge. It was acknowledged that B's right to sell the collateral upon default by A is a real right as distinguished from a mere personal right.[53] 'In the contract of pledge, the pawnor invests the pawnee with much more than the mere right of possession. He invests him with a right to deal with the thing pledged as his own, if the debt be not paid and the thing redeemed at the appointed time.'[54]

---

[48] The prefixes re-, on- and sub- appear to be used interchangeably in the English doctrine to denote the case when B uses collateral extended by A as security in a transaction with C.

[49] Goode 226; see also Bridge 177.

[50] Goode 226.

[51] Palmer and Hudson 631.

[52] *Donald v Suckling* (1865–66) LR 1 QB 585.

[53] cf Blackburn J *Donald v Suckling* (1865–66) LR 1 QB 585 and Story 328; Goode 31.

[54] See judgment by Cockburn CJ *Donald v Suckling* (1865–66) LR 1 QB 585.

Goode notes in his book Commercial Law that a transfer of a mortgage, and presumably also a charge, which contains no reference to the underlying obligation, nevertheless carries with it by necessary implication of law a transfer of the underlying obligation.[55] Where the debt is transferred without mention of the mortgage, the transferor holds the mortgage as trustee for the transferee, who is entitled to it in equity.[56] In his work Legal Problems of Credit and Security, Goode states that in each case of sub-mortgage, sub-charge and sub-pledge, what is involved is the security transfer of or charge of the security interest coupled with an assignment of the debt secured by that interest. In contrast to Swedish and US law, it thus appears that under English law, it is not possible to grant a sub-security independently from the underlying debt. It should be noted, however, that Regulation 16 of the Financial Collateral Arrangements Regulations makes no such requirement, see further Sect. 5.3.2.

It is not possible to repledge on more stringent conditions, i.e. on more severe terms, than those under which B holds the collateral.[57] In other words, B may not grant a sub-security interest greater than its own or grant security for an amount exceeding the original debt or for a later maturity. C cannot acquire an interest beyond that held by B.[58] The idea is that A must be able to restore the collateral by paying off its debt. As a result, a chargee cannot sub-mortgage its interest, since it involves the transfer of legal title to an asset that it does not own.[59] It also means that the sub-security disappears once the original debt has been paid off, although C should be able to assert a security interest over the proceeds of payment. Thus C cannot refuse to allow the original security to be redeemed under the contract with B.[60] However, if A has knowledge of the sub-security and still pays B, A risks having to pay twice in order to redeem the collateral from C.[61]

Like any type of security interest, a repledge must be perfected. The requirements for perfection of a sub-mortgage, sub-charge or sub-pledge are the same as for an ordinary mortgage, charge or pledge. The type of measure that must be completed – possession, registration, notice to the debtor, etc. – depends on the type of asset and security involved.[62]

As mentioned, it was previously uncertain whether a right to repledge existed under English law. Benjamin notes that these doubts were due to some equitable

---

[55] Goode (2004) 645–646 with reference to *Jones v Gibbons* (1804) 9 Ves 407. See also s114 Law of Property Act 1925.

[56] Goode (2004) 645–646 with reference to *Morley v Morley* (1858) 25 Beav 253.

[57] Goode 31. See also Palmer and Hudson 630–631; and Story 324.

[58] Story 288.

[59] Goode 49.

[60] I am grateful to Andrew McKnight, Visiting Professor of Law, London School of Economics and Political Science and Queen Mary, University of London for clarifying this.

[61] cf F Oditah, *Legal Aspects of Receivables Financing* (Sweet & Maxwell 1991) 131 with reference to *Burrows v Lock* (1805) 10 Ves 470 at 475–476. B holds the payment as trustee, but if the money is not recoverable, A would have to pay C again. I am grateful to Roy Goode, Emeritus Professor of Law, St John's College, Oxford University, for clarifying this.

[62] Goode 73 ff.

principles designed to protect the collateral-provider. These equitable rules include the rule against clogs on the equity of redemption, the rule against collateral benefits and the equitable maxim 'once a mortgage, always a mortgage'.[63]

The principle 'once a mortgage, always a mortgage' refers back to the case law developed to protect mortgages of land.[64]

> "Whenever a transaction is in reality one of mortgage, equity regards the mortgaged property as security only for money, and will permit of no attempt to clog, fetter, or impede the borrower's right to redeem and to rescue what was, and still remains in equity his own."[65]

Together with the principle 'equity of redemption', it prevents the mortgagor from giving up its rights by contract.[66] Any waiver of the rights is considered to be a clog on the equity of redemption and will therefore be ineffective.[67]

It should be noted, however, that Goode, when discussing the effects of rehypothecation, states that it is open to the parties to agree that the mortgagee is to have a power of sale even without default, and that such an agreement does not impair the equity of redemption which simply attaches to the proceeds of sale.[68] In light of the implementation of the Financial Collateral Directive, it is now safe to presume that an agreed power of sale is effective for transactions falling within its scope, cf Sect. 5.3.2.

The equity of redemption represents A's – i.e. the owner's – property rights in the collateral.[69] Hence, the equity of redemption is recognised as a beneficial ownership in the asset. Accordingly, A has a right to redeem the property upon payment of the amount due.[70] B's special interest is then terminated. The equity of redemption lasts beyond the date of default of repayment, and is, unless agreed otherwise, exercisable at any time before B has entered into a binding contract with C.[71]

B retains its security interest in the collateral regardless of A defaulting on the payment of the underlying debt.[72] If, however, at the time when A applies to redeem the collateral, it has been sold without notification thereof to A, A is relieved from its duty to honour the contract with B.[73]

There has also been some debate over whether the rule against collateral benefits restricts the possibilities to repledge. This rule restricts B from obtaining

---

[63] Benjamin 111.

[64] Benjamin 112. Benjamin notes that the rule was developed for legal mortgages, but that there is persuasive authority that it also applies to other types of security interests.

[65] *Marquess of Northampton v Pollock* (1890) 45 Ch D 190 per Bowen LJ at 215.

[66] Benjamin 112–113.

[67] *Ibid.*

[68] Goode 225 with references to *The Maule* [1997] 1 WLR 528; *Langton v Waite* (1868) LR 6 Eq 165.

[69] Benjamin 116.

[70] Palmer and Hudson 637–638.

[71] Palmer and Hudson 643.

[72] Story 308–311.

[73] *ibid.*

any benefits apart from the payment of interests, cost and principal.[74] It has been assumed, however, that the possibility for this rule to apply to repledge of indirectly held securities is limited.[75]

The equity of redemption does not affect the rights of bona fide purchasers of legal interest for value without notice.[76] Hence, where C acquires a legal interest in an asset that belongs to A without knowledge of it, it takes it free of A's right to redeem the asset.[77]

It is clear that the rules on repledge under English law are ill-suited to the developments in the securities markets.[78] Due to the equitable principles that protect the collateral-provider, the practice in England and Wales has been to use title transfer structures instead of repledge. Following the implementation of the Financial Collateral Arrangements Regulations, however, the use of repledge is expected to increase.

It should also be pointed out that the meaning and effects of a repledge under English law to a large degree are unclear. Should a repledge be restricted to a pledge of the collateral together with the underlying debt (cf Goode above), it can be questioned whether it would conflict with the equitable principles as stated by Benjamin.

5.3.2 A Right of Reuse under the Financial Collateral Arrangements Regulations

The Financial Collateral Directive was implemented by the Financial Collateral Arrangements Regulations, which came into force on 26 December 2003.[79] The United Kingdom did not exercise any of the opt-out possibilities provided under the Financial Collateral Directive. Instead, the scope was expanded to cover all financial collateral arrangements as between two corporate bodies, i.e. non-natural persons. "Non-natural person" is defined as any corporate body, unincorporated firm, partnership or body with legal personality, thus excluding individuals. This means that UK partnerships, whether limited or general, are included, as well as local authorities and governmental departments. Private persons, whether acting on their own behalf or as trustees, are excluded.

The Financial Collateral Arrangements Regulations apply to financial collateral arrangements where the collateral is transferred into the possession or control of the collateral-taker or a person acting on its behalf. "Financial collateral arrangements"

---

[74] Benjamin 116.

[75] Benjamin 117.

[76] However, due to the increase of intermediation and the reduction of parties' rights to equitable rights, arguably only equitable rights are created with the result of eliminating bona fide purchases, cf *Benjamin* 117.

[77] cf *Bridge* 177.

[78] cf Chaps. 3 and 4.

[79] The original version of the Regulations (No1) was revoked before it came into effect due to a drafting error.

is defined as a title transfer financial collateral arrangement or a security financial collateral arrangement whether or not these are covered by a master agreement or general terms and conditions.[80] The definition of "financial collateral" includes cash and financial instruments. As long as the collateral-taker is given control, it will not matter whether the charge is fixed or floating (although control by the collateral-taker is quite contrary to the nature of the floating charge). Rights to substitute equivalent financial collateral or withdraw excess collateral will not prevent the financial collateral from being in the possession or under the control of the collateral-taker.

The scope of the Financial Collateral Arrangements Regulations is further limited by the definition of "financial instruments" which includes shares in companies and other securities equivalent to shares in companies; bonds and other forms of instruments giving rise to or acknowledging indebtedness if these are tradable on the capital market; and any other securities which are normally dealt in and which give the right to acquire any such shares, bonds, instruments or other securities by subscription, purchase or exchange or which give rise to a cash settlement (excluding instruments of payment); and includes units of a collective investment scheme within the meaning of the Financial Services and Markets Act 2000, eligible debt securities within the meaning of the Uncertified Securities Regulations 2001 (SI 2001/3755) (as amended), money market instruments and claims or rights in relation to any of the financial instruments referred to above.[81]

Regulation 16, which has the heading 'Right of use under a security financial collateral arrangement', sets out the conditions under which a reuse of financial collateral can take place. A collateral-taker under a security financial collateral arrangement may use the collateral as if it were the owner of it if the arrangement provides for such right of use. Regulation 16 thereby prevents any equitable principle being applied by the courts to override such a term in a financial collateral agreement.[82]

Under the Financial Collateral Arrangements Regulations, if a collateral-taker exercises a right of use, it is obliged to replace the original financial collateral by transferring 'equivalent financial collateral' on or before the due date for the performance of the relevant financial obligations. Regulation 3 defines 'equivalent financial collateral' as, in relation to cash, a payment of the same amount and in the same currency, and, in relation to financial instruments, financial instruments of the same issuer or debtor, forming part of the same issue or class and of the same nominal amount, currency and description or, where the financial collateral arrangement provides for the transfer of other assets following the occurrence of any event relating to or affecting any financial instruments provided as financial collateral, those other assets.

The uncertainties that previously impeded repledge were linked to the equitable principle 'once a mortgage, always a mortgage', the rule against clogs on the equity of redemption and the rule against collateral benefits.[83] The introduction of the

[80] Regulation 3.

[81] *ibid.*

[82] HM Treasury Report 36.

[83] cf Sect. 3.1.

Financial Collateral Arrangements Regulations should have removed these doubts. However, the implementation of a right to reuse financial collateral has created other problems. Although Regulation 16 has the heading 'Right of use under a security financial collateral arrangement', it can be questioned whether this provision concerns title transfers and not security arrangements. Since the collateral-taker is allowed to use the financial collateral as if it were the owner and can replace the original collateral by transferring the equivalent collateral, elementary aspects of property are neglected. By allowing a replacement of the collateral, the tie with the equity of redemption in the asset – which represents the collateral-provider's ownership rights – is broken. If the connection is removed there is nothing that upholds the distinction between security and title transfers. Before the acquisition of the equivalent collateral by the collateral-taker, the rights of the collateral-provider will most probably be reduced to a right *in personam*, which is often worthless in the event of the insolvency of the collateral-taker.[84]

It should also be noted that a right of reuse as the owner may run counter to the general rule of *nemo dat quod non habet*. In accordance with this rule, it is not possible to alienate something that belongs to someone else.[85] There are, however, exceptions to this rule, for instance bona fide purchase for value without notice.[86] Also, the implementation of Regulation 16 puts any reservation beyond doubt.

Another problem is that the right of use allows the mortgaged securities to be used to create multiple obligations between different parties. In a report prepared by the City of London Law Society Financial Law Sub-Committee, it is recognised that the resulting obligations will amount to a corresponding multiple of the value of the securities. In other words, an extensive practice of reuse may lead to the same financial instrument being registered on different entitlement holders' accounts with the risk of distorting the property law system. In this light, the Committee recommends that the Treasury should hold discussions with the FSA to ensure that, where the rights of use become available, the FSA has in place systems for monitoring and controlling the extent to which institutions that it supervises have exposures under financial collateral arrangements entered into by them to the multiple use by collateral-takers of financial collateral provided by them.[87]

Another obstacle that seems to have been removed is the restriction of not allowing the collateral-taker to repledge the collateral separately from the underlying obligation.[88] Considering that a reuse of financial collateral as the owner is allowed under the financial collateral arrangement, nothing should prevent the parties from agreeing that the collateral is repledged separately.

A number of other questions are left unanswered. Can repledge take place on more severe conditions than under the initial security agreement? A right to reuse the financial collateral under the Financial Collateral Arrangements Regulations

---

[84] cf Chap. 6.3.2.

[85] Austen-Peters 33–34.

[86] *Burgis v Constantine* [1908] 2 KB 484, 501 per Farwell LJ.

[87] City of London Law Society Report 15.

[88] cf Sect. 3.1.

indicates that this would be possible. This is because ownership, i.e. a transfer of beneficial title, conveys a greater bundle of rights than a security interest. On the other hand, Regulation 16(3) states that the equivalent financial collateral shall be subject to the same terms as under the original financial collateral arrangement, which implies that this interpretation is incorrect.

Moreover, does A keep its equity of redemption, and if so, for how long does it last? Is there a point upon which the right to redeem has been so diluted that it ceases to exist? And how is priority established between B's and C's creditors?[89]

From a regulatory law perspective, it should be noted that different regulatory treatments apply to different situations.[90] Under FSA's Handbook CASS 3, assets that are used as security with a right for the firm to use them as its own provide a lower degree of protection for the client.[91] Under a so-called 'bare security interest arrangement' – i.e. where the firm lacks a right to reuse the collateral – the collateral continues to belong to the client until the firm's right to realise the collateral materialises upon the client's default. By comparison, under a 'right of use arrangement', the client transfers the legal title and associated rights in the collateral to the firm, so that when the firm exercises its right to treat the asset as its own, the collateral ceases to belong to the client and in effect becomes the firm's asset. The collateral is thus no longer subject to the full range of client asset protection. This also means that the firm may book the assets as its own on its records.[92] The different regulatory treatment shows that there are fundamental differences between security and title transfers, something which the Financial Collateral Arrangements Regulations ignore.

5.3.3 *Repos*

Prior to the implementation of the Financial Collateral Arrangements Regulations, the use of repos and title transfer structures were the preferred technique in the United Kingdom. This is because repos give the collateral-taker an increased freedom to deal with the collateral. Another benefit is that mandatory rules on perfection and enforcement do have to be complied with. Repos are, for instance, not subject to the registration requirement under Section 395 of the Companies Act 1985.

---

[89] cf Myrdal; Law Commission, 'Registration of Security Interest: Company Charges and Property Other than Land' (Law Com No 164, 2002); Law Commission, 'Company Security Interests (Law Com No 176, 2004).

[90] FSA's Handbook, CASS 3.

[91] Principle 10 requires firms to arrange adequate protection for their clients' assets when they are responsible for them. The rules are designed primarily to restrict the commingling of the client's and the firm's assets and minimise the risk of the client's safe custody investments being used by the firm without the client's agreement or contrary to the client's wishes, or being treated as the firm's assets in the event of its insolvency. Special rules apply when the firm acts as a trustee.

[92] FSA Handbook, CASS 3.1.7G.

The typical structure of a repo involves a transfer of bare title to the collateral from A to B, together with a right for A to re-acquire assets of the same kind. B commits to retransfer the equivalent amount of collateral as was transferred to it. There is no obligation to return the same assets that were used as security and there are no limitations on B's use of the collateral. The element of security consists of the possibilities to net and set off the value of the collateral against the underlying obligation. Upon default by either party, a close out netting provision converts the obligation to retransfer securities into a money obligation that is set-off against the loan/purchase price.[93]

It is estimated that the liberalisation of the rules on reuse of financial collateral under the Financial Collateral Arrangements Regulations will increase the use of repledge as opposed to repos.[94] What was previously regarded to be disadvantageous to security arrangements has been removed by the Financial Collateral Arrangements Regulations, whereas some of the disadvantages of title transfer arrangements – the credit risk of the collateral-taker and uncertainties in relation to tax, accounting and regulatory capital treatment – still remain.[95]

Recharacterisation risk, which is especially relevant in cross-border transactions and which was previously regarded as one of the main disadvantages with repos, has been addressed in the EU through Art. 6 of the Financial Collateral Directive. In the United Kingdom, through the implementation of the Financial Collateral Arrangements Regulations, it is ensured that title transfer financial collateral arrangements can take effect in accordance with their terms.[96] There is, however, no specific counterpart to Art. 6 of the Financial Collateral Directive in the Financial Collateral Arrangements Regulations. The general view appears to be that this is due to the fact that it was not considered necessary to specifically address recharacterisation risk. Even before the implementation recharacterisation risk was not perceived to be a major issue under English law. As long as the parties intend that the title to the securities shall pass from the collateral-provider to the collateral-taker and the collateral-taker is free to do what it wants with the transferred securities, recharacterisation risk is generally remote.[97]

Should recharacterisation nevertheless take place, Section 101 of the Law of Property Act 1925 may have to be complied with. Under this provision, unless the parties have agreed that an outright transfer of the collateral can take place or a power of sale has become exercisable by statute, B is not allowed to make an outright disposal of the collateral. General practice in the markets is, however, to include a clause to that effect in the documentation. This provision, therefore, does not usually pose any problem. The parties' agreement that B shall have a right to dispose

[93] Goode 220.

[94] HM Treasury Report 16. See also IBA, 'Banking Law Newsletter: Implementation of EU Financial Collateral Directive' (United Kingdom) Vol 12 No 2 (September 2004) 35.

[95] Allen & Overy Briefing Note 'New Law on Financial Collateral' (January 2004) 7.

[96] cf Regulations 4 and 8.

[97] cf *Welsh Development Agency v Export Finance Co Ltd* [1992] BCC 270 and *Agnew v Commissioner for the Inland Revenue* [2001] 3 WLR 454.

of the collateral is binding regardless of whether the sale is preceded by default by B. Such agreement is thus not void for impairing the equity of redemption.[98]

5.4 The Doctrine of Specificity

Reuse of financial collateral under the Financial Collateral Arrangements Regulations entails a right for B to use the collateral as its own and to return equivalent collateral. As pointed out, such right of use infringes on A's equity of redemption.

In many civil law jurisdictions, the scope of the right of use transforms the security interest into a claim, or a so-called *pignus irregulare*. This is due to the extensive right to deal with the collateral. After the dispossession by B the identity between what was extended as security and the replacement is broken. As a consequence, A loses its ownership rights in the collateral.[99] Below follows an examination of the requirement for specificity and the circumstances under which substitutions and mixtures can take place under English law.

5.4.1 Identification

Identification of the subject matter under English law is, as in most jurisdictions, a requirement for the acquisition of property rights. An asset, regardless of whether it is a tangible or an intangible,[100] needs to be identified for a person to have an interest in it – a right *in rem*. Identification is a sensible element where the law coincides with what is practically feasible. As Lord Mustill stated in *Re Goldcorp Exchange Ltd*:[101]

> "It makes no difference what the parties intended if what they intend is impossible as is the case with an immediate transfer of legal or equitable title to goods whose identity is not yet known [. . .] it is impossible to have title to goods, when nobody knows to which goods the title relates."[102]

The requirement of specificity is applicable both in common law and in equity. Both acquisition of real rights and possession depend on identification of the asset.[103] Identity of the subject matter is also relevant in relation to a whole range of other

---

[98] Goode 225; *The Maule* [1997] 1 WLR 528; and *Langton v Waite* (1868) LR 6 Eq 165.

[99] cf Sect. 6.3.

[100] Goode (1987) 459.

[101] [1995] 1 AC 74 at 90 and 92.

[102] cf Lord Blackburn, *The Effect of the Contract of Sale* (1845) 122–123.

[103] Goode (2004), 207.

issues such as risk, frustration and wrongful conversion.[104] The degree of identification varies though, depending on the circumstances.

The need to identify the collateral means that a proprietary interest cannot take effect until it is ascertained. The asset which is to be the subject of a security interest must be identified for the interest to attach.[105] For the collateral to be ascertained, the collateral agreement must describe the collateral so unambiguously that it can be identified without the involvement of the contracting parties.[106] In the case of fungibles, however, it is sufficient if the assets are ascertained at a later stage as the result of an unconditional act of appropriation of the assets to the agreement.[107] The same applies to a security interest in unidentified assets held in an identified bulk – the collateral needs to be appropriated to the agreement for the interest to take effect.[108] From a practical perspective, this means that the assets need to be separated from the rest of the assets in the bulk or need to be marked as constituting the collateral under the collateral agreement.

The same requirement of identification that applies to the acquisition of a security interest applies to the sale of goods.[109] Under Section 16 of the Sale of Goods Act 1979, a buyer cannot assert property rights over goods that are not ascertained.

> "[Subject to Section 20A below] where there is a contract for the sale of unascertained goods no property in the goods is transferred to the buyer unless and until the goods are ascertained"

Section 16 of the Sale of Goods Act is a mandatory rule of law and cannot be altered by the contracting parties through an agreement. Under Section 17(1) property in specific or ascertained goods is transferred when intended.[110] Appropriation is therefore crucial in determining when the legal title passes.[111]

Section 16 of the Sale of Goods Act does not distinguish between wholly unascertained and quasi-ascertained goods.[112] It has therefore been criticised,

---

[104] Goode (2003), 382. See also Goode (2004), 207, who points out that identification may also be relevant to the availability of specific performance (cf *Re Wait* [1927] 1 Ch 606).

[105] Goode 60.

[106] Goode 63. See also U Drobnig, 'The Law Governing Credit Security' in the European Parliament Directorate General for Research Working Paper 'The Private Law Systems in the EU: Discrimination on Grounds of Nationality and the Need for a European Civil Code' (June 2000) 173.

[107] Goode 63.

[108] *ibid.*

[109] Goode 62.

[110] The definition of "specific goods" in Section 61(1) of the Sale of Goods Act includes an undivided share, specified as a fraction or percentage, of goods identified and agreed on at the time the contract of sale is made, cf AG Guest and others (eds), *Benjamin's Sale of Goods* (6th edn Sweet & Maxwell 2002) 192.

[111] The risk is passed from the seller to the buyer when the property is transferred, regardless of whether delivery has been made or not. Where specific or ascertained goods are lost or damaged without fault on the seller's side while in the seller's possession, the buyer bears the risk, Goode (2004), 242.

[112] See McKendrick 386 ff, who elaborates on the possible exemptions from Section 16 of the Sale of Goods Act 1979 that were available prior to the Sale of Goods (Amendment) Act 1995. The

primarily by the commodity trade industry, which claimed that commercial reality and the expectations of contracting parties required that a co-ownership of prepaid goods held in a bulk should pass to the buyer without being marked or separated in relation to each buyer.[113] Subsequently, Section 16 was amended through the Sale of Goods Amendment Act 1995, which introduced Sections 20A-B in the Sale of Goods Act 1979. Sections 20A-B give the prepaying buyer ownership in common of unidentified goods kept in an identified bulk. The buyer's share is proportionate in relation to the total quantity, i.e. where the aggregate of shares in the bulk exceeds the whole the share of each buyer is reduced in proportion.[114]

5.4.2 Substitution

English law is, in comparison with Swedish law, liberal in relation to substitution of collateral.[115] A security interest can often be asserted in the proceeds of the original asset. 'Tracing' is the technique through which the proceeds are identified and 'claiming' the process through which the claimant's proprietary rights are established.[116] Tracing and claiming should also be distinguished from 'following', where the original asset is followed into the hands of the acquirer.

The requirements for substitution – under which circumstances it can take place, etc. – are anything but certain.[117] Tracing and claiming are complex features that still require much analysis in order to understand their foundations and the rules and principles they invoke.[118] As an example, the House of Lords has just recently clarified that an interest in proceeds is a property right derived from the ownership of the original asset and does not stem from unjust enrichment (i.e. the law of restitution), which was previously argued by some academics.[119]

---

exemptions covered are Section 18 Sale of Goods Act 1979 (subsequent ascertainment of goods); exhaustion; co-ownership through agreement by the parties (i.e. intention); and intervention of equity through *(i)* the trust, *(ii)* estoppel, and *(iii)* tracing.

[113] McKendrick 395 ff.

[114] Section 20A(3)-(4) Sale of Goods Act 1979.

[115] cf L Smith, 'Property Transferred in Breach' in P Birks and A Pretto (eds), *Breach of Trust* (Hart Publishing 2002) 130.

[116] cf Millett LJ in *Boscawen v Bajwa* [1996] 1 WLR 328; see Goode 42.

[117] Goode 41.

[118] cf P Birks (ed.), *Laundering and Tracing* (Clarendon Press 1995) x: 'For all its utility tracing is one of the least perfectly understood areas of the law of restitution. It is caught on the horns of a dilemma. The longer its reach and therefore the greater its potency against fraud, the more difficult it is to describe exactly how it works; and the more one insists on the need for an accurate and intelligible account of how it works, the greater the danger of shortening its reach. But there is no real doubt as to how this dilemma must be resolved. The law cannot tolerate figures which are beyond rational description. If there turn out to be limits to what can intelligibly be done by tracing, other weapons will have to be invoked.'

[119] See Goode 42 with reference to *Foskett v McKeown* [2001] 1 AC 102 per Lord Millett at 127 etc. Goode notes that the claimant is entitled to the proceeds as of right in accordance to fixed

Under English law, substitution often provokes the question whether a right to substitute or withdraw collateral converts the security interest into a floating charge, which is subject to registration requirements under Section 395 of the Companies Act 1985.[120] Through the implementation of the Financial Collateral Arrangements Regulations, this uncertainty has been removed.

As a general rule, a security interest in an asset will almost invariably carry through to the proceeds in the case of an unauthorised disposition by the debtor or a third party.[121] The security interest will also extend to proceeds of an authorised disposition where it is effected on behalf of the creditor rather than for the debtor's own account.[122] It should be noted that should these rules be applied to a right of reuse under the Financial Collateral Arrangements Regulations, tracing would be excluded, as in this case the disposal is authorised and B disposes of the collateral as the owner, i.e. on its own account.[123]

Tracing does not distinguish between different types of assets and applies similarly to tangibles and intangibles. It involves three minimum requirements: (1) one asset must be exchanged for another; (2) the substitute must be identifiable; and (3) the substitute must still exist.[124] In addition, proprietary interest must be established for the defendant to have a legitimate proprietary claim.[125]

The proceeds represent the exchange value of the original asset and can be any asset (goods, money, etc.) that is received in exchange for the original asset.[126] There is no need to show any physical correlation between the asset the claimant lost and the asset the defendant received; it is sufficient to show a loss of value by the claimant and a receipt of value by the defendant.[127] The claiming rules determine whether the proceeds of an asset are sufficiently linked to give a proprietary right.[128]

The first step is to assert a "proprietary base" for the tracing claim to be successful.[129] The next step is to establish transactional links, i.e. links between the original property and the substitute.[130] These links rest on rules of evidence and onus. What

principles and is not dependent on the exercise of the court's discretion as to what is fair, just and reasonable.

[120] Goode 226–227.

[121] Goode 41. See also Fox 97 ff; and *Space Investments Ltd v CIBC (Bahamas) Ltd* [1986] 1 WLR 1072 (PC).

[122] Goode 41 with references to *Buhr v Barclays Bank Plc* [2001] EWCA Civ 1223.

[123] cf Fox 97 ff who in the case of authorised dispositions categorises the process as 'overreaching'.

[124] Lawson and Rudden 88.

[125] No proprietary rights are created – tracing merely allows them to be asserted in different assets, L Smith 302–303, 320. cf *Re Goldcorp Exchange Ltd (In Receivership)* [1995] 1 AC 74.

[126] Goode 42. Goode states that proceeds do not include income derived by the debtor from assets (such as rentals, share dividends, etc.) or natural produce or natural increase, for these are not given in exchange for the asset. Tracing ends when the assets disappear, cf *Bishopsgate Investment Management Ltd (In Liquidation) v Homan* [1995] Ch 211, where it was held that equitable tracing did not extend to tracing through an overdrawn bank account.

[127] Goode 42. See also *Foskett v McKeown* [2001] AC 102 per Lord Millett at 128.

[128] Goode 43.

[129] Hayton 19.

[130] Hayton 1.

needs to be proven is that the value of one asset stands in place of the value of another asset.

Due to the difficulties of tracing through money and bank accounts, the law has developed certain presumptions, i.e. artificial rules that penetrate evidential impasses.[131] One presumption is that evidential difficulties must be resolved against the wrongdoer who created them. Two other basic presumptions used in relation to bank accounts are 'first in, first out' and the 'lowest intermediate balance'. A fourth that applies to mixed funds is that contributions abate *pari passu* among contributors.[132]

Through the tracing process, the claimants can vindicate leading to the imposition of an equitable lien or charge upon the traced assets or an equitable interest in the whole or an appropriate proportion of the traced assets.[133] Tracing identifies the substitute and claiming asserts the right *in rem* in the substitute. The insolvency of the debtor is thereby defeated and the owner of the original asset is protected, unless a legitimate defence trumps the claim.[134] There are several defences against tracing and claiming, the most important being bona fide purchases of legal interest for value without notice.[135]

Following *Foskett v McKeown*,[136] it appears that the entitlement holder is entitled to a continuing interest either in the original property or in its traceable proceeds.[137] Accordingly, a claimant cannot assert proprietary rights over the proceeds of an asset and the original asset at the same time.[138] The claimant needs to determine whether to assert a claim over the original asset (i.e. following) or whether to trace and make a claim in its proceeds.[139] Once the decision has been made regarding which technique to pursue, the other remedy expires.[140]

In his work on the subject, Smith discusses tracing and the transfer of proprietary rights in relation to the question of fairness. The starting point is that it is unfair to allow a claimant to assert proprietary rights in traceable proceeds, since some claimants are allowed to trace whereas other claimants are left with unsecured claims. The question of identity is closely connected, as it often serves as the

---

131 Birks (1995), 290, 304.

132 See Birks (1995), 96–297 with references to, *inter alia*, *Lupton v White* (1808) 15 Ves 432, 436, 439–414; *Clayton's Case* (1816) 1 Mer 572; *The Mecca* [1897] AC 286; and *Sinclair v Brougham* [1914] AC 398. See also *Barlow Clowes International Ltd (in liquidation) v Vaughan* [1992] 4 All ER 22; and *Roscoe v Winder* [1915] 1 Ch 62. In *Barlow Clowes International Ltd* the Court of Appeal held that instead of using 'first-in, first-out', alternative methods of distribution should be used if the rule would be impractical, unjust or run contrary to the express or implied intentions.

133 D Hayton, 'Overview' in P Birks and A Pretto (eds.) *Breach of Trust* (Hart Publishing 2002) 380.

134 Wood 81.

135 Other defences that are available are change of position, ministerial receipt, passing on, illegality, incapacity, delay and limitation, etc., Birks (1995), 289 ff.

136 [2001] 1 AC 102.

137 Goode 44.

138 *ibid.*

139 Goode (2004), 54.

140 *ibid.*

establishing factor of a proprietary right. Smith argues that the issue is not whether it is fair to allow tracing or not. 'The important point is that the source of any arbitrariness lies not in the ability to claim traceable proceeds; it derives from the nature of proprietary rights themselves. Proprietary rights always have a specific subject matter.'[141] Smith refers to this theory as the 'Principle of Unfairness'. In accordance with this principle, the specificity of proprietary rights guarantees inequality of treatment among claimants.

> "Thus, the very existence of proprietary rights guarantees inequality of treatment as between those who hold them and those who do not. But the specificity of proprietary rights – the fact that they are rights *in* something, and cannot survive its loss or destruction – guarantees inequality of treatment even among those who never wanted to be unsecured creditors."[142]

Smith argues that tracing does not create property rights; it merely allows them to be transmitted from one asset into another.[143] Even though tracing in effect expands proprietary interests into other assets, it does not alter fundamental property rights to make them non-specific. The requirement for identity must therefore still be upheld.[144]

Although tracing involves a requirement of identity, it cannot be denied that it extends the notion of property. As Matthews puts it, tracing pushes forward the boundaries of the rules concerning acquisition and loss of property interests, by allowing the substitution of one asset for another.[145]

5.4.3 Tracing vs. Mixing

As mentioned, the requirement of identification is relevant in relation to tracing and mixing. In certain cases the lack of identity, or the substitution of one asset for another, can be assisted through the tracing and mixing techniques.

Tracing and mixing should be distinguished from each other.[146] Mixing is when the assets of two or more persons are blended and the assets belonging to each person can no longer be identified. Tracing is, as pointed out, the process used to identify value that has been substituted.[147] Whereas tracing examines the result of substitutions for the original asset, mixing relates to assets that in substance are unchanged.[148]

---

[141] L Smith 303–304.

[142] L Smith 304–305.

[143] L Smith 299.

[144] See L Smith 319.

[145] P Matthews, 'The Legal and Moral Limits of Common Law Tracing' in P Birks (ed), *Laundering and Tracing* (Clarendon Press 1995) 35.

[146] The equivalent phrase in civil law jurisdictions for tracing is real subrogation, Lawson and Rudden 89.

[147] *Boscawen and others v Bajwa* [1996] 1 WLR 328; Birks 228–231; L Smith 3 ff.

[148] Tracing is further dealt with in Sect. 4.2.

Different rules apply to different types of mixtures, depending on the assets involved. Fluid mixtures such as oil generally confer co-ownership. The rule for physical money, i.e. notes and coins, is continuing ownership. For other granular assets, the situation appears to be unclear.[149]

The mixing rules do not apply to bank money. As there is no physical commingling, only the rules relating to substitution and tracing apply.[150] Birks points out the contradiction of applying different rules to different types of assets. He suggests that a single rule – co-ownership for all mixtures in which the constituent units lose their identifiability – should apply. He predicts that, in time, the law will develop so that involuntary co-ownership will be the consequence of all mixtures where the identity is lost without regard to the nature of the substance mixed.[151]

Where value can be derived from different sources, it can be difficult to establish the origins of each contribution. That is why the mixtures rules are sometimes used in connection with tracing.[152] The general rule, however, is that there can be no tracing through mixed funds in common law, although it is possible in equity.[153]

5.4.4 Unallocated Securities

In the 1990s the question of whether fungible securities held on an unallocated basis could constitute a trust was widely discussed.[154] The uncertainty, which was referred to as the allocation question, concerned whether the requirement of certainty of subject matter to establish a valid trust was met. This question is of particular importance since, if the trust is not valid, the client only has a contractual right in the custodian's insolvency.

The discussion was, *inter alia*, concerned, with the famous case *Hunter v Moss*.[155] In this case the defendant, Moss, had declared himself a trustee over 50 shares of the 950 registered shares he held in a company with an issued share capital

---

149 Birks 246.

150 Birks 239.

151 Birks 246–249, 'Involuntary co-ownership will be the consequence of all mixtures without regard to the nature of the substance mixed, provided only that the units have ceased to be identifiable'.

152 Birks 231.

153 *Banque Belge pour l'Etranger v Hambrouck* [1921] 1 KB 321 (CA) at 330; *Re Diplock* [1948] Ch 465 (CA) at 518; Birks 240; and L Smith 160 ff, who rejects this idea. In the case of mixing, the idea behind this maxim is that the ability to trace is lost due to the loss of identification of the substitute, see *Taylor v Plumer* (1815) 105 ER 721.

154 Benjamin 55, who notes that the debate was triggered by the case *Re London Wine (Shippers) Ltd* [1986] PCC 121; Benjamin and Yates 28 ff.

155 [1994] 1 WLR 452; [1993] 1 WLR 934.

of 1,000 shares.[156] The question was whether Moss had made a valid declaration of trust. Moss argued that the trust failed for lack of certainty, as the 50 shares had not been identified or separated.

Judge Colin Rimer QC of the Chancery Division held that a trust made by oral declaration is not void for uncertainty of subject matter merely because it refers to a number, and not to specific shares. It was held that in the case of a trust of intangible assets the requirement of certainty did not necessarily entail segregation or appropriation of the specific property, which was to form the subject matter of the trust. Since the shares were of such nature as to be indistinguishable one from another and were therefore all equally capable of satisfying the trust, it was unnecessary to identify any particular 50 shares.[157]

> "The defendant did not identify any particular 50 shares for the plaintiff because to do so was unnecessary and irrelevant. All 950 of his shares carried identical rights. It mattered neither to him nor the plaintiff which particular 50 shares were to be regarded as held for the plaintiff. The shares were therefore in my judgement of such a nature that each of them could satisfy the trust just as well as any other of them. Why therefore should equity be concerned that 50 particular shares were not identified?"[158]

Moss appealed to the Court of Appeal, which confirmed the judgment by the High Court.[159] The appeal was dismissed: since all the shares were of one class and indistinguishable from one another, they were all equally capable of satisfying the trust. The requirement of certainty of subject matter did not necessarily involve segregation of the asset and there was no problem in declaring a trust over a specified number of shares without identifying any particular shares. The trust was therefore not void for uncertainty of subject matter.[160]

Hunter v Moss has drawn a great deal of criticism, mostly due to the fact that there is no clear basis on which to distinguish between intangibles and tangibles under English trust law.[161] While the requirement for identity of the subject matter, although under different types of situations, has been upheld for wheat,[162] bottles of

---

[156] cf Goode (2003), 380–381, who points out that the actual formulation of the trust did not in fact refer to 50 shares but to 5 per cent of the issued share capital.

[157] [1993] 1 WLR 934.

[158] [1993] 1 WLR 934, see page 946.

[159] [1994] 3 All ER 215; [1994] 1 WLR 452.

[160] *ibid.*

[161] Benjamin 58; D Hayton, 'Uncertainty of Subject-Matter of Trusts' (1994) 110 LQR 335–340. See also Worthington 1–21: 'Even ignoring the initial difficulties associated with the shares being held by a nominee there are problems with the basis upon which *Hunter v Moss* was distinguished from other English authorities.' See also A Underhill and D Hayton, *Trusts and Trustees* (16th edn Butterworths LexisNexis 2003) 78–79; and P Birks, 'Establishing a Proprietary Base' [1995] RLR 83, 87, who argues that *Hunter v Moss* "must be wrong".

[162] *Re Wait* [1927] 1 Ch 606.

wine,[163] money[164] and gold,[165] it was dismissed by the Court of Appeal in relation to shares.[166]

The decision in *Hunter v Moss* was reluctantly followed in *Re Harvard Securities Ltd*[167] where the distinction between having a beneficial interest in an unappropriated interest in chattels and an unappropriated interest in shares was emphasised. It was held that under English law it is possible to have a beneficial interest in the latter, but not the former, type of assets. The decision was also followed in the Hong Kong case *CA Pacific*.[168] In this case the High Court of the Hong Kong SAR Court of First Instance held that each client of a stockbroker holding its clients' assets in a fungible securities account had individual proprietary claims to the securities, rather than as equitable tenants in common.[169]

Benjamin states that two different approaches follow from the discussions prompted by *Hunter v Moss*. The first approach, which she considers prudent, is to view unallocated securities in bulk as being held under a global trust. In accordance with this view, the certainty of subject matter is not met if individual trusts are sought to be established over different groups of securities without separating them or marking them as belonging to the trust (in which case they would no longer be unallocated). That a global trust is created implies that the certainty of subject matter is met in relation to the bulk, and that the owners have co-ownership interests and collateral-takers have co-security interests, in the bulk of securities.[170] One precondition is, however, that the securities are segregated from the intermediary's own positions.

The second approach follows the decision in *Hunter v Moss*. Since the shares held in the pool are intangibles, and the requirement of certainty of subject matter does not apply to intangibles, a valid trust is established despite the difficulties to identify the shares. This argument has been criticised for being illogical, since it is clear that the requirement of certainty of subject matter is upheld in relation to other choses in action, for instance money.[171]

---

[163] *Re London Wine Co (Shippers) Ltd* [1986] PCC 121; cf *Re Stapylton Fletcher Ltd (in administrative receivership)* [1994] 1 WLR 1181; *Re Ellison Son & Vidler Ltd* [1995] 1 All ER 192.

[164] *MacJordan Construction Ltd v Bookmount Erostin Ltd* [1991] BCLC 350.

[165] *Re Goldcorp Exchange Ltd (In Receivership)* [1995] 1AC 74. For an analysis of the case, see E McKendrick, 'Unascertained Goods: Ownership and Obligation Distinguished' (1994) 110 LQR 509.

[166] Worthington emphasises that many critics fail to recognise three different matters which are important when analysing interests in a pool of assets: the problems of identifying the bulk; the type of transaction, i.e. a sale, gift or trust; and the type of assets. She points out that *Hunter v Moss* can be distinguished from many of the preceding cases as there was no difficulty in identifying the bulk, Worthington with further references to *Re London Wine Co (Shippers) Ltd* [1986] PCC 121, *Re Goldcorp Exchange Ltd (In Receivership)* [1995] 1AC 74, *MacJordan Construction Ltd v Brookmount Erostin Ltd* [1991] BCLC 350.

[167] [1997] 2 BCLC 369.

[168] *Re CA Pacific Finance Ltd (in Liquidation) and another* [2000] BCLC 494.

[169] cf K Pullen, 'Fungible Securities and Insolvency' (1999) 14 JIBFL 286 ff; Goode (2002), 105.

[170] Benjamin 56.

[171] *Mac-Jordan Construction Ltd v Brookmount Erostin Ltd* [1991] BCLC 350; Benjamin 55–59.

A third approach is adopted by Goode, who argues that it is not the intangible nature of shares but that they are indivisible that gives them their special character. In accordance with this argument shares are not fungibles, as they are not legally interchangeable.[172]

> "Common wisdom has it that shares are fungible in that any one share is legally exchangeable for any other share and that on a repo transaction what the seller receives on the return leg of the repo is not the shares it transferred but their equivalent in number and kind. As stated earlier, this is a misconception. Fungibility requires the existence of at least two legally interchangeable units. But shares are not like bottles of wine or potatoes, where it is possible to segregate individual units from a bulk and dispose of them separately from the bulk. Individual shares in a company are no more segregable than shares in a racehorse. Just as it is impossible to own a share in a racehorse otherwise than as co-owner of the racehorse itself, so also it is impossible to own a share in a company otherwise than as co-owner of the company's issued share capital. [...] It follows [...] that a sale, mortgage or charge of shares of a particular issue cannot fail for want of ascertainment, for the subject-matter is not individual shares as distinct assets but the issued share capital itself."[173]

Goode claims that in relation to shares in a company it is the entire share capital that constitutes one single asset, not each particular share.[174] This is so even if the securities are numbered, exist in bearer form or are issued in separate issues carrying different rights. Although the certificate represents the ownership and the underlying rights in the share, they only embody title to a co-ownership interest in the securities issue.[175] Goode's approach is further analysed in Chap. 8.

It has been recognised that giving up the requirement for identity creates unclear results in relation to a number of matters. Without identification of any individual shares it can, for instance, be questioned how priority between competing interests should be resolved. Closely related questions are: how to allocate capital gains tax, proceeds and losses due to forged transfers; whether any proprietary interest capable of assignment can be said to exist if the shares cannot be identified; and whether it is possible to obtain an injunction to prevent the sale or mortgage of shares.[176]

Another question is whether there is a difference between creating an equitable interest in a share of the bulk, for instance in 25%, and in a certain quantity, say 250 shares, in a total of 1,000 shares.[177] Some critics claim that it is possible to create an interest in the former case, but not in the latter.[178] When the interest is defined as a share of the whole, all benefits and burdens would be shared on a *pro rata* basis, based on the fact that each entitlement holder holds a proportionate interest, in this

[172] Goode 62–64, 211–212. See also Goode (2002), 97 ff and Goode (2003), 383.

[173] Goode 211–212.

[174] Goode 211 ff; Goode (2003), 384. cf Benjamin 58 n 158.

[175] Goode 212.

[176] D Hayton, 'Uncertainty of Subject-Matter of Trusts' (1994) 110 LQR 335–340; Worthington 1–21.

[177] Worthington 1–21.

[178] A Underhill and D Hayton, *Trusts and Trustees* (16th edn Butterworths LexisNexis 2003) 78–79 who distinguishes the case where the intangibles are shares in a public company whose shares are held by a nominee under the CREST system. See also *Re London Wine Co (Shippers)* [1986] PCC 121 at 137; and K Pullen, 'Fungible Securities and Insolvency' (1999) 14 JIBFL 288.

case 25%, in each share. This would, however, not be possible in a case where the entitlement holder holds an interest in a certain number of shares. In that case it is impossible to determine what shares are covered by the trust and therefore to allocate the benefits and burdens. It has been pointed out that the distinction of having a proprietary interest in a share and a quantity in a bulk of shares is impractical and is often overlooked.[179]

It has also been argued that there is no reason why the rules on tracing and mixed assets should not apply in the case of commingled assets held under a trust structure.[180] Even in a case where the tracing rules would not work, for instance if Moss, in addition to the trust over 50 shares, declared a trust over 475 shares in favour of two different beneficiaries, it has been argued that there is no reason why this should prohibit the creation of a valid trust in the first place.[181] Others argue that the rules relating to mixing and tracing do not apply to commingled securities, since they would only apply if the individual ownership predated the mixing of the assets.[182] It should also be noted that with the practice of holding securities on an unallocated and indirect basis, tracing has proved to be difficult, if not impossible, since it is often not possible to establish the links in the chain of intermediaries and each intermediary only has knowledge of its own customers.[183] Another obstacle that severely impedes tracing is close-out netting and set-off.

Austen-Peters, who discusses substitution of securities held in a pool and the classification of the investor's rights, suggests that there are certain features that can be used to determine whether a property in pooled assets passes to the custodian. One important factor is the existence of an option to substitute the asset for cash or equivalent assets. The reason for this is that the power to determine how the assets are used is an important indicator of who the property resides in. Another feature that may have an impact is the placement of the risk for loss or destruction of the assets between the parties. A third possible factor is the obligation to hold a sufficient number of the relevant assets to meet the demands of the depositors at all times.[184] These features correspond to some of the conclusions made in Chaps. 6 and 7 in relation to the characterisation of the transaction. They are further analysed in Chap. 9.

In conclusion, the established view appears to be that securities held in a fungible bulk constitute co-ownership rights, or – in the case of security – a co-security interest, under a trust and therefore can be ascertained against other creditors.[185] The certainty of subject matter is met as long as the pool of securities is separated

---

179 Worthington 1–21.

180 Worthington 7–8 and Martin 223–227.

181 Martin 223–227.

182 Benjamin 56; L Smith 132.

183 Goode 213 ff; Rogers (1996); and FMLC, 'Issue 3 – Property Interests in Investment Securities' (July 2004) 12.

184 Austen-Peters 51–52.

185 Benjamin and Yates 27 ff; Goode (1998), 78; Benjamin 323. See also FMLC, 'Issue 3 – Property Interests in Investment Securities' (July 2004) 9.

from the intermediary's assets.[186] Thus, a global trust over all the assets held in the pool is established. The intermediary acts as a trustee and the account holders have beneficial interests in the pool, although not in specific securities.[187] Due to the indirect holding structures, the investor does not enjoy direct rights in the underlying securities but rather equitable "interest in securities".[188] Should a shortfall arise, the claimants are deemed to share *pro rata*.[189]

It is submitted that the idea of preserving the requirement for specificity by identifying the pool as the subject matter is flawed. As securities registered on accounts are fungible intangibles and as such impossible to separate and distinguish from each other, it would be more useful to recognise this.[190]

5.5 Summary and Conclusions

With the implementation of the Financial Collateral Arrangements Regulations, the right to reuse financial collateral has been established through statute. Regulation 16 allows the collateral-taker to use and dispose of the collateral in accordance with the terms of the financial collateral agreement as if it were the owner of it. If the collateral-taker exercises such right, it is obliged to replace the original collateral with the equivalent before or on the due date of the performance of the underlying obligation, or, if the arrangement so provides, it may set off the value of the equivalent financial collateral against, or apply it in discharge of, the relevant financial obligation in accordance with the terms of the arrangement.

Following the implementation of the Financial Collateral Arrangements Regulations, any doubt about the collateral-taker's right to repledge financial collateral is removed. The previous uncertainties concerned some equitable principles that were considered to put a clog on the equity of redemption, i.e. the collateral-provider's right to redeem the collateral upon discharge of the underlying obligation.

One issue that hitherto has not been highlighted is whether the right to reuse under the Financial Collateral Arrangements Regulations concerns outright transfers, security interests or both. As the Regulations allow the collateral-taker to reuse the collateral as if it were the owner of it, it can be questioned whether they concern title transfer and not security arrangements. Simply, after conceding the equity

---

[186] Goode (1996), 172–173.

[187] Benjamin 56.

[188] Benjamin and Yates 250; Austen-Peters 77–78.

[189] Benjamin and Yates 33–35; cf *Spence v Union Marine Insurance Co* (1868) 3 LRCP 427, 439 per Bovill CJ. Another rule that that possibly could be used is that if a mixture is wrongfully brought about by one of the parties claiming to have an interest in the pool of assets, for instance if the intermediary has mixed its client's securities with its own proprietary positions, the pool is forfeited to the innocent party. The forfeiture shifts the onus of proof on to the wrongdoing party to show what belongs to it in the pool, Austen-Peters 47 with reference to *Warde v Aeyre* (1614) 2 Bulstrode 323, 80 ER 1157. This should be compared with UCC 8–503.

[190] cf Sect. 3.2.4.

of redemption, there is nothing that upholds the distinction between ownership and security.

The equity of redemption, which represents the owner's property rights in the collateral, is closely connected with the requirement for identity. The requirement for identity is a vital criterion for the acquisition of proprietary rights under English law, as well as in most legal systems. Identification is a requirement for the acquisition of proprietary rights regardless of whether the asset is a tangible or intangible and regardless of whether the right is legal or equitable. If the collateral-provider cannot identify its asset upon discharge of the underlying obligation, it is, under traditional property law rules, difficult to claim a property right in it.

It may be that the tracing, mixing and claiming rules will assist the claimant in asserting a proprietary claim in the substitute or in the commingled pool of assets. Thus, upon the reuse of the financial collateral, it is possible that these techniques can be used by the claimant in identifying the equivalent collateral and asserting its proprietary right.[191] However, also in the case of tracing, identification is an important element in establishing in what proceeds a claim can be asserted. Should there be a shortfall of assets, for instance, in the case of insolvency of B, a decision on how to allocate the assets of B's estate still needs to be made. Moreover, due to the practices in the securities markets, tracing in investment securities may be both theoretically, as well as practically, impossible.[192]

There are indications that English law is moving away from traditional property and security law structures. In relation to the requirement for identity, these developments imply that a relaxation is taking place. Collateral is increasingly taken over a mass of assets where each individual piece is unidentified in relation to the collateral-taker. Not only the floating charge, but also the trust, provide a technique whereby security interests can be created over a fluctuating group of assets.[193] The retreat of the requirement for identity has also been embodied in the mixing and tracing rules through which proprietary rights are extended in proceeds and commingled assets.

It is submitted that in time, a single rule which provides co-ownership for commingled assets held in an identified bulk is likely to develop in English law.[194] The decision in *Hunter v Moss* supports this outcome, although only indirectly.[195] The exemption from the requirement of ascertainability under Sections 20A-B of the Sales of Goods Act 1979, which gives the prepaying buyer ownership in common of unidentified goods kept in an identified bulk, is another example. It should, however, be recognised that intermediated securities evidenced in book-entry form are fungible intangibles and as such impossible to separate and distinguish from each

---

[191] However, it may also be argued that there can be no continuing security interest, as the reuse extinguishes the original security interest, cf Benjamin and Yates 55 n 1; and Sect. 6.3.2.

[192] cf Schroeder (1994), 332. 'Under netting, financial intermediaries do not, in fact, transfer every investment security individually [...].'

[193] cf Goode (1987), 437.

[194] cf Birks 246–249.

[195] cf *Hunter v Moss* [1994] 1 WLR 452; see also *Re Harvard Securities Ltd* [1997] 2 BCLC 369 and *CA Pacific Finance Ltd (in Liquidation) and another* [2000] BCLC 494.

other.[196] Therefore, to speak of these assets as being 'pooled' is not only inaccurate, but also a legal construct.[197]

The developments in English law clearly support the main argument of this book: that unallocated and intermediated securities have outgrown the existing property and security law system and that there is a need to design a separate set of rules for these assets.

---

[196] That is unless the registration of the securities is given constitutive effect, cf Sect. 8.3.

[197] cf Sect. 3.2.4.

Chapter 6
Property Rights in Securities and the Doctrine of Specificity under Swedish Law

"The requirement for identification of the pledge object is [further] deemed to mean, that a pledge right does not arise if the pledgee has a right to use the pledge object by himself and also has done so. An agreement of this type is sometimes referred to as 'pignus irregulare' ".[1] *(freely translated)*

6.1 Introduction

Reuse of financial collateral is also a common feature of the securities markets in Sweden.[2] This Chapter examines repledge and repos under Swedish law and the implementation of the Financial Collateral Directive which came into effect in Sweden on 1 May 2005. It discusses the requirement for substitution and the possibilities to trace assets under Swedish law. An analysis of the doctrine of specificity is also provided with particular focus on unallocated securities.

6.2 Interest in Securities

6.2.1 Introduction to Swedish Security Law

Due to the influences from Germany in the nineteenth century and the legal thinking and attitude that have developed over time, Swedish law bears more resemblance to the laws on the European continent than to those of the Anglo-Saxon tradition.[3] However, in contrast to German law, Swedish commercial law remains to a large degree uncodified.

---

[1] Rodhe 439.

[2] Myrdal 22.

[3] As several of the major characteristics of common law such as equity and trust are absent, it is clear that Swedish law does not belong to the common law family. It can, instead, be said to belong to the Roman-German legal tradition, S Strömholm, 'General Features of Swedish Law' in M Bogdan (ed.), *Swedish Law in the New Millennium* (Norstedts Juridik 2000) 40–41; cf K Zweigert and H Kötz, *An Introduction to Comparative Law* (3rd edn OUP 1998) 63 ff, 276 ff, who distinguish the laws of the Nordic countries as a legal family of its own.

E. Johansson, *Property Rights in Investment Securities and the Doctrine of Specificity*,

© Springer-Verlag Berlin Heidelberg 2009

There is no principal code on security interests. Rather, the rules and principles are scattered in a variety of legislation and have also developed through case law.[4] For this reason the legal literature is of particular importance in establishing and developing the law.[5] The main factors determining which rules apply are the type of assets over which the security is taken and the type of transaction.[6]

A distinction can generally be made between the following types of security: "*panträtt*", "*säkerhetsöverlåtelse*", "*retentionsrätt*", "*legal panträtt*"[7] and "*företagsinteckning*". Title transfers in various forms are also often used as security.

"*Panträtt*" ("pledge") is the main form of security and can be taken over a variety of assets. The pledge is not limited to chattels but can also cover intangibles. Thus, in contrast to English law, it is not dependent on possession. Should the collateral-provider not fulfil its obligations, the pledge object can be sold. The collateral-taker can use the proceeds to make sure the underlying obligation, for instance a loan, is paid. The pledge can, therefore, be viewed as a special type of property even though the right in itself only gives a preference right.[8] Upon sale of the collateral, the collateral-taker must return any surplus to the collateral-provider.[9]

"*Säkerhetsöverlåtelse*" ("security transfer") should be distinguished from outright transfers. In the case of a security transfer, the ownership structure is used to secure an underlying obligation, although the purpose is to use the asset as collateral. The parties agree that the collateral-provider, i.e. the vendor, shall have a right to repurchase the collateral. In the legal literature it is presumed that the collateral-provider's right to repurchase the collateral is valid and enforceable even if the collateral-taker is subject to bankruptcy proceedings and the collateral is in the collateral-taker's possession.[10] A special form of security transfer is regulated in the Bills of Sales Act (1845:50 s 1).[11]

The classification of the transaction has, naturally, legal effects. Should the transaction be characterised as a security transfer and not as an outright transfer, §37 of the Contracts Act §37 (1915:218) comes into play. Thereby any surplus remaining after a sale of the collateral must be returned to the collateral-provider. The classification of the transaction may also affect the application of voidable preferences rules under Ch. 4 of the Bankruptcy Act (1987:672).

"*Retentionsrätt*" and/or "*legal panträtt*" ("lien") can be described as a legal pledge as it only is created by law. There are numerous rules creating liens for various situations.[12] In some cases the rules provide a right for the creditor to sell

---

[4] G Millqvist, 'Swedish Credit Security Law: A Case for Law Reform?' [2004] 15 EBLR 861.

[5] cf Persson 52.

[6] cf Millqvist 21.

[7] In this book "lien" is used as a summarising term for both "*retentionsrätt*" and "*legal panträtt*".

[8] §4 para 2 Preferential Rights Act; cf Walin (1998), 15 ff.

[9] §37 of the Contracts Act.

[10] Håstad 443; Karlgren (1952, 1958) 155; Hessler 450 ff; Rodhe 196.

[11] See also NJA 1912 p 156, and Håstad 217.

[12] See for instance Ch. 11 §3 and Ch. 12 §8 Commercial Code, §75 Sales of Goods Act, §§6, 31–37 and 39 Commission Agency Act, §§15–16 Commercial Agency Act (1991:351), §§49–50

the collateral should the underlying obligation not be fulfilled; in other cases the creditor is only entitled to retain it.

A new Act (2003:528) on Company Charges came into effect on 1 January 2004. It replaced the old act and brought with it a number of changes.[13] The main change is that the "*företagsinteckning*" ("floating charge") has been transformed into a general preference right in 55% of the value of the assets that remain in the enterprise after creditors with better preference rights have received their share.[14]

6.2.2 Security over Investment Securities

Securities can generally be issued in either registered or bearer format. All Swedish securities registered in the VPC system are dematerialised and, from a legal perspective, held either on owner or nominee accounts.[15] Under the Financial Instruments Accounts Act (1998:1479)(FIAA) registration has been equated with possession of bearer documents. This means that the registration confers similar legal effects as possession of a bearer document.[16]

A registration on an owner account gives the account holder the "legitimate capacity" to act as the owner of the securities on the account even though the registration lacks constitutive effect and only evidences title to the securities.[17] A person registered as the owner has the right to dispose of the securities as long as the disposal does not interfere with the limitations set forth on the account. As for nominee accounts, a custodian – who is normally an authorised bank or a broker – holds the securities on behalf of the owner. The owner's holdings are registered in the books of the custodian who keeps the account with VPC.[18] Thus, it is the custodian who is registered as the holder on the VPC account and who is presumed to have the right to dispose of the securities.[19]

A security interest in investment securities is, regardless of whether the securities are in registered or bearer format, usually created by way of pledge. Another method is to use title transfer structures. For securities registered in the VPC system,

---

Consumer Services Act (1985:716), Act on Entrepreneurs' Right to Sell Chattels that are Uncollected (1985:982), Ch. 3 §§36, 39 and 43, Ch. 13 §20, Ch. 15 §11 Sea Act (1994:1009).

[13] It should be noted that this reform is about to be revoked due to the negative effect it has had on commercial credit.

[14] §11 Preferential Rights Act; Prop 2002/03:49.

[15] cf Sect. 3.3.1. Foreign securities can however be immobilised, cf Ch. 4 §§4–5 FIAA.

[16] cf Ch. 6 and Ch. 3 §10 FIAA; Afrell, Klahr and Samuelsson 92–93.

[17] cf Ch. 6 §§1–4 FIAA. See also Afrell and Wallin-Norman 279.

[18] cf Ch. 3 §10 FIAA; and Afrell and Wallin-Norman 279. Only authorised institutions are permitted to act as account keeping institutions and thus to book transactions on accounts, Ch. 3 §§1–6 FIAA. If a nominee is not authorised to act as an account keeping institution, it will have to have an arrangement with such institution or with VPC who makes the registrations on the account.

[19] cf Ch. 3 §10 FIAA; Prop 1997/98:160 118; Afrell and Wallin-Norman 279.

transfers and pledges take place via book entry on the register.[20] A pledge is created by designating the collateral to the collateral-taker on the securities account of the collateral-provider.[21] Title transfers involve the transfer of the collateral to the account of the collateral-taker. A security interest in securities held by a custodian is registered in its books.

6.2.2.1 Perfection

For the agreement between the collateral-provider and the collateral-taker to be effective in relation to third parties, the security interest must be perfected.[22] The method of perfection is determined by the type of assets over which the security is taken and the type of transaction. The same type of measure usually applies to both security and title transfer arrangements.[23]

Generally, a security interest is perfected when the possibility for the collateral-provider to use or dispose of the collateral is cut off.[24] In relation to chattels, this requirement is usually met when the possession of the collateral is transferred to the collateral-taker (*traditio*) or a person acting on its behalf.[25] For other types of assets and situations, other measures apply, for instance notice to the third party when the collateral is in its possession or to the debtor when dealing with ordinary claims.[26] Another example is registration in public registers.[27] In a few limited cases, perfection is achieved through the agreement only, i.e. without any separate measures.[28]

For securities registered on owner accounts in the VPC system, transfers and pledges become effective when registered.[29] Perfection is thus achieved through

---

[20] Ch. 6 §§1–4 and 7 FIAA.

[21] VPC Rules 'Account Keeping and Clearing' (14 February 2005) 47.

[22] There is no requirement to attach a security interest under Swedish law.

[23] In contrast to many other jurisdictions outright transfers must generally be perfected to be valid and enforceable.

[24] cf NJA 1996 p 52; NJA 1995 p 367 I; NJA 2007 p 413.

[25] cf NJA 1925 p 130; NJA 1997 p 660; NJA 1998 p 379; NJA 1987 p 4; §§10 and 22 Promissory Notes Act (1936:81); and Ch. 6 §8 Companies Act (2005:551). The requirement for *traditio,* which has been subject to criticism in recent years, is based on the argument that it prevents shams and other fraudulent transactions, Håstad 286. It has, *inter alia,* been questioned whether the risk of shams and similar fraudulent transactions constitutes a real problem, cf E Johansson, 'The Law Commission's Consultation Paper No 164: Some Reflections regarding the Exclusion of Securities' (2004) 15 EBLR 835 ff. It has moreover been questioned if it is not sufficient with the voidable preferences rules under the Bankruptcy Act, see Millqvist 89. See also U Göransson, *Traditionsprincipen* (Iustus Förlag 1985). *Traditio* as perfection requirement was abandoned in 2002 for consumer purchases of goods, see §49 Consumer Sales of Goods Act; SOU 1995:11 p 133 ff, and Prop 2001/02:134.

[26] cf NJA 1949 p 164; NJA 1980 p 197; §§10 and 31 Promissory Notes Act; and Act (1936:88) on Pledge of Chattels Held by a Third Party.

[27] cf Ch. 12 Patents (1967:837) Act; §§34 a-j Trademark (1960:644) Act; and Ch. 6 §1–4 FIAA.

[28] cf §49 Consumer Sales of Goods Act (1990:932); NJA 1985 p 159; NJA 1998 p 545; NJA 1952 p 407; and NJA 1979 p 451.

[29] Ch. 6 §§1–4 and 7 FIAA.

registration which protects the collateral-taker from the creditors of the collateral-provider and other third parties.[30] As for nominee accounts, notification to the custodian has the same effect as registration on the account; the notification gives the collateral-taker protection in relation to third parties.[31]

In relation to bearer instruments, the security is perfected by taking the documents into possession.[32] Should the instruments be in the possession of a third party, perfection is achieved by notification to the third party.[33]

6.2.2.2 Priority

In the bankruptcy of the debtor, priority between different creditors' claims is determined under the Preferential Rights Act (1970:979). There are two types of preference rights: special and general preference rights. Whereas special preference rights cover the assets over which the security is taken, general preference rights cover all the debtor's assets. Naturally the former group is given precedence over the latter in the distribution of the debtor's assets. Pledge and lien give the collateral-taker a special preference right whereas the floating charge gives the collateral-taker a general preference right (cf above).[34] Priority outside bankruptcy is mainly established under the Good Faith Acquisitions of Chattels Act (1986:796), or, where special regulations apply, those regulations.

6.3 Reuse of Financial Collateral

Repledge and reuse of collateral has been discussed in the Swedish legal literature to a broader extent than in the United Kingdom and the United States. In the discussions, at least three different scenarios related to repledge and reuse of collateral can be distinguished: (1) the case where the collateral-taker pledges the collateral together with the underlying obligation that it secures (i.e. not a strict repledge); (2) a strict repledge, i.e. a repledge of the collateral only; and (3) a disposal of financial instruments deposited with a custodian (i.e. not a pledge in the first case).[35]

Sect. 6.3.1 below, for the most part, discusses scenario 2 i.e. a strict repledge, whereas Sect. 6.3.2 discusses the implementation of Art. 5 of the Financial Collateral Directive and the problems it conveys. A legal analysis of 'repos' is provided in Sect. 6.3.3. Since the amendments made through the implementation of the

[30] cf Ch. 6 FIAA.

[31] Ch. 3 §10 FIAA.

[32] cf §§10 and 22 Promissory Notes Act; and Ch. 6 §8 Companies Act.

[33] cf NJA 1949 p 164; NJA 1980 p 197; §§10 and 31 Promissory Notes Act; and Act (1936:88) on Pledge of Chattels Held by a Third Party.

[34] §§4, 9, 11 and 14 Preferential Rights Act (1970:979).

[35] cf Prop 2004/05:30 p 126; Myrdal 411 ff; and Lennander 153, 171 ff.

Directive are limited to certain institutions, the analysis under A and C applies to the cases falling outside the scope of the Directive.

6.3.1 Repledge

The starting point is that the collateral-taker to a collateral agreement, unless explicitly excluded, has an independent right to repledge. A distinction can generally be made between an agreed right of use and an independent right to repledge.[36]

Ch. 10 §6 of the Commercial Code (1736:0123) provides an independent right for collateral-takers to repledge collateral, i.e. it regulates the cases that are not covered by an agreement. As this provision, which dates back to 1736, is very old certain parts of it are deemed to be obsolete. Its contents are also uncertain.[37] The most important condition – which is not obsolete – is that a repledge cannot take place for a larger debt than the original debt or on more stringent conditions than under the original agreement between A and B. However, since this rule can be modified by agreement, the parties can agree on a more extensive right of use.[38] Another requirement is that the owner of the collateral shall be notified about the repledge. However, this condition is not considered to have constitutive implications and so failure to notify the owner does not affect the validity of the repledge as such.[39]

Where the collateral consists of financial instruments, the Trade with Financial Instruments Act (1991:980) applies. Under Ch. 3 §1 of the Act, institutions under the supervision of the Swedish Financial Services Authority shall clearly specify in a special agreement the conditions where they have the right to dispose of their clients' financial instruments (i.e. scenario 3). The type of disposal shall be carefully specified and, for example, include a right to sell or pledge the financial instruments to a third party. The same applies if the institution takes part or facilitates such an arrangement between other parties. As already mentioned, this provision concerns for the most part the case where a custodian uses its client's assets (*depositum irregulare*).[40]

Ch. 3 §3 of the Trade with Financial Instruments Act provides a right to repledge or transfer the pledge right, either together with the underlying debt or in some other way (i.e. scenarios 1–2). If a company under the supervision of the Financial Services Authority has received financial instruments as security, the company is permitted to pledge or transfer the pledge right only together with the underlying obligation that it secures. A repledge or transfer detached from the underlying obligation requires the same type of special agreement as set out under Ch. 3 §1 of

[36] Prop 2002/03:107 p 45.

[37] Prop 2002/03:107 p 43.

[38] Prop 2004/05:30 p 41–54;Håstad 300.

[39] Prop 2004/05:30 p 41–54; Ds 2003:38 82; Håstad; and Walin (1998), 52.

[40] The effect of this arrangement is that the depositor lacks a right of separation in the depositee's bankruptcy as the depositee's right of use transforms the depositor's property right into a claim, cf Undén 61, S Lindskog, *Preskription* (2nd edn Norstedts Juridik 2002) 89 ff.

the Act. Moreover, a repledge or a transfer cannot take place for a larger amount or on more stringent conditions than under the original agreement between A and B.

The rules under Ch. 3 of the Trade with Financial Instruments Act have been said to be of regulatory nature, and thus, do not govern private law matters.[41] One factor that supports this view is that the Financial Services Authority may order an institution that does not comply with the rules to stop its trade subject to a fine.[42] It should be pointed out, however, that the contents of many of the rules are of substantive law character. It can therefore be questioned whether the above statement is correct. It should also be pointed out that even if the Act only has a regulatory effect, Ch. 10 §6 of the Commercial Code is still applicable.[43]

Similarly to the rule in Ch. 10 §6 of the Commercial Code, the contents of the rules under Ch. 3 of the Trade with Financial Instruments Act are unclear.[44] Since the rules are of a regulatory character, it is also unclear whether an agreement that is contrary to the rules will be invalid or will result in other legal consequences. It is deemed possible that an agreement that is in conflict with the rules may be modified under §36 of the Contract Act.[45]

The government, or following authorisation by the government, the Financial Services Authority, may provide additional regulations as to the agreements covered by Ch. 3 §§1 and 3 of the Trade with Financial Instruments Act.[46] Previously the regulations FFFS 1998:21 were issued. They were, however, abolished in 2002.

VPC has also included a few provisions on repledge in its terms and conditions (VPC Rules). The VPC Rules are binding through accession to the VPC system. Under these regulations a repledge shall be marked on the pledge account with a designated number referring to the collateral-taker C and the collateral-provider B's pledge number.[47] When a nominee is repledging nominee-registered securities, the pledge is registered on a special nominee-account to which the collateral is transferred. When the repledging nominee is also the account operator, the registration of the repledge may not be carried out by the same operator. Instead, the repledge will need to be registered by another account keeping institution to which the collateral is transferred. The repledging nominee is, however, registered as the holder of the repledged collateral.[48]

---

[41] Myrdal 445 ff.

[42] Ch. 6 §2 Trade with Financial Instruments Act; Prop 2004/05:30 p 48; Ds 2003:38 p 72–73.

[43] Myrdal 445 ff.

[44] cf Myrdal.

[45] Prop 2004/05:30 p 48; see also Myrdal 445–447.

[46] Ch. 3 §4 Trade with Financial Instruments Act. Such authority was provided through 1:3 Ordinance (1991:1007) on Trade and Services in the Securities Markets.

[47] VPC Rules *Account Keeping and Clearing* (14 February 2005) 48.

[48] VPC Rules *Account Keeping and Clearing* (14 February 2005) 48: cf Myrdal 465 who notes that due to the complications of transferring nominee registered securities to the account of another institution, common practice is to transfer the securities directly from B to C's account.

There are only a few cases that concern repledge. Most of them deal with the questions of repledge under stricter conditions or good faith purchases of the collateral (cf below).[49]

From the above, it is clear that unless it has been excluded in the pledge agreement, B has a right to repledge the collateral. This right can be said to spring from B's rights as a pledgee.[50]

If B repledges the collateral under stricter conditions or for a larger debt than under the agreement with A, the repledge agreement will be invalid – at least in relation to the extent that the amount exceeds the original amount or as for those clauses that go beyond the provisions of the original agreement.[51] As part of the prohibition on repledging collateral on stricter conditions, C cannot realise the collateral before B would have been able to do so or use the collateral on conditions other than those under the agreement between A and B.[52] A bona fide purchaser can, however, acquire the collateral free from adverse claims, i.e. free from A's property rights. The same applies to collateral arrangements; a bona fide collateral-taker can acquire a security interest in the collateral free from any claims.[53]

There is no explicit rule that requires B to return the collateral to A. Rather it is a matter of course. Since B has not cancelled its contract with A, it is still obligated to return it.[54] B's obligation to return the collateral derives from A's ownership rights in the collateral; as the owner of the collateral A has a right to separate its asset in the bankruptcy of B.[55]

As for perfection, the same requirements that apply to a normal pledge ought to apply to a repledge of collateral, i.e. the collateral-provider shall be cut-off from controlling the collateral (cf Sect. 6.2.2.1).[56]

One of the main questions that has been discussed is whether Ch. 10 §6 of the Commercial Code and the rules under Ch. 3 §3 of the Trade with Financial Instruments Act refer to repledge of the *collateral* or to B's *pledgee-right*.[57] Should these provisions only cover repledge of the pledgee-right, C's right has been deemed to not constitute an independent right.[58] Myrdal, who wrote his doctoral thesis on 'Repledge: On Pledging Collateral and Pledgee-rights', concludes that if the object of the repledge is B's pledgee-rights, B cannot repledge on more stringent conditions

---

[49] See for instance NJA 1912 p 122; NJA 1930 p 134 and NJA 1961 p 2. For a more comprehensive analysis, see Myrdal 71 ff.

[50] cf Prop 2004/05:30 p 43–44.

[51] Ch. 10 §6 Commercial Code.

[52] Walin (1998), 327 f.

[53] cf Prop 2004/05:30 p 54.

[54] Walin (1998), 310.

[55] cf Ch. 4 §§17–19 Code of Execution (1981:774) and Ch. 3 §3 Bankruptcy Act.

[56] Håstad 240, 299. For a different opinion on perfection of repledge, see Myrdal who argues that notification to A best achieves the purpose of preventing B from controlling the collateral as it limits A's incentive of paying its debt to B.

[57] Prop 2004/05:30 pp 43, 46; Myrdal.

[58] Ds 2003:38 p 69.

than under the agreement with A, as B cannot repledge anything but its own rights. Moreover, in this case, i.e. a repledge on more stringent conditions, it would be impossible for C to make a good faith purchase of the pledgee-rights.[59] Even though Myrdal finds it more natural that a repledge would concern B's pledgee-rights, based on statements made in case law and in the preparatory works that repledge can take place on more stringent conditions and that a good faith purchase can be made, he draws the conclusion that the object of a repledge is most probably the collateral.[60]

This whole discussion is an unfortunate result that arises from the separation of the pledgee-rights from the collateral. A repledge concerns the collateral-taker's repledgee-rights and at the same time, the object of the pledgee-right is the collateral.[61] One simply cannot talk about a right to repledge without having something to repledge. Should the collateral be destroyed, it would be difficult to argue that B's pledgee-rights remain if the object of the pledge and ownership rights are extinguished.[62] As a result, unless agreed otherwise, a repledge on more stringent conditions than under the original pledge agreement between A and B cannot take place unless C is in good faith. Moreover, since the object of the repledgee-rights is the collateral, a bona fide purchase can take place even though the object of the repledge is the repledgee-rights.

Another question which has been discussed and which is also unclear is whether A can pay off the underlying debt to B and then redeem the collateral from C if A knows that the collateral has been repledged to C.[63] If this is possible, it undermines C's security right as A would then ultimately have the right to redeem the collateral without paying C's claim against B.[64] A closely related question is whether the repledge ceases to exist once the original debt has been paid off.

It is also questionable whether a joint repledge, i.e. a repledge of assets belonging to several parties, for a larger amount than the smallest for which the collateral was originally pledged, is a repledge on stricter conditions. For instance, where A and A1 each has pledged collateral worth GBP50,000 to B for a loan of GBP90,000 and GBP80,000 respectively, if B repledges the same collateral to C for a loan of GBP110,000, it is possible that this transaction would constitute a repledge for a

---

[59] Myrdal Ch. 11.3 and 507 ff.

[60] Myrdal 507 ff.

[61] cf Lennander 156; and G Millqvist, 'Recension Staffan Myrdal, Återpantsättning. Om pantsättning av pant och panträtt, Norstedts Juridik, Stockholm 2005, 594 s' JT [2005–06] 460.

[62] It could, of course, be argued that the pledge right remains through the right of *surrogation* to the insurance compensation, cf Ch. 9 Insurance Agreements Act (2005:104); and Act (2005:105) on Security Rights in Insurance Compensation. Even though the collateral-taker has a right of separation to the compensation, the right is principally derived from the insurance contract covering the interests of third parties rather than through *surrogation*, cf Håstad 166.

[63] Myrdal 253 ff.

[64] cf Prop 2004/05:30 p 126; Myrdal 253 ff. It should be noted that this is not possible under English law, i.e. A would in this case risk having to pay twice (cf Sect. 5.3.1).

larger debt, i.e. on stricter conditions. This is because A or A1 would have to pay the whole debt of GBP110,000 if either one of them wanted to redeem the collateral from C.[65]

6.3.2 A Right of Reuse under the Financial Collateral Directive

The Financial Collateral Directive was finally implemented in Sweden on 1 May 2005.[66] Through the implementation two new paragraphs have been added to Ch. 3 §§1 and 3 of the Trade with Financial Instruments Act respectively; the rules in each paragraph shall not apply if, in relation to §1, the counterparty, one of the parties to an agreement that the institution has facilitated, or, in relation to §3, the collateral-provider, are one of the following institutions: a company under the supervision of the Financial Services Authority or a foreign company from the EES area which in its home country can conduct similar operations and is under the safe supervision of a similar authority; the Swedish National Debt Office or a similar authority from within the EES; the Swedish Central Bank (*Riksbanken*) or a foreign central bank from within the EES including the European Central Bank; a multilateral developing bank or the IMF, BIS or the EIB; or a credit institution listed in Art. 2.3 of the Directive 2000/12/EC of the European Parliament and of the Council of 20 March 2000 relating to the taking-up and pursuit of the business of credit institutions. The amendments mean that the protection given to the owner in Ch. 3 §§1 and 3 of the Trade with Financial Instruments Act through the condition that the use of financial instruments should be specified in a special agreement, does not apply to the above parties. The condition that a repledge cannot take place for a larger amount or under stricter conditions does not apply either. However, as Ch. 10 §6 of the Commercial Code applies, the parties still need to specify this condition in the collateral agreement (cf Sect. 6.3.1).

A right of reuse under Art. 5 of the Directive is not deemed to be a repledge but is rather characterised as a *pignus irregulare*, which gives the collateral-taker a right to use the collateral as the owner.[67] It embraces the case where the creditor, who has received collateral, has a right to dispose of it and is only obligated to return the equivalent asset.[68]

Walin describes *pignus irregulare* as a term, which lacks practical importance and notes that it is not normally considered to be a pledge.[69] Since *pignus irregulare* is not regulated in Swedish law, its legal effects are deemed to depend on the contents of the agreement and also follow from general principles in property law.[70]

---

[65] Myrdal 458–459.

[66] The Directive was not implemented through one single statutory instrument but rather by making a few amendments to the relevant statutes.

[67] Prop 2004/05:30 p 42; Ds 2003:38 p 63. See also Myrdal.

[68] cf Prop 2004/05:30 p 42; see also Undén 172.

[69] Walin (1998), 23.

[70] Prop 2004/05:30 p 42; Ds 2003:38 p 70; Walin (1998), 310.

Prop 2004/05:30 emphasises that the right of use under the Financial Collateral Directive is a complicated matter. Not only does the Directive create problems in relation to existing property law structures but it is also contradictory in itself. Read together, Art. 5 and Art. 2(1)(m) provide a right for the collateral-taker to use the collateral as the owner under the security financial collateral arrangement. At the same time Art. 2(1)(c) defines a 'security financial collateral arrangement' as an arrangement under which a collateral-provider provides financial collateral by way of security to a collateral-taker and where the full ownership of the financial collateral remains with the collateral-provider.[71] As a result, a situation arises where the collateral-provider keeps its ownership rights and, at the same time, the collateral-taker is permitted to use the collateral as if it were the owner. In the worst case, the collateral-provider who grants an extensive right of use can lose its financial instruments as it may not be protected in the event of the collateral-taker's bankruptcy. The collateral-taker, on the other hand, is deemed to be fully protected.[72]

Prop 2004/05:30 points out that a possible solution to this problem is to interpret the Directive as if the ownership rights remain with the collateral-provider when the security interest arises. According to this interpretation, the parties would enter into a special type of agreement whereby the ownership of the collateral would, at some point in time, pass to the collateral-taker. It further points out that there are reasons not to categorise agreements covered by Art. 5 as normal pledge agreements. Instead the interpretation should be made objectively.[73]

Myrdal, who is of the opinion that Art. 5 does not cover repledge, suggests that the arrangement could be interpreted as a pledge agreement with an option for B to transform the agreement into a *pignus irregulare* or an ordinary claim, i.e. a title transfer arrangement.[74]

The question of the collateral-provider's right to redeem the collateral and the protection of its ownership rights may vary depending at what stage the rights are analysed. At least four different phases can be identified: (1) before the collateral-taker has reused the collateral; (2) when the collateral-taker reuses the collateral (without having reacquired the equivalent assets); (3) when the collateral-taker has acquired the equivalent assets; and (4) when the collateral-taker transfers the collateral back to the collateral-provider. These phases are analysed in chronological order below.

With reference to stage (1), i.e. before the collateral-taker has reused the collateral, Prop 2004/05:30 states that the collateral-provider probably (Sw: *torde*) has a right to separate the collateral on the basis of its ownership rights.[75] It is acknowledged that there are different opinions on whether the collateral-provider is entitled to a right of separation during the time the collateral-taker has not used the collateral. This question is deemed to be dependent on whether the collateral can be

---

[71] Prop 2004/05:30 p 41.

[72] Prop 2004/05:30 p 41, 52.

[73] Prop 2004/05:30 p 42.

[74] Myrdal 496.

[75] Prop 2004/05:30 p 53.

identified and whether it has been mixed with the collateral-taker's other assets. It is further acknowledged that a right to redeem the collateral can occur by applying the Accountable Funds Act by analogy.[76]

The Accountable Funds Act (1944:181) provides different alternatives for protecting ownership to funds entrusted to or received by another person (the "accountable"). Under the Act, the principal is protected even if the accountable has used the money or commingled them with its own.[77] Thus, the principal has a right to separate the funds in the bankruptcy of the accountable in the cases covered by the Act.

The first paragraph of the Accountable Funds Act provides that funds that the accountable receives from a principal with a duty to account for them are protected in the insolvency of the accountable if the funds are kept separate and if the separation took place without delay. The same applies if the funds are separated at a later stage as long as the accountable is not insolvent when the separation takes place. The second paragraph provides an exception to the above: what the accountable has immediately available to be separated is also protected in its insolvency as long as the separation is made without delay. The last paragraph states that if the fund consists of funds from several principals, the fund is to be shared amongst the principals in proportion to their respective claims.

The Accountable Funds Act provides several exceptions from the requirement that funds belonging to someone else must be kept separate on a continuous basis for the ownership not to be lost.[78] That the funds should be received from a principal means that the Act covers funds in the hands of a person who has received them with a duty to treat them as someone else's; excluding ordinary loans and claims. The receipt of the funds could for instance be due to an assignment or an employment but could also be a mistaken payment, or be the result of a crime or a legal provision.

The accountability requirement is disputed and unclear.[79] It is deemed to mean that the person holding the funds is obliged to treat them as someone else's and on a continuous basis should be able to account for them and pay them to the principal. If a person can be charged with the criminal offences of embezzlement or unlawful disposal under Ch. 10 §§1 and 4 of the Penal Code (1962:700), that person is deemed to be accountable under the Act.[80] Through the requirement a distinction is made between ordinary loans and funds that the person holding them is obliged to treat as a foreign value, i.e. as belonging to someone else and thus not allowed to endanger.[81] It is not deemed possible to create accountability which gives the principal a right

[76] Prop 2004/05:30 p 53; and Ds 2003:38 p 76 ff.

[77] T Håstad, 'Property Rights regarding Movables' in M Bogdan, *Swedish Law in the New Millennium* (Norstedts Juridik 2000) 419.

[78] NJA II 1944 p 404.

[79] Millqvist 78; and Wennberg 88 ff; Hellner 233 ff; Walin (1997), 99.

[80] It should be emphasised that it is not clear that it is the same accountability requirement that applies under the Accountable Funds Act as applies under the Penal Code, cf. Hessler 479, Hellner 234.

[81] SOU 1940:20 p 172.

to separate the funds through contractual provisions only; such an agreement must be supported by law to be effective.[82]

In the preparatory works to the Accountable Funds Act it is stated that the Act applies by analogy to fungible assets other than money.[83] The governmental reports Prop 2004/05:30 and Ds 2003:38 argue that the Act applies even if the collateral-taker has a right to use the collateral as the owner until the actual use or disposal has taken place, and that it is a precondition that the assets are received with a duty to account for them. It is recognised that it is open to question whether the collateral is received on behalf of the collateral-provider or the collateral-taker.[84]

The Council on Legislation, which provides opinions on legislative proposals before they are submitted to the Swedish Parliament (*Riksdagen*), declared in its opinion on the implementation of the Financial Collateral Directive that the question of the collateral-provider's right to separate the collateral – in contrast to what is claimed in the above reports – is clear; if the collateral-taker has a right to use the collateral as if it were the owner without responsibility for embezzlement (*förskingringsansvar*), if it is unable to return the equivalent asset, it follows that the collateral has not been taken and kept for the collateral-provider with a duty to account for it under the Accountable Funds Act (cf above). The case in question is therefore not a repledge but a claim, a *pignus irregulare*. As a consequence, the collateral-provider lacks a right to separate the collateral in the insolvency of the collateral-taker.[85] It is also recognised that this conclusion is in line with the Nordic principle that a right of use makes title retention clauses invalid from the commencement of the transaction. Another effect is that the substitute cannot be subject to a right of separation. The fact that the collateral-taker has a right to dispose of the collateral immediately puts the ownership rights of the collateral-provider at risk and is difficult to reconcile with the accountability requirement.[86]

In the legal literature different opinions have been expressed. Undén argues that the collateral-provider has a right to separate the collateral until the use as the owner has taken place. It should be noted, however, that his statements were made in the 1920s, i.e. prior to the implementation of the Accountable Funds Act.[87]

Walin seems to be of the opinion that the accountability requirement is met if the collateral-taker is obliged to account for what he has acquired as a substitute for the entrusted asset. He presumes, however, that the collateral-taker must keep the collateral separate or remain solvent for the Accountable Funds Act to apply.[88]

Håstad, who was one of the Supreme Court Justices in the Council of Legislation giving the above opinion on the proposed legislation, notes in his monograph from 1996 that the accountability requirement is only fulfilled if the assets are entrusted

---

[82] Hellner 247.

[83] Prop 1944:81 p 31.

[84] Prop 2004/05:30 p 53.

[85] Prop 2004/05:30 p 122.

[86] *ibid.*

[87] Undén 172; cf Karlgren (1951), 74.

[88] Walin (1998), 116–117.

as a foreign value, i.e. with an obligation to treat them as someone else's, which the receiver is not allowed to endanger as set out in the preparatory works to the provision on embezzlement under the Penal Code.[89] He thus implies that the accountability requirement under the Accountable Funds Act and the criminal offence of embezzlement under the Penal Code are the same. As the purpose of *pignus irregulare* is that the collateral-taker should be able to use the collateral as if it were the owner regardless of when the use takes place and without an obligation to stay solvent, Håstad seems to be of the opinion that the arrangement is incompatible with the accountability requirement. If, on the other hand, the collateral-taker is only allowed to use and dispose of the collateral in the interests of the collateral-provider, or to use and dispose of it in its own interest as long as it stays solvent, the security interest in the collateral remains if it can be identified.[90] The collateral-provider has, following the disposal, moreover a right to separate the substitute in the bankruptcy of the collateral-taker if the collateral-taker has separated the substitute on behalf of the collateral-provider while remaining solvent.[91]

Rodhe notes that the requirement for identification of the collateral is considered to mean that a security interest does not arise if the collateral-taker has a right to use or dispose of the collateral and in fact does so. This type of agreement can instead be characterised as a *pignus irregulare*. He acknowledges that the security interest is deemed to be valid and enforceable as long as the collateral-taker keeps the original collateral without commingling it with its own assets. As soon as the commingling has taken place or the collateral-taker has in some other way used or disposed of the collateral, we are no longer dealing with a pledge but with an obligation to provide assets of the same kind or compensation (i.e. a claim).[92]

Myrdal states that the position under Swedish law is unclear.[93] The fact that Undén and many of the other distinguished authorities in the field have presumed that A should have a right to separate the collateral and that the developed custom has been to rely on their statements is in his opinion important.[94] He acknowledges that §53 of the Commission Agency Act (1914:45) is probably not applicable as A does not provide its securities to B for sale in commission. As for the applicability of the Accountable Funds Act, Myrdal notes that the conclusion that A lacks a right of separation is made by applying the Act by analogy and by drawing the conclusion *e contrario*.[95] Accordingly, just because a right of separation is denied by applying the Act, it is not clear that A is without a right of separation on the basis of some other rule or principle. With reference to NJA 1994 p 506 (see Sect. 6.4.3) it is acknowledged that a right of separation could be possible in cases other than those

89 SOU 1940:20 p 172.

90 cf NJA 2007 p 413.

91 Håstad 347–348, cf 155 ff.

92 Rodhe 439.

93 Myrdal 503 ff.

94 *ibid* with references to Undén 172, Rodhe 439, Hessler 155 ff, Karlgren (1951), 74, Millqvist 65 and Walin (1998), 117.

95 cf NJA 1994 p 506 where it is declared that the Accountable Funds Act not is intended to be applied *e contrario*.

covered by the Act. A natural starting point would, however, be to make the right of separation dependent on the application of the Act. Myrdal concludes that A ought to have a right to separate the collateral before B has used or disposed of it. The ownership should pass from A to B upon B's use or disposal.[96]

With reference to stage (2), i.e. when the collateral-taker has reused the collateral, it is clear that the collateral-provider loses its ownership right and the right to redeem the collateral (if it has not already lost it). The collateral-provider is left with a personal claim – a right *in personam* – against the collateral-taker which is unprotected in the event of the bankruptcy of B to the extent set-off against the underlying debt is not possible.[97]

In relation to stage (3), the question is whether the collateral-provider is entitled to the equivalent assets, i.e. the substitute. Again, this depends on whether the substitute can be identified and separated from the rest of the collateral-taker's assets. A condition for a right to redeem the substitute, i.e. the equivalent collateral, is deemed to be that the Accountable Funds Act is applicable.[98]

Prop 2004/05:30 questions whether the Accountable Funds Act is applicable in this case,[99] and points out that a clarification is desirable. It is however concluded that a revision is not needed as Recital 19 of the Directive states that the rules on reuse of financial collateral should be without prejudice to national legislation about the separation of assets and unfair treatment of creditors and, therefore, that the rules on a right of separation, i.e. including the Accountable Funds Act, do not need to be amended. This analysis is obviously unsatisfactory. In the worse case, i.e. if the Accountable Funds Act is not applicable and the right to separate the equivalent collateral is lost, the result is that the collateral-provider is left without any protection on the insolvency of the collateral-taker.[100]

Another issue that has been discussed is as follows. Under Art. 5(2) of the Directive, if the right of use is exercised, the collateral-taker has an obligation to transfer the equivalent collateral at the latest on the due date for the performance of the relevant financial obligations covered by the security financial collateral arrangement. In the preparatory works and the legal literature it has been questioned whether the word transfer (Sw: *överföra*) under Art. 5(2) means acquisition of the equivalent collateral from the collateral-taker from a third party or the transfer of possession of the equivalent collateral by the collateral-taker to the collateral-provider.[101] This question is, *inter alia*, of importance in relation to the question whether the collateral-provider has a right to separate the equivalent collateral on the bankruptcy of the collateral-taker. Should transfer be interpreted to mean a transfer of the collateral

---

[96] Myrdal.

[97] Prop 2004/05:30 p 53.

[98] *ibid*; Ds 2003:38 p 76 ff.

[99] Prop 2004/05:30 p 53.

[100] Prop 2004/05:30 p 54.

[101] Prop 2004/05:30 p 43; Ds 2003:38 p 63–65; and Myrdal 494 f.

to the collateral-provider, it could possibly have the consequence that the collateral-provider would not be protected until it has the collateral in its possession.[102]

One cannot but agree with those who argue that it is unfortunate if Art. 5(2) would be interpreted in this way. Not only does it contradict the purpose of facilitating security financial collateral arrangements but it also makes little sense. Art. 5(3) states that the equivalent collateral transferred in discharge of an obligation as described in Art. 5(2) should be subject to the same security financial collateral agreement to which the original financial collateral was subject and treated as having been provided at the same time as the original financial collateral. It must therefore be more appropriate and also better suited to the purpose of the Directive to interpret the two provisions so that the right to separate the collateral on the collateral-taker's bankruptcy arises as soon as the equivalent collateral has been acquired by the collateral-taker.[103]

So to the last stage (4), where the collateral-taker has transferred the equivalent collateral to the collateral-provider. There is, of course, a chance that the retransfer could be attacked by the voidable preference rules under Ch. 4 of the Bankruptcy Act. However, as long as the retransfer is normal, these rules are deemed not to apply.[104] Provided that the transaction has been perfected, it should be protected from the creditors of the collateral-taker regardless of whether it is characterised as a pledge, *pignus irregulare*, or an outright transfer.

The scope of the implemented regulations should also be discussed. Through the exemptions from the protection provided to consumers and other holders of financial instruments under Ch. 3, §§1 and 3, the listed institutions are subject to a much more liberal scheme than would normally apply. The amendments have the effect that the protection normally given to owners through the conditions that the use of financial instruments should be specified in a special agreement and that a repledge cannot take place for a larger amount or under stricter conditions do not apply to these institutions. The limitation of the scope of the amendments is motivated by the lower degree of protection that they offer. It is however recognised that a limitation involves disadvantages for certain market participants who may not be able to get access to the same type of services and prices. Moreover, should a reuse of financial collateral not be allowed, this would mean that Swedish financial institutions would have a disadvantage in relation to foreign institutions. The best compromise was, therefore, to make an exemption from Ch. 3 §§ 1 and 3 of the Trade with Financial Instruments Act for the listed institutions. It was further considered important to only exempt parties that are of equal standing. Therefore, the opt-out possibility under Art. 1(3) of the Directive, which provides that agreements where only one of the parties is a listed financial institution and the other is a person other than a natural person (e.g. an ordinary company), was exercised.[105]

---

[102] Myrdal 494 f.

[103] cf Myrdal 494 f.

[104] Prop 2004/05:30 p 54. It has been questioned whether Ch. 4 §10 Bankruptcy Act applies to other performances than money, Håstad 271–272, 392; cf NJA 1950 p 417 and NJA 1988 p 149.

[105] Art. 1.3 and 2(e) Financial Collateral Directive; Prop 2004/05:30 p 47 ff.

Apart from creating a special regime for certain institutions (see Chap. 2) and thereby creating different schemes for different creditors, the implemented changes can be criticised for providing further uncertainty. Many of the provisions under the Financial Collateral Directive are ambiguous and contradictory. Some of the substantive rules are placed in the preamble (see for instance Recitals 14 and 15), whereas others are very general and leave room for the Member States to determine the applicability and the scope of the provisions. This is unfortunate, considering that one of the objectives of the Directive is to establish a Community regime and to improve the legal certainty of financial collateral arrangements.[106]

In relation to the Accountable Funds Act, it should be recognised that the application of the accountability requirement is a difficult matter. As previously mentioned, the content of this criterion is anything but clear.[107] In relation to Art. 5, the main problem is that the collateral is provided both in the collateral-taker's and the collateral-provider's interest. Even if the collateral-taker has a duty to keep the collateral-provider informed of the management of the collateral and is obligated to return the collateral or its substitute at the end of the transaction, it is difficult to argue that the collateral-taker keeps the collateral as a foreign value which it is not allowed to endanger when it has a right to use it as if it were the owner. As soon as the collateral-taker has disposed of the collateral (stage 2), the collateral-provider is left with an unprotected claim, which at best can be set-off against the underlying obligation. Should the parties agree that the collateral-taker only has a right to use the collateral as if it were the owner if it simultaneously replaces it with a substitute which is kept separate the question would probably appear in a different light.[108]

As for the argument that the collateral-taker is allowed to use the collateral in its own interest but only as long as it stays solvent (cf stage 1) and Håstad's opinion above), it can be questioned whether this is sufficient for the accountability requirement to be met.[109] First of all, as the legal effect of the application of the Accountable Fund Act is that the collateral-provider has a right to separate the collateral in the bankruptcy of the collateral-taker, it can be questioned if a contractual provision to stay solvent shall have this result in the bankruptcy of the obligated party. As it is not possible to create accountability which gives the principal a right to separate funds and fungible assets through contractual provisions only, it can also be questioned whether a provision in the agreement between the parties with this content shall have such effect.[110] It is also difficult to interpret such a requirement as being part of the nature of the relationship or assignment as insolvency is the unwanted consequence of the failure of most types of businesses.[111] The requirement to stay solvent can therefore only be relevant together with the condition that the collateral

[106] cf Recitals 3 and 5 Financial Collateral Directive.

[107] cf Walin (1975), 97 ff 98; Hellner 239.

[108] cf Wennberg 95.

[109] Håstad 347–348.

[110] Hellner 247.

[111] cf Law Faculty Committee, Stockholm University, 'Statement on the implementation of the Financial Collateral Directive' (9 August 2003) on the implementation of the Financial Collateral Directive; and *Hellner* 240 who elaborates on the solvency criterion. He argues that it should be

should be entrusted as a foreign value. This is however of little help as it, as Hellner notes, only leads to the question of when this is the case.[112]

In conclusion, it is unclear whether the collateral-provider has a right to redeem the collateral when the collateral-taker has a right to use the collateral as the owner under the security financial collateral arrangement in relation to stages (1) and (3) of the collateral arrangement.[113] The confusion created by statements made in the reports that the Accountable Funds Act probably (Sw: *torde*) applies (cf. stage 1) and the authoritative statement by the Council on Legislation that it is clear that the Accountable Funds Act is not applicable is unfortunate as it only leads to further uncertainties. Considering that EC law is superior to national law in EU Member States and, in light of the aim of the Financial Collateral Directive to facilitate the use of financial collateral, the argument that Swedish law should be interpreted as protecting the collateral-provider's rights is rather strong. A clarification is, however, desirable.

6.3.3 The Use of Repos

There is no special legislation regulating repos under Swedish law so an interpretation of repos has to be made by applying general rules and principles.[114] As previously mentioned, the common purpose of a repo is to use the underlying assets as security. Often the repo is structured as an outright transfer of the collateral from A to B together with an option for A to re-acquire the equivalent assets.[115] As the obligation to return the collateral is not restricted to the original assets, B has an unlimited right of disposal of the collateral.

Under Art. 6(1) of the Financial Collateral Directive, Member States must ensure that a title transfer financial collateral arrangement can take effect in accordance with its terms. Recital 13 states that the aim of this provision is to protect the validity of financial collateral arrangements which are based on the transfer of full ownership of the financial collateral by eliminating recharacterisation risk of repos as security interests. In the Swedish version of the Directive the translation of 'title transfer financial collateral arrangement' specifically refers to "*säkerhetsöverlåtelse*" ("security transfer"). The English version states that 'title transfer financial collateral arrangement' means an arrangement, including repurchase agreements, under which a collateral-provider transfers full ownership of financial collateral to a collateral-taker for the purpose of securing or otherwise

interpreted to mean that the funds should be separated in such a way that illiquidity or insolvency does not affect the principal.

[112] Hellner 246; see also Karlgren (1982), 52.

[113] Prop 2004/05:30 p 53, 122.

[114] cf G Millqvist, 'Swedish Credit Security Law: A Case for Law Reform' [2004] 15 EBLR 865–866.

[115] cf Prop 2004/05:30 p 31 and the discussion on genuine and false repos. It is stated that the latter form does not always require that a retransfer takes place.

covering the performance of relevant financial obligations. It should be noted that both the English and the Swedish versions specifically refer to repurchase agreements.[116]

In the Swedish preparatory works to the Financial Collateral Directive, repos are also characterised as security transfers. It is, however, emphasised that the interpretation of each agreement shall be made based on its substance rather than its form, and that repos under Swedish law do not belong to any special legal category or type of agreement. Nevertheless, in both Prop 2004/05:30 and Ds 2003:38 the assumption is that repos should be classified as security transfers, i.e. contrary to the intention of Art. 6.[117] It is, moreover, presumed that the rules on transfer of title under the Financial Collateral Directive are compatible with Swedish law on security transfers (cf below).[118]

Irrespective of these statements, it can be questioned whether a repo where the collateral-taker has a right to use the collateral as the owner should be characterised as a security transfer. The answer to this question depends, naturally, on the intention of the parties. However, it seems that upon interpretation of these agreements it is insufficient to look only at the intention of the parties when determining whether the transaction is a security transfer or not. Even if A has a right to re-acquire the equivalent collateral, and the intention is to secure the underlying obligation, the intention is also often that B shall have the right to use the collateral as the owner.

If B has an unlimited right of disposal and the requirement for identification of the collateral is not upheld, it is difficult to claim that the transaction is a security transfer.[119] Instead, it would be more appropriate to interpret the arrangement as an outright transfer. Consequently, the only form of security involved would be the possibility to set off the value of the collateral against the underlying obligation.

The characterisation of the agreement has important consequences. Should the agreement be interpreted as a security transfer, A is deemed to have a protected right to repurchase the collateral even if B is bankrupt.[120] Another effect is the applicability of §37 of the Contracts Act (cf Sect. 6.2.1) and the prohibition against forfeiture of collateral, which applies to security arrangements.[121] The characterisation may also affect the application of voidance preference rules under the Bankruptcy Act.[122]

Other possible factors that could be relevant when interpreting the agreement are B's right of disposal, A's right to repurchase the collateral, and which of the parties that bear the risk for the collateral. For instance, if A bears the risk, B has a right to require A to pay the difference between the price received upon sale of the collateral and the required value of the collateral under the agreement should there be a deficit. In this case the agreement should be interpreted as a security agreement. If B bears

---

116 See also Recitals 3 and 13 Directive.

117 Prop 2004/05:30 p 30–31; Ds 2003:38 p 43–44.

118 Prop 2004/05:30 p 28 ff; Ds 2003:38 p 40 ff.

119 cf Karlgren (1936), 165; and Karlgren (1952, 1958) 11–13, 17.

120 cf Håstad 443; Karlgren (1952, 1958), 116–117 and Karlgren (1936), 183 ff; Hessler 450–451; and Rodhe 196.

121 Helander 704; cf NJA 1949 p 744 and NJA 1952 p 256.

122 cf Helander 704.

the risk, the agreement is an outright transfer. In this case, B will bear any loss that may arise as a result of the sale. B also takes the risk that the price of the collateral will go up after the disposal and that it will make a loss upon repurchase of the equivalent collateral. Another factor that may become relevant is whether B has a right and not only an obligation to retransfer the collateral to A.[123]

In conclusion, the legal characterisation and thereby the legal effects of the repurchase agreements discussed in this Section are unclear.[124]

6.4 The Doctrine of Specificity

Art. 5 of the Financial Collateral Directive involves a right for the collateral-taker to use the collateral as its own and to exchange it with the equivalent collateral. Art. 5(3) ensures that the equivalent collateral is treated as having been provided under the same security financial collateral arrangement at the same time as the original financial collateral was first provided. As pointed out, such right of use infringes on the collateral-provider's ownership rights and is contrary to the doctrine of specificity.

Sect. 6.4.1 below examines the requirement for identity under Swedish law. Sect. 6.4.2 examines substitutions, Sect. 6.4.3 mixtures of assets, and Sect. 6.4.4 the question of property rights in unallocated securities.

6.4.1 Identification

Similarly to English and US law, in order to have a protected property right the collateral must, as a general rule, be identified. The requirement for identity applies to all types of assets: tangibles and intangibles as well as fungible and specific assets, and covers both title transfer and security arrangements.[125] It is also applicable irrespective of the type of property right.[126]

The doctrine of specificity means that it is not possible to create property rights in non-identified property.[127] The principle has been said to consist of two elements: (1) that the claim should refer to a specified asset and (2) that the asset should be identifiable at all times.[128] If the asset has been exchanged for another asset or is mixed with other identical assets so it can no longer be identified, the property right

---

123 Rodhe 148; cf Karlgren (1952, 1958), 25–26.

124 Walin (1998), 20–21, 34; cf Law Faculty Committee, Stockholm University, 'Statement on the implementation of the Financial Collateral Directive' (9 August 2003).

125 cf S Lindskog, 'Pant i egen skuld' SvJT [1983] 537; Undén 198 ff and Håstad (1985), 309 ff.

126 As previously mentioned, the floating charge is an exemption.

127 Håstad 152; Undén 59 ff.

128 Håstad 152.

is generally lost.[129] A right of separation can thus only be made in identifiable assets that are not destroyed or which have not otherwise vanished when the claim is made.[130]

Another way of describing the above is that the identification of the asset is a relevant factor that leads to a right of separation in the execution of the asset or the debtor's bankruptcy.[131] Conversely, should the requirement for identification not be met, the owner is left with a claim which is unprotected in the debtor's bankruptcy.

The doctrine of specificity is, however, not without exceptions. Due to practical needs and considerations of reasonability and fairness, it has been departed from in certain cases.[132] In some cases of substitutions and mixtures, the property rights remain in spite of the loss of identity (see further Sects. 6.4.2–3).

Furthermore, in relation to floating charges and other universal forms of security (*universitas rerum*) the collateral is allowed to be exchanged without a loss of the security interest. To argue that the security in these cases concerns a pool of assets and that the doctrine of specificity therefore is upheld is, as Walin points out, only a play on words as it is the individual assets that are covered by the security.[133]

One aspect of the doctrine of specificity is that the debtor cannot use all of its assets as security, i.e. grant a general hypothec in its estate. The requirement has also been deemed to mean that security cannot be granted in terms of quantity or value.[134] However, this view appears to have changed in recent years (see Sect. 6.4.4).

When elaborating on the requirement in relation to pledge, Millqvist notes that the applicability of the principle is uncertain. Generally it is required that the collateral is identified in the agreement, at least by way of interpretation; that the security interest concerns a specific identifiable asset even if the description focuses on a quantity or a value of a larger unit; that the collateral-provider does not have a right to exchange the whole or parts of the collateral on its own; and that the collateral-taker does not have a right to use the collateral as its own and later exchange it with the equivalent asset.[135] As has been shown, the last requirement is particularly relevant in relation to repledge and Art. 5 of the Financial Collateral Directive.

The requirement for identification is often closely connected with perfection of the collateral.[136] Often the identification takes place automatically when the security interest is perfected. It is a logical consequence that the requirement for *traditio*, i.e. that the collateral-taker shall take possession or at least that the collateral-provider shall be cut off from the possibility of disposing of the collateral, involves a certain

---

[129] Håstad 152.

[130] cf Millqvist 61 ff; Undén 60 f; and Rodhe 196.

[131] Hessler 37 ff.

[132] See for instance Ch. 9 §35 Real Estate Code; NJA II 1908 p 79 ff; NJA 1935 p 277; and Håstad 152, 162 ff. See also Ch. 7 §23 Bankruptcy Act; NJA II 1921 p 619 ff and Håstad 165.

[133] Walin (1998), 174.

[134] Undén 60, 198 ff.

[135] Millqvist 133–134; Håstad 152 ff; Undén 60 ff; and Rodhe 439.

[136] cf SOU 1995:11 p 173; and NJA 1910 p 216.

degree of identification of the collateral.[137] The methods of notification and registration also involve elements of identification, although the level of identification depends on the specific situation. To give a few examples, where chattels or bearer instruments are pledged as collateral, the requirement for identification is met when the collateral is handed over from the collateral-provider to the collateral-taker; the transfer of possession individualises the collateral. When the collateral is in the possession of a third party and *traditio* is replaced with notification, the identification of the collateral does not occur with the same ease. In particular, problems may occur when the collateral is fungible and mixed with assets of the same sort. Here, the requirement for identification is deemed to mean that the third party must be notified about the specific assets that the notification concerns. Similarly, when debt is used as collateral, the asset must be sufficiently specified in the notification to the debtor of the pledged debt.[138]

The rules on bona fide purchases also assume that the owner's claim concerns an identified asset. Should A's claim concern generically specified assets, for instance a type of share, and the purchase is not perfected, C would not make a bona fide purchase from B but an ordinary purchase, without interfering with or violating the ownership rights of A.[139]

Identity is, moreover, relevant in relation to sale of goods. Even though the distinction between species and genus was removed in 1990 through the implementation of the new Sales of Goods Act (1990:931) it still fills a function. For instance, the application of the control criterion in §§27 and 40 of the Sales of Goods Act on damages is affected by the question of whether the purchase concerns a specific asset or not. The question of identity is also important in relation to the issue of when the risk for the goods passes from the seller to the purchaser. The main rule, which is established in §13 (first para) of the Act, declares that the risk passes from the seller to the purchaser when the goods, or the document entitling the holder to dispose of the goods, are handed over to the purchaser. In relation to fungibles this means that the assets are individualised through marking, separation or in some other way no later than the time of which the assets are handed over.[140] Also under the Bills of Sales Act the purchased assets must be specified, in a register.

6.4.2 Substitution

In comparison with English and US law, Swedish law is restrictive of allowing substitution of collateral. Tracing, claiming and following as legal concepts do not exist, though, to a certain extent they can be said to be represented by vindication and

[137] cf Rodhe 436; Håstad 163.

[138] Helander 526–527; Rodhe 436–437.

[139] Hessler 164.

[140] cf §§13–14 Sales of Goods Act; and J Hellner, *Speciell avtalsrätt II: Kontraktsrätt* (3rd edn Norstedts Juridik 1996) 40.

substitution. Vindication can be described as a claim or action to redeem an asset in another person's possession (*rei vindicatio*).[141] The acknowledgement of a proprietary right in a substitute is termed "*surrogation*".[142]

In accordance with the principle of vindication the real owner has a right to redeem its asset without paying compensation.[143] Against this principle stands the principle of extinction, which allows a bona fide purchaser to keep the asset it has acquired. Due to the extensive right to make bona fide purchases of chattels under Swedish law, the right of vindication is limited.

The principle of extinction is incorporated in the Good Faith Acquisition of Chattels Act (1986:796). The Good Faith Acquisition of Chattels Act is applicable to bona fide purchases of chattels. It does not apply where there are special regulations in other statutes, for instance §11 Contracts Act, §§54–55 Commission Agency Act, §14 Promissory Notes Act, Ch. 3 §6 Companies Act and Ch. 6 §§3–4 Financial Instruments Accounts Act.

If any of the criteria for a bona fide purchase is not met, the original owner has a right to vindicate the asset without paying any compensation.[144] Moreover, the owner has a right to make a claim for compensation for the value of the property in relation to every purchaser in the chain that is not a bona fide purchaser under the Act.[145]

In 2003, the Good Faith Acquisition of Chattels Act was amended to provide an exemption from the main rule: even if the conditions for a bona fide purchase are met, if the property was acquired through an "unlawful taking of possession", eg theft or robbery, the owner's right to the property remains.[146] Thus, the original owner can redeem the asset without paying any redemption price. One precondition is, however, that the owner vindicates the asset within six months from the time when it gained knowledge of the acquirer's possession.[147] It should be pointed out that the above does not affect the application of the rules on bona fide purchases of promissory notes, shares and financial instruments.[148]

Surrogation can be described as a property right in an asset, which replaces another asset in such way that the claim remains under the same conditions as were

---

[141] It should be noted that the meaning of this term is unclear: Walin (1975), 11–12. cf Undén 66 ff; Rodhe 15 ff; and SOU 1965:14 p 14 ff.

[142] cf Walin (1950), 534 f; SOU 1965:14 p 111, 115 ff; cf NJA 2004 p 52.

[143] SOU 2000:56 p 19.

[144] cf NJA 1963 p 502.

[145] cf NJA 2005 p 425; NJA 1993 p 206; and SOU 2000:56 p 24; Hellner 245 f; and A Agell, 'Skadeståndsansvaret vid obehöriga förfoganden över annans egendom' in *Festskrift till Hellner* (Norstedts Juridik 1984) 56 f.

[146] cf §§3–4 Good Faith Acquisition of Chattels Act; Prop 2002/03:17; SOU 2000:56 p 19 ff; SOU 1995:52; Prop 1997/98:168 and NJA 2004 p 633.

[147] *ibid.*

[148] cf §§13–14 Promissory Notes Act, Ch. 6 §8 Companies Act and Ch. 6 §§3–4 FIAA.

applicable to the original asset.[149] To describe it differently, it is a transfer of a property right from one asset to another.[150] The general principle is that *surrogation* is only allowed in limited cases.[151] It is an exemption from the doctrine of specificity and allows the claimant to assert a proprietary claim in the substitute of the original asset (cf Sect. 6.4.1).

The extent to which *surrogation* can take place is to a large degree uncertain as the legislation is neither clear nor exhaustive.[152] The most important example provided by statute is the Accountable Funds Act. Other examples are Ch. 9 §35 of the Real Estate Code (1970:994),[153] Ch. 12 §8 of the Inheritance Code (1958:637), the Act on Company Charges and Ch. 7 §23 of the Bankruptcy Act.[154] *Surrogation* has also been allowed in a few cases without support by legislation where the correlation between the original asset and the substitute is clear and not too complicated.[155] In comparison with English law, the possibilities for tracing through bank accounts and chains of substitutions are limited.

Surrogation can concern ownership rights as well as limited property rights such as pledge or lien. In order for *surrogation* to be acknowledged the substitute needs to be identified.[156] Should the identity of the asset be lost, for instance through a mixture with other fungible assets, the general rule is that a substitution cannot take place. There are, however, exemptions from this rule, for instance the Accountable Funds Act, and also as provided by case law. It should, moreover, be pointed out that the requirement for identification also requires that the original asset has been identified.[157]

From an economic perspective *surrogation* is important as it prevents the destruction of value. It prevents an arbitrary transfer of value from one person to another without compensation. It also prevents unjust enrichment of one person and its creditors at the expense of another person and its creditors.[158] It has been argued that it would be unjust (Sw: *obilligt*) not to give the owner a right of separation to the substitute and that it correspondingly would be unjust to benefit the general creditors in the bankruptcy (cf Sect. 8.3).[159]

---

149 Walin (1950), 162 ff.

150 cf Rodhe 199.

151 Millqvist 63–65, 134.

152 Hessler 41; Walin (1975), 162 ff; cf Persson 494.

153 cf NJA 1881 p 515.

154 cf also Ch. 9 Insurance Agreements Act (2005:104); and Act (2005:105) on Security Rights in Insurance Compensation.

155 cf Håstad 166 ff, 333 ff, 347, 360; Millqvist 64–65; Walin (1975), 162 ff; NJA 1996 p 624; NJA 1991 p 550; NJA 1990 p 562; NJA 1989 p 781; NJA 1989 p 705 I; NJA 1987 p 105; NJA 1974 p 463; NJA 1956 p 562; NJA 1941 p 711 I-II; NJA 1910 p 413 and RH 1986:63.

156 Hessler 161–162; Walin (1975), 173 ff.

157 cf Millqvist 134; and Hessler 41, 161–162.

158 Walin (1975), 163.

159 cf NJA II 1921 p 619 ff; Håstad 165; and Håstad (1985), 318. cf Walin (1950), 532 ff.

6.4.3 Mixtures

In relation to fungible assets, the requirement for identification means that the collateral must either be marked or separated on a continuous basis as the identity can easily be lost through mixtures with other claimants' assets. One relevant question is whether a claimant can have a right of separation when its assets have been mixed and the claim no longer concerns assets that can be distinguished. Moreover, to what extent can the claimant have a protected property right in fungible assets when the claim concerns a value or a certain quantity?[160]

The starting point is that the right of separation is lost when the claimant's assets have been mixed with the debtor's or with other claimant's assets.[161] The traditional view is therefore that it is impossible to pledge a quantity of a larger pool of assets without separating the collateral.[162] There are, however, exceptions to this rule. The most important exception is the Accountable Funds Act. Under the Act a mixture is permitted if the funds are immediately available to be separated as long as the separation occurs without delay. The right of separation is also preserved if the funds are separated at a later stage if the accountable was solvent and the separation was made for the purpose of accounting for the funds (cf Sect. 6.3.2 above).

Mixtures are also to a certain extent allowed outside the scope of the Accountable Funds Act. In the preparatory works to the Act it is stated that under certain circumstances the owner and the debtor can have co-ownership rights to an amount which is separated from the rest of the debtor's assets even if the Act does not apply. The intention is thus not to violate property rights under general rules.[163]

An old case that is still relevant is NJA 1910 p 216. In this case a debtor pledged a certain quantity of metal scrap, which appeared to be of varied quality, as collateral. The question was whether the pledge was valid and enforceable, as the collateral had not been separated from the rest of the scrap yard and the debtor kept a right to dispose of the parts of the scrap yard that exceeded the quantity of the collateral. The Supreme Court held that as the collateral had not been separated and the collateral-provider was permitted to freely dispose of the exceeding quantities, the collateral-takers lacked a preference right in the collateral in the debtor's bankruptcy. Another troublesome fact was that the collateral was in the possession of a representative of the collateral-provider.[164] Justice Sjögren, who voted with the majority, developed an opinion that is renowned. He declared that it is a general principle that each property right must be tied to an individually specified thing. A quantity which is part of a larger warehouse or the like – a half generically specified thing – can, as such, be the object of a claim, but not a property right. A mixture of different things or of similar things of different qualities – for instance a warehouse – cannot to a non-individualised part be the object of a property right. The basis for this is

[160] Myrdal 479 ff; cf Håstad 152 ff; and Håstad (1985), 309 ff.

[161] cf NJA 1976 p 251.

[162] Undén 60 ff; Rodhe 196 f; Håstad 335 f; Myrdal 480 f.

[163] NJA 1944 p 411, 419; cf NJA 1959 p 590, NJA 1994 p 506; and NJA 1995 p 367 II.

[164] cf S Lindskog, 'Om sakrättsligt misstroende' JT [1991–92] 275 ff.

especially clear in the case of pledge of chattels. In the interest of proper business relationships one has to demand that the collateral is individually specified and that the creditor, or a third party on his behalf, acquires the possession of the object. The former is a precondition for the latter; the acquisition of possession cannot take place without the object being an individually specified thing. Nevertheless, under certain circumstances a pledge of a quantity which is part of a larger warehouse should be valid and enforceable. That a co-owner generally can pledge its share cannot be disputed. If the share that is pledged is expressed to be a fraction or a certain quantity, this is apparently irrelevant. It may be possible for a certain share to be pledged even when the whole is not the object of a co-ownership right, although this is not very common. However, in the interest of proper business relationships, the creditor or a third party on his behalf must acquire possession of the warehouse for the pledge agreement to be enforceable. Thus, even if one could approve of a pledge of a quantity of a larger warehouse it could not be done in this case as the condition – that possession of the warehouse as a whole had passed – was not met. Justice Sjögren also pointed out that co-possession of a warehouse between the debtor and the creditor in certain cases would be sufficient, but only if the creditor could prevent the debtor from disposing of the assets on its own.

Following NJA 1910 p 216 it was deemed more or less impossible to pledge a quantity of a larger pool of fungible assets without separation of the collateral.[165] This view has, however, been softened in recent years.[166] It has been argued that in cases where it is practically meaningless and also costly to separate the collateral that is a quantity of a larger part, the security arrangement ought to provide a protected property right regardless of whether the collateral-provider has a right to dispose of the exceeding quantity (see further Sect. 6.4.4).[167]

One case where a right of separation was provided despite there being a mixture of the owner's and the debtor's assets is NJA 1994 p 506.[168] In this case the question was whether Carl-Gustav R had the right to separate an equivalent amount of grain to that which he had left for storage in the depositee Swedcorn AB's (Swedcorn) silo even though the mixture of Carl-Gustav's grain with the other depositors' and Swedcorn's grain had led to a loss of the identity of his grain. The Supreme Court stated that it was undisputed that a quantity of the grain corresponding to what had been stored by the different depositors remained when Swedcorn became bankrupt. It was, moreover, undisputed that the mixture had taken place for practical reasons. The Court acknowledged that the inquiry did not show that the agreement between Carl-Gustav and Swedcorn included a right for Swedcorn to dispose of the grain, nor that the agreement should be interpreted as anything but a deposit agreement. A right to separate deposited assets in a bankruptcy generally requires that the assets can be identified. This does not exclude a right of separation of fungible assets in certain cases, however, even if the assets have lost their identity as a result of being

[165] Undén 60 ff; Rodhe 196 f; Håstad 335 f; Myrdal 480 f.

[166] Håstad 335–336; cf Håstad (1985), 309 ff.

[167] Håstad 335 ff.

[168] See also NJA 1995 p 367 II.

mixed with other assets. As the mixture in this case had not only been made from the different depositors' assets but also the depositee's assets, the Accountable Funds Act did not apply. It was nevertheless recognised that a right of separation could exist on some other ground. Thus it was acknowledged that the Act is not intended to be interpreted *e contrario*. Based on the above, and taking into account the fact that Carl-Gustav's grain was part of a pool of assets that was clearly separated from Swedcorn's other assets, the Supreme Court came to the conclusion that the grain was sufficiently identified and that Carl-Gustav's right of separation was not lost.

NJA 1994 p 506 provides some guidance as to the extent to which the principal can have a protected property right in fungible assets that are mixed with the debtor's assets.[169] It is, however, difficult to ascertain a general principle from it. Nevertheless, it is argued that where the circumstances and practical needs require a mixture and this is made with a separated part of a debtor's assets, a right of separation to the share or quantity is probable. When a mixture concerns different principals' assets the situation is clearer; the principals are deemed to have a co-ownership right in the pool of assets.[170] Should a shortfall arise, the deficit is deemed to be shared on a proportionate basis in relation to each principal's stake. It can also be established that where the mixture is made with the general assets of the debtor, the principal's property rights are lost.[171]

6.4.4 Unallocated Securities

It is common practice that securities held in custody are used as security.[172] A custody arrangement can be described as an account to which one or more sub-accounts may be linked and by which securities are registered.[173] Often a bank account is linked to the custody account and included in the collateral arrangement. This way the collateral arrangement facilitates the trade in, substitution and top-up of collateral. One problem is that the collateral concerns fungible assets that are not specified in relation to the collateral-provider or the collateral-taker.[174] Another issue is that securities belonging to different owners are often mixed on nominee accounts.

The question of property rights in mixtures of assets becomes especially relevant in relation to securities that are unallocated. In the legal literature there has been discussion over whether it is possible to have a protected property right in fungible securities when the claim concerns a quantity or value of a pool of assets. This

---

[169] See also NJA 1995 p 367 II.

[170] cf Accountable Funds Act; NJA 1994 p 506; Håstad 177; Rodhe 196–197, Hessler 158 and Walin (1998), 88.

[171] NJA 1994 p 506; and NJA 1995 p 367 II; Rodhe 196–197; Håstad 168 ff.

[172] cf Myrdal 474–475.

[173] cf Swedish Securities Dealers Association, General Conditions Governing Custodian Services, Bank (May 2003); and General Conditions Governing Custody & Cash Account Services, Securities Company (May 2003).

[174] Ds 2003:38 p 141 ff.

question arises, *inter alia*, when the collateral-provider only pledges a part of the assets held in the custody.[175] Is it possible to pledge a part of the custody without separating the collateral from the other assets? Moreover, is it possible for the collateral-provider to dispose of the excess value or quantity? It should be noted that the discussion was initially based on the premise that securities were issued in bearer format and thus existed in physical form (cf below).

NJA 1910 p 216, summarised in Sect. 6.4.3, provides a good starting point. To recall, as the collateral, consisting of a quantity of metal scrap from a larger amount, had not been separated and the collateral-provider was permitted to freely dispose of the exceeding quantities, the Supreme Court held that the collateral-taker did not have a protected security interest in the collateral. The question of a security interest in a quantity or value of a larger pool of assets has thereafter been discussed in the legal literature, where different opinions have been expressed. Some academics who have discussed the doctrine of specificity in relation to securities held in custody have come to the conclusion that in cases where it is practically meaningless and also costly to separate the collateral, the collateral-taker ought to have a protected property right in the custody over which it has control even if the collateral is only established to be a certain value or quantity of the whole, i.e. the assets are not specified as such.[176] Håstad, for instance, argues that a pledge of a quantity of a pool of homogeneous securities ought to be valid and enforceable without separation even if the collateral-taker is allowed to dispose of the excess quantity.[177] Even where a certain value of a custody consisting of heterogeneous securities is pledged the collateral arrangement ought to be valid and enforceable, at least as long as the collateral-provider lacks the right to dispose of the collateral.[178] Walin and Lindskog also appear to be of the opinion that a security interest in a quantity of a heterogeneous pool of assets ought to be valid and enforceable.[179] As for security interests specified in terms of value, the views appear to differ. Walin is of the opinion that a pledge of a value of a larger total is not a valid collateral arrangement, regardless of whether the pool consists of homogeneous or heterogeneous assets. As custody arrangements can be pledged as a whole, i.e. with reference to the specific custody arrangement and with a provision stating that the security interest covers a certain amount, he argues that there is no need to allow a pledge in respect of the value.[180] Håstad argues that a pledge of a value of a pool of assets ought to be protected, at least as long as the collateral-provider lacks a right to dispose of the exceeding value. Should the collateral-provider have a right to dispose of the excess value, it can either harm the collateral-taker by withdrawing the most valuable assets or benefit the collateral-taker by withdrawing the most worthless assets. In Håstad's opinion, the collateral-provider's right to dispose of the excess

[175] Håstad (1985), 312 ff.

[176] Ds 2003:38 p 54; Håstad 334–338; Walin 116; and Myrdal 479 ff. The word "valid" is used here to mean that the collateral-taker has a protected security interest.

[177] Håstad 336; cf Håstad 328.

[178] Håstad 336 ff.

[179] S Lindskog, 'Om sakrättsligt misstroende' JT [1991–92] 280; and Walin 38 n 2.

[180] Walin 115–116.

value is, however, more a question of perfection of the collateral, i.e. whether the collateral-provider has been cut off from disposing of the collateral, than a question of specificity.[181] Moreover, Håstad notes that a pledge of securities held in custody specified in relation to a certain value appears to mean that all securities kept in the custody arrangement are pledged with the restriction that the collateral-taker's right is limited by the underlying claim and the agreed value of the pledge.[182] It should also be noted that a share of a homogeneous asset or pool of assets can be used as collateral on the condition that the collateral-provider is cut off from disposing of the asset or the pool.[183]

One closely related question is whether the collateral-provider has a right to substitute the collateral with an equivalent asset.[184] Another related question is whether the collateral-provider has a right to sell the collateral if the funds received are deposited into a bank account included in the collateral arrangement.[185] The current view appears to be that this ought to be possible as long as the collateral-provider is cut off from disposing of the collateral, and that general statements in the legal literature prohibiting substitutions of collateral should be ignored.[186]

A situation where the whole custody is pledged should also be acknowledged. Where the collateral-provider pledges all securities that are held in custody X (i.e. with a reference to the specific custody arrangement) without being restricted in respect of the disposal of the assets, it can be questioned whether a valid and enforceable security interest actually arises.[187] Should the collateral-provider not be cut off from disposing of the assets, it can also be questioned whether the interest has been properly perfected.[188]

It should be noted that the above is only a summary of quite a detailed discussion and that Swedish law in this area is unclear. It should also be recognised that the discussion is based on the fact that until quite recently securities have been issued and traded in bearer format and so could easily be separated and identified. To a large degree this discussion is no longer relevant. As has been shown, intermediated securities are held on a fungible basis; i.e. they are unidentifiable in relation to their entitlement holders. This is a result of the development of the securities trading and holding systems (cf Chap. 3). Another important fact is that securities registered on accounts are fungible intangibles. Unlike grain in a silo or oil in a tank they cannot be separated as they do not exist in the physical world. Only if the registration of the securities by the intermediary with a direct relationship with the ultimate investor is given constitutive effect, or alternatively a similar legal effect to possession of a document of title, can the legal construct that securities are able to be separated be

181 Håstad 337.

182 cf Håstad 336–337.

183 Walin 115; Rodhe 437; Håstad 163; Håstad 316.

184 cf Myrdal 475 n 1611.

185 Håstad 334 f.

186 cf Arts. 2(2) and 8(3)(b) and Recitals 5, 16 Financial Collateral Directive; Walin (1998), 114–115; Håstad 334 f; Myrdal 474–477; cf Helander 526 f and Rodhe 436 ff.

187 cf Walin (1998), 112–113; Håstad 333–334.

188 Håstad 334 f. cf Undén 198 ff.

upheld. The question that preferably should be asked is whether this is necessary or whether the desired legal effect with protected property rights can be achieved by some other means (cf Chaps. 8–9).

In relation to securities held in the VPC system it should be noted that since the registration of securities in the VPC system does not have constitutive effect, it does not establish that the registered person is the true owner.[189] Difficulties arise as securities evidenced by book entry in respect of owner and nominee accounts are fungible intangibles and as such are impossible to distinguish. Another troublesome fact is that the investor's right is indirect; there is at least one party standing in between the investor and the issuer. Since the investor is dependent on the act by an intermediary the right bears more resemblance to a personal right than a property right; the right is a claim on a person to perform in a certain way.[190] Nevertheless, as the Financial Instruments Accounts Act gives the registered person the right to act as the owner, i.e. as the one having the right to dispose of the financial instruments, it is argued that even if the financial instruments are unallocated and the register only evidences title, the person registered as the owner ought to have a property right in the instruments.[191] In relation to securities mixed with other entitlement holders' securities on nominee accounts, the entitlement holders are deemed to have at least co-property rights in the securities.[192] Should a shortfall arise, the securities ought to be shared on a *pro rata* basis.[193] It should also be noted that nominees are obligated to separate their owner accounts from their nominee accounts and that commingling of their own securities with the securities of their customers is prohibited.[194]

As for the question of claims against higher tier intermediaries, it should be noted that VPC would not recognise a claim in shares held in the VPC system from someone not authorised to dispose of the shares. For instance, should a nominee become bankrupt, the owner of the shares would have to make its claim against the bankruptcy estate to have its rights recognised.[195]

As shown in Sect. 6.4.2, tracing is much more restricted in Swedish law than in English or US law. The possibility of tracing unallocated and intermediated securities outside the VPC system is therefore limited. The practices of close-out netting and the difficulties in identifying securities registered on accounts also reduce the possibilities of tracing these assets.

It can be concluded that it is unclear whether an interest in securities identifiable through its value or a certain quantity is valid and enforceable under Swedish law. Considering the statements made in the preparatory works to the Financial

[189] Prop 1997/98:160 p 177.

[190] Afrell and Bogdan 523; cf Lundstedt 334 f.

[191] cf Ch. 6 §§1 and 7 FIAA. cf also Afrell, Klahr and Samuelsson 93; and Answer to Q7 Legal Certainty Group Comparative Survey.

[192] cf Håstad (1985), 311 f.

[193] Due to the lengthy procedures in relation to the administration and sale of co-owned assets under the Co-ownership Act, custody agreements often state that the Act not shall apply.

[194] cf Prop 1997/98:160 p 121; and Prop 1987/88:108 p 30.

[195] I am grateful to Karin Wallin-Norman, Senior Legal Adviser, VPC AB, Stockholm, for clarifying this.

Collateral Directive and in the legal literature, it appears as if this question would be determined in favour of the entitlement holder.[196] It is evident that there is a pressing need to allow such security arrangement. Should the judiciary try this question it would, however, be surprising if it was held that a right of separation was lacking as it would undermine the structure of the Swedish securities holding system.

6.5 Summary and Conclusion

Also under Swedish law the collateral-taker has a general right to repledge collateral. This right can be said to follow from Ch. 10 §6 of the Commercial Code and, in relation to financial instruments, Ch. 3 §3 of the Trade with Financial Instruments Act. As a general rule, unless the parties have agreed otherwise, the collateral-taker may not repledge the collateral for a larger debt or on more stringent conditions than under the original pledge agreement between A and B.

The implementation of Art. 5 of the Financial Collateral Directive was made through revisions of Ch. 3 §§1 and 3 of the Trade with Financial Instruments Act. The amendments imply that the protection given to the owner through the condition that the use of financial instruments should be specified in a special agreement does not apply to certain institutions. Moreover, a repledge can, in respect of the listed institutions, take place on more stringent conditions or for a larger amount. The limited scope is motivated by the lower degree of protection that the implemented provisions involve. The opt-out possibility under Art. 1(3) of the Directive is thus employed.

As in many other European jurisdictions a right of use under Art. 5 of the Directive conflicts with the property law structures and the division between rights *in rem* and rights *in personam*. Under Swedish law a right to reuse financial collateral as the owner is not deemed to be a repledge but rather characterised as a claim or a *pignus irregulare*. It embraces the case where the collateral-taker has a right to use or dispose of the collateral and is only obliged to replace it with an equivalent asset. Under the traditional analysis the right to dispose of the collateral transforms the property right into a claim. One consequence is that the collateral-provider who grants an extensive right of use may not have a protected interest in the collateral-taker's bankruptcy.

In the preparatory works it is pointed out that a possible solution to the problem inherent in Art. 5 is to interpret the Directive as if the ownership rights shall remain with the collateral-provider when the security interest arises. At some point in time the ownership of the collateral passes to the collateral-taker. The collateral-provider's right to redeem the collateral and the protection of its ownership rights may thus vary depending on the stage at which the right is analysed. At least four different phases can be identified: (1) before the collateral-taker has reused the collateral; (2) when the collateral-taker has reused the collateral; (3) when the

[196] Prop 2004/05:30 p 36; Ds 2003:38 54.

collateral-taker has acquired the equivalent assets; and (4) when the collateral-taker transfers the collateral back to the collateral-provider.

In relation to stage (1) the right of separation is deemed to depend on whether the collateral can be identified and whether it has been mixed with the collateral-taker's other assets. It is acknowledged that the Accountable Funds Act may apply even if it is uncertain if the accountability requirement under the Act, i.e. that the collateral shall be received on behalf of someone else, is met. With respect to stage (2) it is established that the collateral-provider loses its ownership rights and the right to redeem the collateral when the collateral-taker reuses the collateral, thereby being left with a personal right that at best can be set-off against the underlying debt. As for stage (3), the analysis is again deemed to depend on whether the substitute collateral can be identified and separated from the rest of the collateral-taker's assets. It is also recognised that it is unclear whether the Accountable Funds Act applies. In relation to stage 4), as long as the retransfer is normal the voidable preference rules under Ch. 4 of the Bankruptcy Act are not deemed to apply. The collateral-provider's ownership rights are thus protected. It can be concluded that it is unclear whether the collateral-provider has a right to redeem the collateral when the collateral-taker has a right to use the collateral as the owner under the security financial collateral arrangement in relation to stages (2) and (3).

The great degree of uncertainty in relation to Ch. 3 §§1 and 3 of the Trade with Financial Instruments Act, the applicability of the Accountable Funds Act and the collateral-provider's ownership rights is most unfortunate as the objective of the Financial Collateral Directive is to establish a Community regime and improve the legal certainty in relation to financial collateral arrangements. Considering the position of EC law as being superior to national law and in light of the aim of the Financial Collateral Directive to facilitate the use of financial collateral, the argument that Swedish law should be interpreted in favour of the collateral-provider is rather strong. Nevertheless, there is a pressing need for clarification.

Another problem is that the rules on repledge under Ch. 10 § 6 of the Commercial Code and Ch. 3 §3 of the Trade with Financial Instruments Act are ill-suited to the developed practices in the securities markets. Securities registered on accounts are held on a fungible basis and securities on nominee accounts are often mixed. These practices often make it impossible to identify the securities in relation to their respective entitlement holder (cf the analysis above in relation to stages (1) and (3)). Another concern is that the collateral is often specified as a value. Since the requirement for collateral under the collateral agreement, the extended credit and related derivatives positions often fluctuate from time to time, the situation easily occurs where collateral is repledged on more stringent conditions (cf Chap. 4).

As has been shown the right of reuse is closely related to the requirement for identification of the collateral as the disposal effectively destroys the identity in the asset. Also the characterisation of repos is dependent on the identity of the collateral. In the Swedish version of the Financial Collateral Directive the translation of 'title financial collateral arrangement' specifically refers to security transfer. In the preparatory works it is emphasised that repos do not belong to any special legal category and that the classification depends on the interpretation of the agreement. At the same time it is presumed that repos shall be characterised as security transfers. It can, irrespective of this, be questioned whether a repo where the collateral-taker has a right to dispose of the collateral should be characterised as a security transfer. If the collateral-taker has an unlimited right of disposal and is only obliged to retransfer the equivalent collateral to the collateral-provider the requirement for specificity is not met. Instead the transaction bears more resemblance to an outright transfer. As the characterisation is of great significance in relation to the legal effects that come into play further clarifications are desirable.

The requirement for identification also causes concern in relation to substitutions, mixtures, the classification of investors' rights, assertions of claims against higher tier intermediaries, good faith acquisitions, negotiability, etc. This is because the legal system, including the Financial Instruments Accounts Act, is designed for assets that are identifiable. The rules on securities are based on the fact that until quite recently these assets have been issued and traded in bearer format. The legal construct that the bearer document is the carrier of the rights against the issuer facilitates the identification of these assets. Problems arise as securities registered on accounts are held on a fungible basis; i.e. they are unidentifiable in relation to their entitlement holders. Another problem is that securities registered on accounts are fungible intangibles. As such they are impossible to separate and distinguish from each other.

The analysis and conclusions presented above support the main argument of the book that intermediated securities have outgrown the existing property and security law structures and that there is a clear need to revise the laws in this area.

Chapter 7
Property Rights in Securities and the Doctrine of Specificity under US Law

The notion that wise government rules actually can somehow prevent any and every derivatives calamity is incurably romantic because government regulation, at best, can deal only with the last reported disaster. New and totally unanticipated potential forms of disaster are evolving all the time! In fact, as I have argued in the past [. . .] many of the innovations we see are introduced precisely to get around regulatory restrictions. The regulators are always behind the curve. And just as well. Can you imagine the size of the Federal Register if the regulators really believed they could anticipate problems and not just react to them?[1]

7.1 Introduction

When it comes to law reforms in the area of investment securities it is clear that the US has surpassed other nations. The US was quick to recognise the problems inherent in the indirect holding system and the difficulties of applying traditional property law rules to unallocated securities. UCC Arts. 8-9 provide alternative solutions to issues that England and Sweden have recognised but yet failed to solve. The American system also provides a framework that is flexible enough to adapt to changes in the financial markets.[2] The US legal system is therefore of great interest not only in relation to this book but also for the legislator seeking to amend existing laws.

This Chapter examines reuse of financial collateral under US law. It examines repledge and the use of repos and discusses the circumstances under which substitutions and mixtures can take place. An analysis of the doctrine of specificity is provided with particular focus on unallocated securities.

7.2 Interests in Securities

7.2.1 Introduction to US Security Law

Secured transactions in personal property were subject to extensive law revisions at an early stage in the US. In 1940 William A Schnader and Karl N Llewellyn

[1] M H Miller, *Merton Miller on Derivatives* (John Wiley and Sons 1997) x.

[2] ALI Report Art. 8, 5.

© Springer-Verlag Berlin Heidelberg 2009

persuaded the National Conference of Commissioners on Uniform State Laws (NCCUSL) to prepare the Uniform Commercial Code (UCC). In 1942 NCCUSL and the American Law Institute (ALI) commenced their work on drafting the UCC which took the shape of a model law with Karl N Llewellyn as its Chief Reporter and his spouse Sofia Mentschikoff as Associate Chief Reporter.[3]

The UCC is not federal law and had to be adopted by the US Member States to come into effect. Today it has been enacted by all 50 states and by the District of Columbia and Puerto Rico.[4] It consists of nine articles. Art. 9 regulates secured transactions and Art. 8 concerns investment securities.

The original version of Art. 8 was based on possession and delivery of certificated and bearer securities. Ownership was recognised by possession and transfer by delivery of the physical document.[5] Following the so-called paperwork crunch in the late 1960s, the problems concerning transfers and holdings of certificated securities were recognised. In 1977 NCCUSL proposed a revision of Arts. 8-9 in relation to property interests in investment securities.[6] There was a need to replace physical securities with uncertificated securities and possession and delivery with electronically recorded ownership and transfers of securities. In 1978 the proposed amendments were approved.[7] The amendments were severely criticised, however, for ignoring the indirect holding system in the securities markets and for still being based on the idea that ownership is represented by physical possession of the object.[8] As Schroeder notes 'Fictive physicality was to replace actual physicality'.[9] The only difference from the traditional system was that ownership was not evidenced by physical certificates – a change in the register of the issuer was still required.[10]

In 1994, in the aftermath of the market crash in October 1987, the Commissioners proposed new changes to Art. 8 with conforming amendments to Art. 9. The major concern that necessitated the revision was the indirect holding system of securities.[11] Another issue was the lack of uniformity in the various states' versions of old Art. 8. Due to uncertainties in relation to applicable law, this caused significant problems.[12] A third concern was the complexity and non-accessibility of old Art. 8.[13]

One of the objectives of the revision of Art. 8 was to make it neutral and sufficiently flexible to respond to market and regulatory changes. Previous experience had shown that it was impossible to predict how the practices of trading and holding

[3] White and Summers 3 ff.

[4] Rocks and Bjerre vii.

[5] ALI Report Art. 8, 1.

[6] Schroeder (1994), 295.

[7] ALI Report Art. 8, 1.

[8] Schroeder (1994), 295, 303.

[9] Schroeder (1994), 312.

[10] ALI Report Art. 8, 1.

[11] *ibid.*

[12] Rogers (1996), 1542.

[13] Rogers (1996), 1447.

securities would evolve. After the paper-crunch the predictions were that a system of uncertificated securities would develop. Instead a system with certificated securities – often in the form of a global note placed in custody and held indirectly through chains of intermediaries – was the preferred solution.[14] Another aim was to accommodate both direct and indirect holding systems.[15]

The same year, 1994, ALI and NCCUSL approved the revision and the enactment process began.[16] Through the revision, the rules on security interests in investment securities were moved from Art. 8 to Art. 9.

A number of amendments were also been made to Art. 9 with conforming changes to Arts. 1, 2, 5 and 8.[17] The basic rules governing security in personal property were, however, established through the revisions of Art. 9 promulgated in 1972.[18]

7.2.2 Article 9 of the Uniform Commercial Code

Security interest in investment propertyis governed by UCC Art. 9. The broader scope of Art. 9 is security interests in personal property.[19] Many important aspects in relation to securities and financial assets are, however, placed in Art. 8.

Art. 9 generally applies to consensual security arrangements between debtors and secured parties where collateral in the form of personal property or fixtures is used to secure an underlying obligation. It uses a functional approach in relation to security interests and does not only cover traditional charges but also some transactions that are structured to have the function and effect of security, so called quasi-security (e.g. consignments and leases). Instead of taking a formalistic approach, the purpose of the transaction is recognised.

One example of the functional approach of the UCC is the transformation of the different types of security interests such as the mortgage, charge, lien and pledge into one single security device. This transformation has been described as the grand invention of the UCC. A single set of terms such as 'debtor', 'secured party', 'security agreement', 'collateral' and 'security interest' replaces previous terminology and types of security.[20]

The primary aims of Art. 9 are to provide notice of property interests and to solve priority issues.[21] Through electronic filing of financial statements information is provided to third parties and the perfection order is established. By searching

---

[14] ALI Report Art. 8, 4.

[15] FMLC, 'Issue 3 – Property Interest in Investment Securities (July 2004)' 5.

[16] Rogers (1996), 1432.

[17] ALI Report Art. 9, xxix; Hakes xv.

[18] ALI Report Art. 9, xiii.

[19] Art. 1–201(35).

[20] White and Summers 710.

[21] Hakes 12.

the internet information can be obtained regarding a security interest created in the debtor's property.

To attach, i.e. to create, a security interest and make it enforceable between the parties three requirements must generally be met: (1) the parties must have an adequate security agreement which is authenticated by the debtor and which provides a description of the collateral; (2) the secured party must give value; and (3) the debtor must have the right or the power to transfer rights in the collateral.[22] The security interest does not only become enforceable in relation to the contracting parties but also in relation to third parties upon attachment. Priority is however usually based on the perfection order.[23]

A certain measure needs to be taken to perfect the security interest. The measure required depends on factors such as the type of the collateral and the transaction. Filing is promoted as the preferred method of perfection and is generally available to most types of collateral.[24] In a few cases collateral is perfected automatically, i.e. upon attachment. Possession and control are also common methods of perfection. For instance, investment property, deposit accounts, letter-of-credit rights and electronic chattel papers may be perfected by taking control.[25] Sale of payment intangibles and promissory notes may be perfected automatically while goods, instruments, money, negotiable documents or tangible chattel paper may be perfected by possession.[26]

If more than one party is asserting claims in the same asset, either a cut-off rule or a priority rule applies. Cut-off rules allow a purchaser or a collateral-taker to take the collateral free from adverse claims. If a cut-off rule is not applicable, the conflict is solved through a priority rule. It determines the priority order between two parties with competing claims. Once the claim of a winning party has been satisfied the enduring value will go to the competing claimant.[27]

The primary rule for determining the priority order between two security interests is that first-in-time to file or perfect prevails.[28] The first-in-time rule gives the secured party an incentive to file as it then is likely to achieve protection from competing claims. It thereby supports the main objective of the scheme of providing information to third parties.[29] An even more basic rule is that a perfected security interest prevails over an unperfected interest.[30] A security interest that has been perfected through any other method than filing succeeds if it was done before the filing took place. When two competing interests are unperfected, priority is given

[22] Art. 9-203; Hakes 17 ff.

[23] Hakes 33.

[24] Art. 9-310(a). Hakes 34.

[25] Hakes 54.

[26] Hakes 33–79. Perfection by possession is limited for goods covered by a certificate of title, Art. 9-313(b).

[27] Hakes 79.

[28] Hakes 81, 88.

[29] Hakes 81–82.

[30] Smith 24.

to the first in time to attach.[31] Exempted from the first-in-time to file or perfect rule are, *inter alia*, qualifying buyers, lessees, and licensees of collateral, qualifying purchase-money security interests[32] and persons with special rights in negotiable collateral.[33]

In general a security agreement is effective against purchasers of the collateral.[34] Nevertheless, customers of the debtor who buy goods in the debtor's ordinary course of business take them free from any security interest even if they had knowledge of the interests.[35]

Art. 9 does not recognise the floating charge. However, to a certain extent Art. 9 has a similar effect to a floating charge. Art. 9 is structured in a way that makes it possible for the debtor to retain possession of and use the collateral and keep the power to transfer the collateral notwithstanding the security interest. Thus, similarly to the floating charge, Art. 9 allows the debtor to continue to deal with the assets in its business and extend collateral over a shifting class of assets.

7.2.3 Security over Investment Securities

UCC Art. 8, which concerns transfer, settlement and holding of interests in securities and other investment property,[36] updates the law to the practices of indirect holdings in the securities markets by recognising that book-entry forms of securities accounts record ownership.[37]

Under Art. 8 directly and indirectly held securities are separated by different rules. Art. 8(2) concerns certain aspects of the obligations of issuers in the direct holding system. Registration in the direct holding system is governed by Art. 8(4). Art. 8(5) deals with indirectly held securities and questions relating to securities accounts and acquisition of security entitlements from securities intermediaries. Transfers of certificated and uncertificated securities are regulated by Art. 8(3).

The UCC makes it possible for an indirect holding to be converted into a direct holding and vice versa. This is important as different levels of protection are given to the holders of securities in the two systems, which exist simultaneously and do not conflict or interfere with each other.[38]

Essential to the scope and the contents of Art. 8 are the terms 'security', 'financial asset', 'securities entitlement', 'entitlement holder', 'securities intermediary' and 'securities account'. The definition of security covers securities and other financial

---

[31] Hakes 81.

[32] Art. 9-324.

[33] Hakes 88–89.

[34] Arts. 9-201(a) and 9-315(a).

[35] Art. 9-320(a).

[36] White and Summers 866. Rocks and Bjerre 5.

[37] ALI Report Art. 8, xi.

[38] ALI Report Art. 8, 12.

assets normally dealt with or traded on securities exchanges or on the securities markets. It includes obligations of an issuer or a share participation, or other interest in an issuer or in property or an enterprise of an issuer which is represented by a security certificate in bearer or registered form or the transfer of which may be registered on books maintained by the issuer which is one of a class or series of shares, participations, interests or obligations.[39] 'Financial assets' includes securities, tradable obligations, participations and other interests which are dealt in or traded on the financial markets, or that are recognised as a medium for investment. Property held in a securities account by a securities intermediary who has agreed with its customer to treat it as a financial asset under Art. 8 is also included.[40] Thus, the definition of financial assets is much broader than the definition of securities. Financial assets that are not securities are only covered by the scheme if they are held in a securities account, i.e. in an indirect holding system.[41]

Central to the system of indirect holdings is the concept of security entitlements. An investment held through the indirect holding system is not analysed as a direct property interest in any specific underlying security regardless of whether any security is individually identifiable or held in a fungible bulk.[42] A security entitlement is instead defined as the rights and property interest of an entitlement holder with respect to a financial asset.[43] The term is used to describe the rights and the property interest, including the right to receive the benefits of ownership and the right to direct the disposition of the interest of a person who holds a security or financial asset through a securities intermediary.[44] It also covers the entitlement holder's personal rights against the securities intermediary. A security entitlement is protected in the insolvency of the intermediary and is only enforceable in relation to the intermediary with whom the investor has a direct relationship.

The entitlement holder is the person identified on the books of the securities intermediary as the person having a security entitlement against the securities intermediary.[45] Securities intermediary means either a clearing corporation or a person, including a bank or broker, that in the ordinary course of its business maintains securities accounts for others and is acting in that capacity.[46] A securities account is an account to which a financial asset is credited in accordance with an agreement under which the securities intermediary undertakes to treat the entitlement holder as entitled to exercise the rights that comprise the financial asset.[47]

[39] Arts. 8–102(a)(15) and 8–103. See also Rocks and Bjerre 5 ff.

[40] Art. 8–102(a)(9) and 8–103.

[41] Rocks and Bjerre 6–7, 41.

[42] Schroeder (1994), 362.

[43] Art. 8–102(a)(17).

[44] ALI Report Art. 8, 9.

[45] Art. 8–102(a)(7).

[46] Art. 8–102(a)(14).

[47] Art. 8–501(a).

The investor's securities entitlement under Art. 8 is a *sui generis* interest.[48] It represents both the personal rights against the securities intermediary and the interest in the assets held by the intermediary.[49] It is generally acquired by the entitlement holder when the securities intermediary credits financial assets to its securities account.[50]

Another important definition in relation to the creation of collateral is 'investment property'. Section 9-102(49) defines it as a security, whether certificated or uncertificated, security entitlement, securities account, commodity contract, or commodity account. 'Securities account' is included in the definition to simplify the drafting of the rules on security interests. By including this term, Art. 9 allows the debtor to create a security interest in the whole account.[51]

7.2.3.1 Creation and Perfection

Rocks and Bjerre note that there are four means of creating or attaching a security interest in investment property: (1) through obtaining a security agreement and giving value with respect to the collateral; (2) by obtaining control of the collateral pursuant to an agreement and giving value with respect to the collateral; (3) through delivery of a security certificate in registered form pursuant to an agreement; or (4) automatically.[52] The latter two forms of attachments are only relevant in relation to certificated securities and so called brokers' lien.[53]

A security interest in investment property is usually perfected either by taking control over the collateral or by filing a financial statement.[54] Filing is common when a security interest is granted in all the debtor's assets. As control grants priority over other methods of perfection, the prudent collateral-taker may, however, want to use this method.[55] A security interest in investment property created by a broker, securities intermediary or clearing corporation is perfected automatically.[56] Certificated securities may be perfected by delivery.[57]

In general, control means taking the steps necessary to place the secured creditor in a position where it could have the collateral sold off without further cooperation of the debtor.[58] Control over a security entitlement can be established by different

48 Schroeder (1994), 363.

49 Official Comment 17.

50 Rocks and Bjerre 40.

51 ALI Report Art. 8, 9.

52 Rocks and Bjerre 78–79.

53 The term broker's lien refers to the situation where a broker is granted a security interest in financial assets that are purchased on behalf of its customer, securing the customer's obligation to pay the purchase price, cf Art. 9-206 and Rocks and Bjerre 78–79.

54 See Arts. 9-312; 9-314 and 8–106.

55 Rocks and Bjerre 78–79.

56 Art. 9-309(10).

57 Art. 9-313.

58 Official Comment 1, Art. 8–106. See also Art. 8–106 and 9-106(a).

methods. The secured party can for instance become the entitlement holder or, in the case where the debtor remains as the entitlement holder, obtain a control agreement from the securities intermediary, i.e. an agreement that obliges the intermediary to comply with orders from the secured party without further consent from the debtor. If the collateral is granted to the intermediary by its own entitlement holder, control is achieved automatically.

A security interest remains perfected by control until the secured party loses control and the debtor acquires possession of the security certificate or, if the collateral is an uncertificated security, the issuer registers the debtor as the registered owner or the debtor becomes the entitlement holder if the collateral is a security entitlement.[59]

7.2.3.2 Priority

The priority between competing interests is determined in accordance with certain principles. Many of these depend on factors such as whether the security interest is perfected, when the interest was perfected, what kind of perfection method the parties used and the identity of the debtor and the secured party.[60]

The most general priority principle is that 'first in time, first in right' prevails. This means that in a conflict between two security interests perfected by filing, the interest that was perfected first takes priority. An important exemption is that a security interest perfected by control trumps a security interest perfected by any other method regardless of when it was perfected.[61] Thus, even if a security interest is perfected by filing before a security interest is perfected by control in the same asset, the latter prevails. Another principle is that a security interest held by a securities intermediary and maintained by the same securities intermediary, has priority over a conflicting security interest held by another secured party.[62]

In relation to the indirect holding system, Section 8-511 governs priority disputes between entitlement holders and creditors with security interests in the same financial asset. If a securities intermediary does not have sufficient financial assets to satisfy both its obligations to the entitlement holder and the creditor, the claim of the entitlement holder has priority over the claim of the creditor. However, a creditor with an interest in the same financial asset as the entitlement holder has priority if it has control over the asset.[63] Another exemption is when a clearing corporation is acting as intermediary: in this case the clearing corporation's creditors take priority over the entitlement holders.[64]

[59] Art. 9-314.

[60] Rocks and Bjerre 91.

[61] Art. 9-328(1). See also Rocks and Bjerre 92.

[62] Arts. 9-328(3).

[63] Art. 8–511(b).

[64] Art. 8–511(c).

7.3 Reuse of Financial Collateral

Even though the term repledge is not directly used in the legislative text of the UCC, it is used in the Official Comments to denote the case where the secured party uses the debtor's collateral to secure its own obligation in relation to a third party.[65] It has also been used in prior versions of the UCC.[66] The term rehypothecation is also used in the Official Comments.[67] It appears as the use of this term, however, is made in the broader sense, i.e. to describe both repledges and outright transfers. This Chapter, as in the rest of the book, avoids the term rehypothecation to prevent misunderstandings and confusions of the different meanings it has obtained.[68]

7.3.1 Repledge

UCC Art. 9-207(c)(3) gives a secured party having possession or control of the collateral a right to create a security interest in the collateral. It applies to all forms of collateral and not exclusively to investment property. It does not apply, however, if the secured party is a buyer of accounts, chattel paper, payment intangibles, or promissory notes or is a consignor; Art. 9-207(d).

Unless the parties have agreed otherwise, Art. 9-207(c)(3) gives the secured party an unlimited right to repledge the collateral.[69] It does not require approval from A. As long as B has possession or control of the collateral as required under Arts. 9-104 to 9-107 it can repledge the collateral.

Former Art. 9-207(e) required that the repledge should not impair the debtor's right to redeem the collateral. A repledge on more stringent conditions, for instance, for a larger amount or for a later maturity than under the original loan is considered to impair the debtor's right to redeem the collateral. This is because it enhances the risk that the debtor is impeded or delayed in getting its property back upon repayment of the loan.[70] This qualification has been removed under revised Art. 9-207. The revised version of Art. 9-207(c)(3) thus appears to provide B with an extensive statutory right to reuse the collateral. The Comments to Art. 9-207 state that the change is primarily for clarification. Thus, there is no basis on which to draw any interference concerning the debtor's right to redeem the collateral.[71]

---

[65] See Official Comments 5–6, Art. 9-207 and Official Comment 4, Art. 9-623.

[66] See Prior 9-207(2)(e), which remained unchanged from 1958 until Revised Article 9. Prior 9-207(2)(e) read: "Unless otherwise agreed, when collateral is in the secured party's possession [...] the secured party may repledge the collateral upon terms which do not impair the debtor's right to redeem it", Kettering (1999–2000), 68–69.

[67] See for instance Official Comment 2, Art. 8–504.

[68] cf Kettering (1999–2000), 51.

[69] Kettering (1999–2000), 176 ff.

[70] Gilmore 1160.

[71] Official Comment 5, Art. 9-207(c)(3).

Former Art. 9-207(e), which embodied the pre-UCC common law, prohibited the parties from impairing A's equity of redemption by repledging on more stringent conditions. The courts have also traditionally shown little sympathy toward creditor-inspired attempts to weaken the equity of redemption.[72] Nevertheless, both former Art. 9-207(e) and the common law allowed the parties to contract out of this condition without recharacterising the transaction as an outright sale.[73]

As stated in the Comments to revised 9-207(c)(3), the intention is not to impair the debtor's equity of redemption. On the other hand, the Comments acknowledge that as Art. 9-207 does not prohibit the secured party from repledging the collateral on more stringent conditions, it may be that the equity of redemption is weakened. This issue is not further elaborated upon. Instead, the Comments bury the problem by stating that, as this matter normally would have been dealt with in the agreement between the parties, any change from the prior version of Art. 9-207(c)(3) would have had very little effect.[74]

The Comments further explain that A's unimpaired right to redeem the collateral nevertheless may not be enforceable against the new secured party C.[75] Through the statutory power provided, in the vast majority of cases where the repledge rights are significant, the security interest of C will be senior to A's interest. Thus, C will typically cut off any claim from A or be immune from them.[76] A would retain a right to redeem the collateral from B upon satisfaction of the secured obligation. However, in the absence of a traceable interest, A would retain only a personal claim against B. Even in the unlikely event that A could trace a property interest in the context of the financial markets, normally the operation of Art. 9-207(c)(3), A's explicit agreement to permit B to create a senior security interest, or legal rules permitting C to cut off A's rights or making C immune from A's claims, would effectively subordinate A's interest to C's security interest.[77]

From the Official Comments it can be concluded that, at least theoretically, the effect of Art. 9-207(c)(3) is that where the parties have not limited B's right to extend a security interest in the collateral and a repledge can be made on more stringent conditions, the security interest is transformed into a title transfer. In other words, where B repledges the collateral and C's rights in the asset would cut off A's claim, in effect, A's property right is transformed into a contractual claim – a right *in personam*. The result is that A loses its equity of redemption in the collateral, i.e. the right to have the property back, when B can fulfil its obligation by returning the equivalent collateral.[78] At the best A can set-off its claim against the underlying

[72] The majority of repledge cases occurred during the 1920's and 1930's in connection with the failures of stockbrokers. After 1940 they have been almost nonexistent, Gilmore 1159.

[73] Kettering (1998–2000), 5.

[74] Gilmore 1160.

[75] Official Comment 5, Art. 9-207(c)(3).

[76] *ibid.*

[77] Official Comment 6, para 3, Art. 9-207(c)(3).

[78] It can also be questioned whether the right to repledge under Art. 9-207(c)(3) does not infringe the secured party's duty of care of the collateral under Art. 9-207(a).

obligation. To the extent set-off is not possible, A will have to share *pari passu* with the unsecured creditors.

Leading US scholars have analysed Art. 9-207(c)(3), former versions of the provision and the common law on repledge and made arguments that support the above conclusion.[79] From their analyses the following can be deducted: where A has "consented" to an impairing repledge, either through agreement, statute or otherwise, in the insolvency of B, A is in most cases left with a contractual claim against the insolvency estate. Moreover, A's right in the collateral after a repledge by B to C, is most often subordinated to the rights of C.

Kettering distinguishes between the case where B has sold the collateral free of A's interest and immediately accounts for the proceeds, either by holding them as substitute collateral, applying them to reduce the secured debt or remitting them to the debtor, and the case where B has the right to use the proceeds of sale for its own purposes, so that the *res* to which the security interest has attached is gone but the obligation which it secures still remains. He refers to the latter situation as a non-accountable sale, implying that it is a pre-default sale authorised by the debtor in which the debtor's rights in the asset have been cut off or subordinated and where the secured party is not obligated to account for the proceeds in the ways described above.[80] Kettering argues that the former situation does not necessarily interfere with the classification of whether it is a secured transaction or an outright transfer whereas the latter situation causes severe classification issues.[81]

Like repos, the latter transaction blurs the distinction between secured loans and outright sales.[82]

> "[...] the problem is whether the relationship between the pledgor and the secured party after such a sale (or, perhaps, even before the sale, if the secured party is authorised to sell) ought to be characterised as a secured transaction at all. The core of the definition of "security interest" is "an interest in personal property or fixtures which secures payment or performance of an obligation." If there is no *res*, there can be no security interest."[83]

Kettering, suitably, refers to this classification issue as "the case of the missing *res*".[84] The former situation, i.e. where B is accountable for the proceeds in relation to A, resembles the solution argued for under Swedish law in Prop 2004/05:30 and Ds 2003:38 with the application of the Accountable Funds Act by analogy.[85]

Kettering notes that prior to the UCC, when this issue was dwelt upon by the courts in connection with brokers' defaults, most notably in the 1940s, the courts tended to respect the label of repledge as a secured transaction, regardless of how squeezed the repledge was as long as it was traceable.[86] Kettering also notes that

---

[79] Kettering (1999–2000), 193–194; Johnson (1997), 973 ff; and Schroeder (1996), 1023.

[80] Kettering (1999–2000), 193–194.

[81] Kettering (1999–2000), 192 ff.

[82] Kettering (1999–2000), 194; cf Sect. 6.3.2.

[83] Kettering (1999–2000), 196–197.

[84] Kettering (1999–2000), 201.

[85] cf Chap. 6.3.2.

[86] Kettering (1999–2000), 205.

despite the textual and conceptual difficulty of characterising a relationship as continuing to be a secured transaction after a non-accountable sale, security agreements used in connection with capital markets transactions, for instance securities lending arrangements, permit such sale as well as repledge and continue to refer to the relationship as being a secured transaction.

If the above analysis is correct and the transaction rightfully should be characterised as an outright transfer, one question that is prompted is *when* the transformation of the security interest into a sale takes place. As previously discussed, there are several alternatives to choose between: (1) before the collateral-taker has reused the collateral; (2) when the collateral-taker reuses the collateral; (3) when the collateral-taker has acquired the equivalent assets; or (4) when the collateral-taker transfers the collateral back to the collateral-provider. This question is further discussed in Sect. 9.2.1.

Clarification is also needed as to the cases in which a transformation of the repledge into a title transfer take place: does an authentic repledge on the same conditions as the initial pledge between A and B have this effect or is it limited to the case of an outright sale of the collateral by B? Does a repledge on more stringent conditions, e.g. for a larger debt or later maturity, lead to a reclassification from repledge to an outright sale even though B only repledges the asset and thus, does not sell it to C?[87]

Art. 9-623 regulates the debtor's equity of redemption. Under this provision the debtor may redeem the collateral when all obligations secured by the collateral and certain expenses and attorney's fees have been tendered.[88] The debtor may generally redeem the collateral at any time before a secured party has collected, disposed of, or accepted the collateral as satisfaction of the obligation it secures. If the secured party fails to permit the collateral-provider to exercise its equity of redemption, it is liable for conversion.[89]

The Official Comments to Art. 9-623 state that the debtor's equity of redemption does not impair a repledge by the collateral-taker. The wording used is that the debtor's right – as opposed to its practical ability – to redeem collateral is not affected by and does not affect the priority of a security interest created by the debtor's secured party.[90] By making the distinction between the debtor's right vs. its practical ability to redeem, the conclusion can perhaps be drawn that it is recognised that the right to redeem may be weakened in the case of a repledge. As has been shown, in the case of an impairing repledge, the collateral-provider's equity of redemption is not worth much. Due to the cut-off rules under Arts. 8-9, in most cases, upon repledge of the collateral, A's property rights vanish. Moreover, because of the difficulties of tracing in the indirect holding system the question whether the collateral-provider has a right to redeem the collateral does not really make sense.[91]

---

[87] Kettering (1998–2000), 5.

[88] Art. 9-623(b).

[89] Johnson (1997) 975, Gilmore 1158–1159; 1165 ff; and G Glenn, 'The Pledge as a Security Device' (1937–1938) 24 Va L Rev 363.

[90] Official Comment 4, Art. 9-623.

[91] cf Sect. 5.4.4.

Another provision that is relevant in relation to repledge of investment property is Art. 9-314(c). It provides that once a secured party has control, its security interest remains perfected by control until the secured party ceases to have control and either, if the collateral is a certificated security, the debtor has or acquires possession of the security certificate; if the collateral is an uncertificated security, the issuer has registered or registers the debtor as the registered owner; or if the collateral is a security entitlement, the debtor is or becomes the entitlement holder. In relation to repledge or sale by the collateral-taker, Art. 9-314(c) thus clarifies that the security interest will remain perfected by control. However, regardless if B creates a security interest in the collateral or sells it outright, typically C's interest will cut off any interest or be more senior to the interest of A. The Official Comments state that if the investment property is used as collateral, A normally would retain no interest in the collateral following C's purchase from B. A's claim against B for redemption or otherwise with respect to the collateral would be a purely personal claim. The Comments thus acknowledge that A is left with a contractual claim.

The Comments develop a theory which Kettering refers to as the "Doppelganger Theory": 'If the investment property transferred by B is a financial asset in which A had a security entitlement credited to a securities account maintained with B as a securities intermediary, A's claim against B could arise as a part of its securities account notwithstanding its personal nature.' The comments suggest that this claim would be analogous to a "credit balance" in the securities account, which is a component of the securities account even though it is a personal claim against the intermediary.[92] The Comments thus present a theory by which the relationship between A and B may continue to be a secured transaction after B's sale of the collateral. The contractual right for redemption that A has against B pursuant to a sale of the collateral is under this theory viewed as the *res* of the security arrangement between A and B.[93] The example of investment securities kept in a securities account maintained by B as securities intermediary is given. If the investment securities are sold by B to a third party, B's contractual obligation is deemed to be part of the account to which the security interest attaches. As a result, the security arrangement between A and B, including B's security interest and A's equity redemption, stays alive notwithstanding that the collateral has been sold outright to a third party who takes full ownership over the asset.[94] The security entitlement is perceived to continue in the collateral-taker's redemption obligation. Whether the collateral-taker's redemption obligation is property is a "nice metaphysical question" as Kettering puts it.[95]

One argument in favour of treating a personal obligation as a property right is that it is already now possible for a bank to take a charge back over a customer's bank account, i.e. its own contractual obligation towards the customer.[96] A similar

---

[92] Official Comment 3, Art. 9-314(c).

[93] Kettering (1999–2000), 212.

[94] Kettering (1999–2000), 212 ff.

[95] Kettering (1999–2000), 219.

[96] Kettering (1999–2000), 220. See also Arts. 9–109 and 9–340(b), and B A Markell, 'From Property to Contract and Back: An Examination of Deposit Accounts and Revised Article 9' (1999) 74 Chi-Ken L Rev 963.

example arises when a charge is taken by a financial institution over debt instruments of its customer issued by the same institution. Also in this case the chargee has a security interest in its own contractual obligation.

It should be recognised, however, that in B's insolvency, regardless of whether the Doppelganger Theory applies or not, what A is left with is in most cases nothing more than an unsecured claim that at best can be set-off against the underlying obligation.[97] It should also be pointed out that the Doppelganger Theory, as presented in the Comments, only applies to certain cases. The Theory is limited to the situation when B is acting as A's securities intermediary and the financial assets are held in a securities account maintained by B. Moreover, as Kettering shows, under the existing UCC, due to problems with perfection and priority, the theory is limited to the cases where a security interest is taken over the whole account.[98]

A relevant question in relation to the Doppelganger Theory is how it relates to the debtor's equity of redemption. Kettering points out that both the prior and revised Art. 9 precludes the debtor from waiving the right to redemption before default. On the other hand, as has been demonstrated, the Comments to revised Article 9 and especially the Comments on the continuation of control under Art. 9-314(c), describe the equity of redemption as a personal right against the secured party for the return of the equivalent property.[99] Thus, the Comments implicitly show that once it is accepted that B may make an impairing repledge, either through statute, agreement or otherwise, A's property rights in the collateral can easily be wiped out.[100]

Kettering also presents another hypothesis in relation to the issue of characterisation of repledge and outright transfers. He proposes that the characterisation issue should be determined against a "Consent to Impairment Test". If B has the right to impair A's redemption right, either in the form of an impairing repledge[101] or a nonaccountable sale, then A has given B rights which are too extensive to be consistent with A's continuing ownership of the collateral, and the transaction should be characterised as a sale.[102] It is pointed out that the leading scholar in the US on repos, Jeanne L. Schroeder, argues that the sale label attached to repos should be respected if the repo buyer, i.e. B, has the right to dispose of the security (cf Sect. 7.3.2).[103] The Consent to Impairment Test is thus consistent with Schroeder's proposal. Kettering acknowledges, however, that despite the attractiveness and simplicity of the proposed rule, it probably will not win ground as it would overthrow the precedent of allowing A to authorise impairing repledges without recharacterisation. In addition, it would require a revision of Art. 9-207(c) since the current drafting, in effect, would recharacterise all repledges as outright sales.[104]

---

97 Kettering (1999–2000), 221.

98 For a more detailed description, see Kettering (1999–2000), 214 ff.

99 Kettering (1999–2000), 226.

100 Kettering (1999–2000), 227.

101 Kettering (1998–2000), 5.

102 Kettering (1999–2000), 205.

103 Kettering (1999–2000), 193 n 331 and 206; and Schroeder (1996).

104 Kettering (1999–2000), 205–207.

Another provision that is important in relation to repledge is Art. 8-504(b). It concerns the securities intermediary's right to repledge its customer's assets and is connected with the obligation to obtain and maintain financial assets in a quantity corresponding to the aggregate of all security entitlements that the intermediary has established in favour of its entitlement holders under subsection (a) (see further Sect. 6.4.4). Subsection (b) provides that a security interest may not be granted by the securities intermediary in the financial assets it is obligated to maintain pursuant to subsection (a) except to the extent agreed by the entitlement holder.[105] It should be emphasised that Section 8-504(b) concerns securities intermediaries' rights to repledge financial assets and is thus narrower in its scope than Art. 9-207(c), which gives an unlimited right to repledge.

In respect to priority rights, under Art. 8-511 a secured creditor of the intermediary has priority over entitlement holders who have security entitlements with respect to the financial asset if it has control over the financial asset. Thus, C has an interest that is superior to the entitlement holder A. A is thereby normally left with a recourse against intermediary B.[106] If, however, C acted in collusion with B in violating B's obligation to A, A could recover the interest from C.[107]

As to the possibility of pledging the security without assigning the underlying debt, it should be reasonably clear from the analysis above that this is possible.[108] A security interest can also be transferred outright together with the underlying debt.[109]

In relation to perfection there is no difference between perfecting a repledge and an ordinary security interest. The same applies to priority rights. Priority between B's and C's creditors in the collateral is established in accordance with ordinary priority rules.

As already mentioned, in most cases C's interest in the collateral cuts off the claim of A. The main rule is that no adverse claim can be asserted against a person who acquires a security interest for value, obtains control, and does not have notice of any adverse claim.[110]

It can be concluded that similarly to English and Swedish laws, a right to use financial collateral under UCC Art. 9-207(c) risks the distortion of the property law system and the distinction between property and claims. An extensive practice of reuse also risks the legal construct that securities are property that can be held on accounts (cf Chap. 5, 6 and 9).

From a regulatory law perspective it should be noted however that the US Securities and Exchange Commission's (SEC) rehypothecation rules prohibit broker-dealers from commingling and rehypothecating fully paid customers' securities.[111]

---

[105] Art. 8–504 (b).

[106] Rocks and Bjerre 49.

[107] Art. 8–503(e). See also Art. 8–511, Official Comment 1.

[108] Gilmore 1157.

[109] Hakes 50–51; Gilmore 1156.

[110] cf Arts. 8–303, 8–502 and 8–510.

[111] Schroeder (1994), 338. Rehypothecation is also subject to self regulation by the various exchanges, see Johnson (1997), 967–968.

Moreover, federal securities laws require that brokers obtain the explicit consent of customers before pledging customer securities or commingling different customers' securities. Federal regulations also limit the extent to which brokers may rehypothecate their customers' securities to 110% of the aggregate amount of the borrowings of all customers.[112]

7.3.2 The Use of Repos

In the US, the question of the legal characterisation of repos has received a great deal of interest. The question, which has prompted numerous cases, is whether repos should be characterised as secured transactions or as outright transfers.[113] Since repos, for economic purposes, are equivalent to secured loans, they are often referred to as collateral by market participants.[114] The seller of the repo is, accordingly, the debtor and the buyer the creditor.[115] Should repos be classified as secured loans, UCC Art. 9 applies. Should they, on the other hand, be classified as outright transfers, Art. 8 applies.[116] Different rules under US bankruptcy laws and federal regulation would also come into play depending on the classification.

The repo market is one of the largest and most important sources of credit in the US. It is based on the assumption that the ownership of the underlying security passes to the repo buyer in accordance with what is agreed between the parties. Should the repo be characterised as a secured transaction, it would have disastrous effects on the industry.[117] For instance, the remedies of Article 9 rather than the contractual remedies under the repo agreement would apply. This means that any surplus of the market value of the security would have to be returned to the seller upon a foreclosure sale.[118] Moreover, should a repo be deemed to constitute a security interest, it would have to be perfected to avoid the trustee's strong arm power under the Bankruptcy Code.[119] A closely connected issue is whether the assets transferred under the repo is part of the repo seller's bankruptcy estate and therefore subject to the automatic stay.[120] The characterisation issue is also relevant in relation to regulatory, accounting, tax and securities law.

Unfortunately the US courts have failed to develop consistent principles that distinguish between the two devices, even though the courts – contradictory to the elementary spirit and principle of the UCC that commercial transactions should be

---

112 ALI Report Art. 8, 127. See also Official Comment 2, Art. 8–504.

113 See for instance 2005 ISDA Collateral Guidelines 39.

114 Schroeder (1996), 1006–1007.

115 *ibid.*

116 Schroeder (1996), 1003–1004.

117 Schroeder (1996), 1008.

118 cf Schroeder (2002), 572–573.

119 *ibid.*

120 Schroeder (2002), 612.

interpreted against their substance rather than form – have tended to rely on the litigants' intent to characterise repos as outright sales.[121] Through amendments to the Bankruptcy Code adopted in 1984, which had the purpose of minimising the importance of the characterisation issue for bankruptcy purposes, some of the problems were dealt with.[122] The scope of the amendments, however, is limited to only cover certain types of securities and entities. Moreover, the amendments do not eliminate the problem of how to classify repos as such.[123]

Jeanne L. Schroeder argues that repos are *sui generis* transactions as they do not fit the traditional categories of title transfer and security interest. Rather, repos are hybrids as they share elements with both categories but also have their own unique characteristics.[124] She suggests that the characterisation issue should be determined against the substance of the transaction. Thus, if a repo is a concealed security agreement, it should be treated as such and Art. 9 should apply.[125] Schroeder points out that the question must be whether there are any material substantive legal differences between outright transfers and secured loans. She distinguishes between a true repo, i.e. an outright sale, and a disguised repo, i.e. a secured transaction.[126] In a true repo the buyer has the power and right of possession, enjoyment and alienation over the underlying security. The security is delivered to the repo buyer and the repo buyer has the right to collect payments under the repo. The buyer is also permitted to sell the original security and is only required to acquire and sell an equivalent security to the repo seller at the last moment in time. Thus, the buyer has no obligation to maintain the original security or any substitute security for the account of the seller.[127]

Schroeder proposes that the characterisation issue, i.e. whether a repo involving investment securities should be classified as a secured transaction or as an outright sale, should be determined against the so-called "Debtor Equity Test". Under this test a repo should conclusively not be considered to be a security interest if the buyer has a right to return equivalent securities rather than the securities which it originally received.[128] If the seller loses its equity of redemption in the collateral, the transaction shall not be deemed to be a secured transaction but an outright transfer.[129] Schroeder's thesis supports the conclusion presented in Sect. 7.3.1 in that where B has the right to transfer the repledge outright to a third party and replace it with an equivalent asset, and effectively does so, the transaction is no longer a repledge (i.e. a secured transaction) but an outright transfer.

---

[121] Schroeder (2002), 566.

[122] Schroeder (1996), 1028–1033; Schroeder (2002), 574–575.

[123] Schroeder (2002), 574–575.

[124] Schroeder (2002), 577–578.

[125] Schroeder (1996), 1007, 1018.

[126] Schroeder (2002), 572.

[127] Schroeder (1996), 1020 ff.

[128] Schroeder (2002), 601.

[129] Schroeder (2002), 583.

7.4 The Doctrine of Specificity

As previously pointed out, the scope of the right to repledge financial collateral, including the right for the collateral-taker to use the collateral as the owner and exchange it for the equivalent collateral, infringes on the collateral-provider's equity of redemption. In some civil law jurisdictions the broad powers and rights of the collateral-taker transform the security interest into a claim. Under the common law it is possible that the property right remains and can be established in the proceeds of the collateral through tracing. Below is an examination of the requirement of identification under US law and the circumstances under which substitution and mixtures can take place.

7.4.1 Identification

Identification of the subject matter is also a requirement for the acquisition of real rights under US law. Identification of the asset is a general requirement to convey a security interest or transfer property regardless of whether the asset is tangible or intangible, fungible or specific. As in all other jurisdictions the requirement is a matter of practical necessity. Rogers notes that '[...] any rule about transfer of property presupposes a theory of identity of objects. We cannot talk about "my thing" and "your thing" unless we can distinguish "same thing" from "different thing".'[130] In relation to certain types of asset and situations, however, for instance in the case of fungible and commingled securities, the requirement has been relaxed (cf Sect. 6.4.4).

As for goods, they must both exist and be identified before any interest in them can pass.[131] Art. 2-501 gives the buyer a special property in goods by identifying them as the goods referred to in the contract. The special property is obtained even though the identified goods are non-conforming or the buyer has an option to return or reject them.[132]

A security agreement must describe the collateral to be enforceable.[133] The purpose of the identification requirement is evidentiary, i.e. to minimise future disputes.[134] Alternative evidentiary tests are possession, delivery or control, as required pursuant to the security agreement. These alternatives are substitutes for the debtor's authentication of the security agreement and the description of the collateral.[135]

---

130 Rogers (1990–1991), 484.

131 See Art. 2–105(2).

132 See also Arts. 2–402 and 2–502.

133 Art. 9-203(b)(3), including Official Comment 3.

134 Official Comment 3, Art. 9-203. cf SS Curley, 'Problems as to the Degree of Specificity of Descriptions under the Uniform Commercial Code' (1976–1977) 22 N Y L Sch L Rev 679; cf Sect. 8.3.

135 Art. 9-203(b)(3)(A)-(D).

Also, the financial statement in the case of notice filing requires a certain degree of specification.[136] However, the notice indicates only that a person may have a security interest in the collateral.[137] Further inquiries are therefore usually required.[138]

Art. 9-108 of the UCC regulates the level of description that must be met in relation to personal or real property. Generally a description is sufficient if it reasonably identifies what is described. Examples of reasonable identification that meet this requirement are if the collateral is identified by specific listing, category, quantity, computational or allocations formula or procedure, or if the identity of the collateral is objectively determinable.[139] Super generic descriptions such as "all the debtor's assets" or "all the debtor's personal property" are insufficient.[140] The purpose is to make possible the identification of the collateral described. The idea that a description is insufficient unless it is exact and detailed is, however, rejected.[141] In comparison with Swedish law, US law takes a more pragmatic approach in relation to the requirement for identity.

As for investment property, a description is sufficient if it describes the collateral as a security entitlement, securities account, or commodity account. Investment property can also be described in terms of the underlying financial asset or commodity contract.[142] If a security interest is granted in an account, it means that the collateral that the security is taken over will fluctuate. A security interest in an account would also include a credit balance due to the debtor from the securities intermediary.[143]

Another relevant provision is Art. 9-207(b)(3), which requires that the secured party in possession of the collateral keeps the collateral identifiable, unless the collateral is fungible. If the collateral is fungible it may be commingled.[144] The definition of fungible goods includes goods which by nature or trade custom are treated as fungible or goods that by agreement are treated as equivalent.[145] The result is, naturally, that the duty to keep the collateral identifiable under Art. 9-207 can be altered through agreement.

---

[136] Art. 9-502(a)(3) and 9-504.

[137] The degree of specification in the security agreement and the financial statement has been subject to a substantive amount of litigation, SS Curley, 'Problems as to the Degree of Specificity of Descriptions under the Uniform Commercial Code' (1976–1977) 22 N Y L Sch L Rev 679.

[138] Official Comment 2, Art. 9-502.

[139] Art. 9-108(b).

[140] Art. 9-108(c).

[141] Official Comment 2, Art. 9-108.

[142] Art. 9-108(d).

[143] Official Comment 4, Art. 9-108. In a consumer transaction, however, a description of a security entitlement or account by type of collateral only, is insufficient, see Art. 9-108(e).

[144] Art. 9-207(b) does not apply if the secured party is a buyer of accounts, chattel paper, payment intangibles, or promissory notes or a consignor, see Subsection (d).

[145] Art. 1–201(18).

7.4.2 Substitution

Similarly to English law, US law is generous as to substitutions of collateral. As a general principle the collateral-taker may assert a security interest in proceeds of the collateral that are identifiable. The principle of allowing the secured party to assert a claim in the proceeds of the collateral is embodied in Art. 9-315. This provision replaced previous Art. 9-306, which was one of the more disputed provisions of Art. 9.[146]

Under Art. 9-315(a) a security interest continues notwithstanding a sale or other disposition of the collateral, unless the secured party authorises the disposition free of the security interest. The security interest attaches to any identifiable proceeds of collateral, as defined under Art. 9-102 (see further below).[147] As per English law, the secured party may claim an interest in either the original collateral or the proceeds, but not in both at the same time.[148] Often the transferee of the original collateral will take it free of the security interest, for instance through a purchase in the ordinary course of business. The collateral-taker is therefore often left with a claim in the proceeds.[149]

Art. 9-315 does not explicitly state what is meant by "identifiable proceeds". One question which often arises is whether cash proceeds deposited into a bank account and commingled with other means lose their identifiability.

The question of identifiability of commingled cash proceeds is imperative in a number of different situations. One of the most common situations is when a conflict arises between a bank keeping the account for the debtor and a secured party of the debtor claiming a security interest in proceeds deposited into the account. Often the bank wants to exercise a right of set-off against the account which has the effect of diminishing the secured party's interest. Another example is priority conflicts between secured creditors claiming an interest in the same account. Yet another example is where a bankruptcy trustee defeats a payment by the debtor to a secured party on the grounds that it constitutes a voidable preference. As Diamond notes 'In each instance, the court must initially determine whether the proceeds retained their identifiability after commingling so that the secured party has an interest on which to base his claim.'[150]

Subsection (b) of Art. 9-315 states that proceeds that are not goods that are commingled with other property are deemed to be identifiable proceeds to the extent that the secured party identifies the proceeds by a method of tracing, including the application of equitable principles that is permitted under law other than Art. 9 with

---

[146] See for instance *In re Gibson Products of Arizona* 543 F2d 652, 655 (9th CIR 1976). See also Diamond.

[147] Art. 9-315(a)(2). See also Art. 9-203(f).

[148] cf Sect. 5.4.

[149] Official Comment 2, Art. 9-315.

[150] WH Henning, 'Article Nine's Treatment of Commingled Cash Proceeds in Non-Insolvency Cases'. (1981–1982) 35 Ark L Rev 194.

respect to commingled property of the type involved.[151] The Official Comments mention the equitable rule 'lowest intermediate balance' as one of the rules that may apply.[152]

Proceeds is defined under Art. 9-102(64) as (1) whatever is acquired upon the sale, lease, license, exchange, or other disposition of collateral; (2) whatever is collected on, or distributed on account of, collateral; (3) rights arising out of collateral; (4) to the extent of the value of collateral, claims arising out of the loss, nonconformity, or interference with the use of, defects or infringements of rights in, or damage to, the collateral; or (5) to the extent of the value of collateral and to the extent payable to the debtor or the secured party, insurance payable by reason of the loss or nonconformity of, defects or infringement of rights in, or damage to, the collateral.[153]

The security interest attaches to the proceeds automatically.[154] For priority purposes, the proceeds of the original collateral are treated as if they were continuations of the original collateral.[155] The time of filing or perfection of the security interest in the collateral is the same as the time of filing or perfection of the security interest in the proceeds.[156] The only requirement is that the proceeds can be identified.[157]

Previous Art. 9-306 provided a very technical and complicated solution for determining whether a creditor had an interest in commingled cash proceeds upon the insolvency of the debtor. This did not only cause uncertainty but also led to a great deal of dispute and litigation.[158] Instead of providing a substantive rule defining identifiable proceeds, the revised rule, Art. 9-315, only generally refers to principles and rules developed in common law and equity.[159] The requirement is that the property should be traceable, directly or indirectly, to the original collateral.[160]

As mentioned, one tracing rule that the Comments explicitly refer to is the 'lowest intermediate balance rule'.[161] The secured party's interest in proceeds held in

---

[151] Art. 9-315(b)(2). As for goods, Art. 9-336 applies.

[152] Official Comment 3, Art. 9-315.

[153] Art. 9-102(64).

[154] Art. 9-203(f). Diamond 407.

[155] Rocks and Bjerre 96.

[156] Art. 9-322(b)(1).

[157] Diamond 407.

[158] See especially Diamond 386 who notes that [...] 'section 9-306(4)(d) provides an overly technical and complicated formula for calculating an interest in cash proceeds in the event of insolvency. This artificial formula was intended to replace the general principles of tracing with a more workable method. Despite this goal, many problems have resulted which have caused some severe and harsh consequences to creditors who believed that they had fully perfected security interests in collateral and their proceeds. To combat these problems and many others, the Revised Article 9 was created. Basically, it deleted the artificial formula and in its place, called for the utilization of equitable tracing principles.'

[159] Even though the US rules on tracing differ from those of English law, the scope of this book does not allow a further examination. See instead FOB Babafemi, 'The Proprietary Remedies of Tracing: A Comparative Study of English and American Law' (1973) 2 Anglo-Am L Rev 198.

[160] cf Official Comment 13 d, Art. 9-102.

[161] The leading case is *In Re Hallett's Estate* (1879) 13 Ch D 696; cf Sect. 5.4.2.

an account commingled with other assets is protected as long as the balance of the account does not drop below the value of the secured party's interest. This rule presumes that any withdrawal of funds from the account is of other means than the secured party's interest. If the balance goes below the secured party's interest, even if funds are later on deposited and the balance increases, the difference between the lowest balance and the secured party's interest is lost. However, should there be a clear intent to make restitution, the secured party regains its security interest in the proceeds to its full value.[162]

Another tracing rule that might be applicable is the 'first in, first out' rule.[163] It assumes that the first assets deposited in the account are the first assets withdrawn from the account. Diamond notes that the 'first in, first out' rule makes it more difficult for a debtor to dissipate funds owed to his creditors by commingling them with other money, as funds deposited last are presumed to remain in the account until all other funds have been dissipated. It thereby supports basic insolvency rules and principles set up to prevent preferential transfers and fraudulent conveyances from debtors when the insolvency is imminent.[164] Another closely related rule is 'last in, first out'.

A third possible solution that might be available in the case of conflicting interests in commingled funds is the 'pro rata approach'.[165] Art. 9 does not provide any solution on how to allocate cash proceeds between two competing creditors who both claim an interest in a commingled account.[166] The *pro rata* approach suggests that the creditors should share the funds proportionally in relation to the value of their respective interests in the account. Thus, if creditor X's interest of $1,500 constitutes 75% of the total fund and Y's interest of $500 the remaining 25%, upon a shortfall of half of the fund, i.e. $1,000, X will take $750 and Y $250. Another option that was exercised in *Bombadier Capital*[167] is a combined application of the 'lowest intermediary balance rule' and the 'pro rata approach'.[168]

Diamond also mentions a fourth possibility that brings with it great benefits for creditors as it avoids many of the problems associated with tracing through commingled accounts. Revised Art. 9 allows security to be taken over deposit accounts.[169] By depositing the proceeds into a separate deposit account, the secured creditor avoids the problem of having to identify the proceeds. A closely related technique is to take a security interest directly over the account into which the proceeds from the collateral are deposited.[170]

---

162 Diamond 409.

163 cf Sect. 5.4.2.

164 Diamond 412.

165 cf Sect. 5.4.

166 cf Art. 9-336; and Diamond 413.

167 639 A2d at 1067–68 (1994).

168 Diamond 413–414.

169 cf Art. 9-102(a)(9) and 9-109(d)(13).

170 Diamond 414–415.

7.4.3 Mixtures

The rules on identification are also relevant in the case of mixtures, i.e. commingling of assets. As the Official Comments to Art. 9-336 note: 'By definition, the identity of the original collateral cannot be determined once the original collateral becomes commingled goods. Consequently, the security interest in the specific original collateral alone is lost once the collateral becomes commingled goods, and no security interest in the original collateral can be created thereafter except as a part of the resulting product or mass.'[171]

Art. 2-105(4) gives a prepaying buyer in an identified bulk of fungible goods a co-ownership in the bulk. An undivided share in an identified bulk of fungible goods is sufficiently identified, although the quantity of the bulk is not determined. Any agreed portion of such a bulk or any quantity thereof agreed upon by number, weight or other measure may to the extent of the seller's interest in the bulk be sold to the buyer who becomes an owner in common.

Art. 9-336 concerns commingled goods, i.e. goods that have lost their identity through manufacturing or commingling with other goods of the same sort.[172] Once collateral becomes commingled, the security interest is transferred from the original collateral to the product or mass.[173] The priority order between competing interests is based on perfection. A perfected security interest has priority over an unperfected interest.[174] If more than one security interest is perfected, the interests rank equally in proportion to the value of the collateral at the time they were commingled.[175] The Comments suggests that where a single input is encumbered by more than one security interest, the secured parties should be treated like a single secured party for purposes of determining their collective share. In other words, where two secured parties have a first priority and a second priority interest in the same collateral, they should be treated as a single secured party in relation to the pool of commingled goods and other secured creditors.[176]

Art. 7-207 regulates goods held in a warehouse. It requires a warehouseman, unless the warehouse receipt provides otherwise, to keep the goods separate to permit identification and delivery. Fungible goods may be commingled and are co-owned by the holders of receipts. Rogers makes several interesting remarks in relation to subsection (2).

> "The rules of section 7-207(2) are interesting as an example of the blurring of property rules that comes with loss of discrete identity. The first step – that the owner-bailors of the commingled goods are treated as owners in common – is little more than a rule of necessity. If it is physically impossible to identify each person's property, then there is not much else to do except divide up what is left. The next step – that any holder of a negotiable document

[171] Official Comment 3, Art. 9-336.

[172] Art. 9-336(a).

[173] Art. 9-336(c)-(d).

[174] Art. 9-336(f)(1).

[175] Art. 9-336(f)(2).

[176] Official Comment 6, Art. 9-336.

> covering the goods is also entitled to a share – is somewhat more interesting. The Common Law of confusion deviated from ordinary property rules only to the extent compelled by practical necessity. All who bailed goods to the dishonest or unfortunate bailee would be treated equally, because it makes no sense to ask whose grain was still left in the elevator. Yet in a dispute between the bailors and a pledgee, the Common Law would say that the bailors obviously prevail because the grain in the elevator was theirs at the time the bailee purported to pledge it. Section 7-207(2), by contrast, shows that once we drop "mine and thine" thinking in one setting, it is hard to see why we should apply it in another. If it makes no sense to resolve disputes among the bailors by asking whose grain is whose, why should a dispute between the owners and the pledgee be resolved by asking whether the grain was theirs or hers? The bailors and any transferees from the bailee are all in the same soup – or gruel. They trusted the bailee's assurance that he had enough grain to meet all his commitments. Why, then, not treat them all the same?"[177]

One cannot but agree with Rogers in his analysis that the rule that owner-bailors of commingled goods should be treated as owners in common is little more than a rule of necessity. To treat bailors and pledgees the same, however, may have certain consequences that have perhaps been overlooked. The interest of a bailor is broader and conveys more rights, as the bailor is the owner of the property. To place the two on an equal footing would, in the case of a shortfall, mean that the pledgee's security interest in the collateral is given the same standing as the bailor's, even though a security interest confers a limited property right.

7.4.4 Unallocated Securities

UCC Art. 8 recognises that the source of the investor's rights in relation to a financial asset is the securities account with its own intermediary and not physical certificates or the issuer's register.[178] In relation to the intermediary the investor holds a security entitlement. A security entitlement under Art. 8 is described as a *sui generis* interest. This is because it consists of a bundle of rights giving the entitlement holder certain rights in relation to its intermediary only and not an interest in specific assets. The nature of an indirect holding system is that an entitlement holder has an interest in common with others who hold positions in the same financial asset through the same intermediary. Thus the entitlement holder does not acquire an interest in any specific underlying asset. For this reason one cannot speak of property or identity as a requirement for conferring property rights in the assets held in the pool. Instead, Art. 8 refers to a security entitlement, which is neither a traditional property right nor a contractual claim.[179]

Art. 8-503 regulates the issue of the entitlement holder's property rights in financial assets held by a securities intermediary. To the extent necessary to satisfy all

[177] Rogers (1990–1991), 486.

[178] FMLC, 'Issue 3 – Property Interests in Investment Securities' 8.

[179] Rogers (1996), 1518 cf E Micheler, 'Modernising Securities Settlement in the UK' (Comp Law 2002 23(1) 9-14, who notes that the leading US Supreme Court cases are *Gorman v Littlefield* 229 US 19 (1913) and *Duel v Hollins* 241 US 513 (1916).

entitlement holders' claims, their interests are not property of the securities intermediary and therefore not subject to the claims of the intermediary's creditors.[180] Entitlement holders share *pro rata* with other entitlement holders having interests in the same type of asset held by the same securities intermediary. All entitlement holders have a *pro rata* interest regardless of the order in which their respective interest was acquired.

As a consequence entitlement holders' claims are not subject to the claims of the intermediary's creditors while the intermediary's creditors' rights are subject to the claims of the entitlement holders. Through the asymmetry of the provision the entitlement holders are given preferential treatment over the intermediary's creditors.[181] It should also be pointed out that Art. 8 does not require segregation of the clients' assets and does not distinguish between the clients' assets and the intermediary's assets.[182]

Art. 8-504 is crucial in relation to the question of the nature of an investor's rights in unallocated and intermediated securities. It requires the securities intermediary promptly to obtain and thereafter maintain financial assets in a quantity corresponding to the aggregate of all security entitlements it has established in favour of its entitlement holders.[183] Thus, even if each entitlement holder's interest cannot be identified or traced, the intermediary has an obligation to maintain financial assets corresponding to each entitlement holder's securities entitlement. The securities intermediary may maintain the financial assets directly or through other securities intermediaries.[184]

The securities intermediaries' duty to maintain financial assets reflects the understanding of property rights in indirectly held securities and the parties' expectations of having property interests in the assets.[185] The duty is satisfied, however, if the intermediary acts in accordance with what has been agreed upon by the parties. This means that the intermediary can agree on a threshold lower than that required by Art. 8 with its customers. In the absence of agreement, if the securities intermediary exercises due care in accordance with reasonable commercial standards to obtain and maintain the financial assets, the duty is deemed to have been satisfied.[186] Art. 8-504 also provides that, except to the extent agreed by the entitlement holder, a securities intermediary may not grant any security interest in a financial asset it is obligated to maintain.

---

180 Art. 8–503(a). One exemption is provided in Art. 8–511.

181 Rogers (1996),1518.

182 FMLC, 'Issue 3 – Property Interests in Investment Securities' 8.

183 The Official Comment 1 to Art. 8–504 states that the locution "shall promptly obtain and thereafter maintain" is taken from the corresponding regulation under federal securities law, 17 CFR § 240.15c3–3.

184 Art. 8–504 (a).

185 Rocks and Bjerre 48–49.

186 Art. 8–504 (c). The Official Comment 4 states that the "agreement/due care" provision in subsection (c) is necessary to provide sufficient flexibility to accommodate the general duty stated in subsection (a) to the wide variety of circumstances that may be encountered in the modern securities holding system.

Art. 8 does not recognise any right to 'look through' the intermediary in order to assert a claim against an upper-tier intermediary or the issuer. Due to the difficulties encountered in acquiring information about the intermediary's counterparties and customers, an entitlement holder would find it difficult to hold anyone else responsible for a claim other than its securities intermediary. The structure of the securities holding system, the multilateral netting practices, the fast-moving markets and the practical constraints of tracing through layers of intermediaries make it more or less impossible to assert a claim against anyone but the securities intermediary with whom the entitlement holder has a direct relationship.[187] Also, the concept of a securities entitlement as a bundle of rights is incompatible with the idea of interests in identifiable assets and upper-tier attachments. Arts. 8-112(c) and 8-503(c) recognise these difficulties and provide that an entitlement holder's property interest with respect to a particular financial asset in most cases may only be enforced against the securities intermediary with whom the entitlement holder's securities account is maintained.[188]

Arts. 8-505 to 8-508 regulate certain other duties that embody the entitlement holder's security entitlement. These provisions concern the intermediary's duties with respect to payments and distributions, its duties to exercise corporate and other rights with respect to a financial asset as directed by the entitlement holder, to comply with orders from entitlement holders, and to change an entitlement holder's position from one available form of holding to another or to transfer a position to an account of another intermediary. All these provisions incorporate the same "agreement/due care" formula as that stipulated in Art. 8-504. This formula allows the parties to alter the duties of the intermediary through contractual provisions or by acting in accordance with reasonable commercial standards with regards to the specific duty.

If the substance of a duty imposed upon a securities intermediary by Arts. 8-504 to 8-508 is the subject of another statute, regulation or rule, compliance with that statute, regulation or rule satisfies the duty.[189] This means that compliance with applicable federal regulatory requirements constitutes compliance with those duties. To give one example, the US federal securities laws establish a comprehensive system of regulation of the distribution of proxy material and the exercise of voting rights with respect to securities held through brokers and other intermediaries. Compliance with these rules is analogous to compliance with Art. 8-506.

It should also be mentioned that some of the principles and rules traditionally found in property and securities laws are used in federal regulation to protect entitlement holders. For instance, intermediaries are prohibited from using customers' securities in their own business activities.[190] Securities firms which hold both customer and proprietary positions are not permitted to grant charges to lenders covering all securities that they hold for their own account or for their customers.

187 cf Rogers (1996), 1455.

188 See also Art. 8–503(d).

189 Art. 8–509.

190 Official Comment 2, Art. 8–511.

Rather, they are required to assign those positions in which they are extending security interests.[191] Another example is that customers' securities only can be pledged to fund the customers' loans, and only with the consent of the customers.[192] Moreover, brokers are required to maintain a sufficient amount of securities to satisfy the claims of all their customers for fully paid and excess margin securities.[193]

In conclusion, the main elements of a security entitlement are as follows. The entitlement holder does not take any credit risk in relation to the securities intermediary's business. In other words, the holder's financial assets are not subject to claims of the intermediary's general creditors.[194] In the case of a shortfall, the entitlement holders are allowed to assert claims against the intermediary's proprietary positions. The most important element, however, is the intermediary's obligation to hold financial assets corresponding to the claims of entitlement holders under Art. 8-504.[195] These three elements can be said to be the fundamental components of property rights in indirectly held securities under Art. 8.

Even if the revised Art. 8 limits the protection given to investors through the traditional property law rules, to a certain extent the protection has been increased through the rules provided in Arts. 8-503 and 8-504. The requirement of a one-to-one match of financial assets in relation to entitlement holders' claims, together with the possibility for entitlement holders to assert claims in the intermediary's assets, do not only protect the entitlement holders' securities entitlements but also provide a cushion.

The possibility of altering the duty to obtain and maintain financial assets through agreement and the alternative of holding financial assets through other intermediaries may however undermine the interests of investors. These rules require counterparties of securities intermediaries not only to understand the risks involved in altering the duty but also to supervise its own intermediary and the intermediaries through whom the intermediary holds its financial assets. As the intermediaries higher up in the chain may hold their assets through other intermediaries located in other jurisdictions, this task easily expands into a duty of assessing the soundness and stability of the whole financial system. Needless to say, such undertaking by the investor alone is impossible. Instead the investor has to rely on the regulatory and insurance systems.

It can be concluded that under the US legal system it is inappropriate to speak of a requirement of identity in relation to unallocated and intermediated securities. Art. 8 recognises that it is usually impossible to identify particular securities as

---

[191] Official Comment 2, Art. 8–511.

[192] Official Comment 2, Art. 8–511 with references to SEC Rules 8c-1 and 15c2–1.

[193] Official Comment 2, Art. 8–511 with references to SEC Rule 15c3–3.

[194] See Art. 8–503. See also Rogers (1996), 1449 ff.

[195] Also under federal securities laws, broker-dealers are subject to detailed regulation concerning the safeguarding of customers securities, see Official Comment 5, Art. 8–504 with references to 17 CFR § 240.15c3–3.

the investor's or the firm's own securities.[196] It is also pointless to speak of property rights in relation to these assets. More appropriate would be to regard the entitlement holder's interest as a *sui generis* interest.

7.5 Summary and Conclusions

Under revised UCC Arts. 8-9, viable solutions are provided for many of the issues with which the law-makers in the EU have just started to grapple. For instance, a fresh and innovative approach has been taken in relation to the question of the nature of the investor's rights in indirectly held securities which matches the developments in the markets.

Art. 9-207(c)(3), which covers repledge, provides that a secured party having possession or control of the collateral may create a security interest in the collateral. This right is very broad as it gives the secured party an unlimited right to repledge the collateral unless the parties have agreed otherwise. In comparison with the previous version of Art. 9, the requirement that the repledge shall not impair the debtor's right to redeem the collateral has been removed. This may mean that the collateral-taker B can repledge the collateral on more stringent conditions than under the original security agreement between A and B. The Official Comments state that the purpose is not to impair the debtor's equity of redemption. On the other hand, it is recognised that the new provision may have this effect.

Through the vast statutory powers provided, in the majority of cases, A's interest will be subordinated to the interest of C. It may be that A is able to trace its interest into proceeds held by B. However, in the absence of a traceable interest, A would retain only a personal claim against B. Should the parties not have limited B's right to repledge, it may moreover be that the security transaction is transformed into an outright transfer. A would thereby lose its equity of redemption. It is also possible that in the case of an impairing repledge A's right *in rem* would be transformed into a right *in personam*. The courts have, however, traditionally been hesitant in recharacterising an impairing repledge as an outright transfer.

The question of characterisation is also relevant in relation to repos. Here the question is whether a repo, which is often structured to fill the function of security, should be characterised as a secured transaction or as an outright sale. Recharacterised as a secured transaction, Art. 9 would apply with the formal requirements for perfection for the security interest to be effective. Any surplus would have to be returned to the seller upon a foreclosure sale. A characterisation as a secured transaction would also have implications in relation to tax, regulatory and securities laws.

In relation to repledge there appears to be no case law that has dealt with the question of characterisation after the implementation of revised Art. 9-207(c)(3). As for repos the US courts have failed to develop consistent principles that solve this issue.

---

[196] Official Comment 1, Art. 8–504.

It is submitted that the rules on repledge under US law dilute the difference between claims and property. An impairing repledge (cf above) is an exemption from the fundamental concept of property and the difference between rights *in personam* and rights *in rem*. If most assets held by securities intermediaries are provided as security in separate transactions, it may be that these practices will destroy the property law system, as the protection that the system is supposed to give is, to a broad extent, diminished.[197] This conclusion corresponds with the conclusions made in Chaps. 5–6 in relation to English and Swedish law. If the practices are restricted by standard agreements and federal regulation, this risk may however be counterbalanced.

Under existing US laws, repledges and repos do not fit the traditional classification and division of property vs. obligation. Rather, they live their lives outside the existing property law structures.[198] As for repledge this means that that the protection given to the collateral-provider A is reduced. The prudent investor should therefore restrict the rights to repledge under UCC 9-207(c)(3) or should at least be compensated for assuming the risk that this involves. Moreover, it would be advisable for the investor to monitor its exposures by carefully assessing the value of the collateral it has posted in order to avoid over-collateralisation.[199] Another conclusion is that if one chooses to lower the level of protection this must be made clear to investors. Thus, the system should be transparent and investors should be informed about the risks they take.

As for unallocated securities, it is inappropriate to speak of a requirement of identity in relation to indirectly held securities. A new legal concept – security entitlement – is introduced through Art. 8 of the UCC. A security entitlement can be described as a bundle of rights that give the holder of indirectly held securities certain rights, including corporate and economic rights, in relation to its intermediary. Since these rights do not convey an interest in any specific asset but rather an interest in common with others, it is unsuitable to describe them as property rights. A more correct description would be to characterise them as a *sui generis* interest.

The following can be said to represent the equivalent of property rights in a security entitlement: (1) the securities intermediary is required to obtain and maintain financial assets in a volume corresponding to the aggregate of all security entitlements it has established in favour of its customers; (2) to the extent necessary to satisfy all customers' claims, interests held on behalf of the customers are not the property of the intermediary and, therefore, not subject to the claims of its creditors; (3) should there be a shortfall the customers share *pro rata* with other customers who have an interest in the same type of asset;[200] and (4) the customers can assert claims in the intermediary's positions should there be a shortfall. Another important aspect is that entitlement holders have the right to require that the holdings of

[197] It should be noted that under Art. 8–504 the consent of the entitlement holder is required for the securities intermediary to grant a security interest in the assets it is obligated to maintain.

[198] cf Sect. 3 and Schroeder (2002), 577–578.

[199] Johnson (1997), 992.

[200] Art. 8–503.

their positions are changed from the indirect to the direct holding system, thereby increasing their protection.

The rules set out above have certain exceptions. First of all, the duty to maintain and obtain financial assets can be altered through agreement. This means that the intermediary can agree on a lower threshold with its customers than that which is required by Art. 8. The duty is also satisfied if the intermediary acts in accordance with reasonable commercial standards to obtain and maintain financial assets. Moreover, the intermediary may maintain financial assets through other securities intermediaries.

Together these exceptions limit the protection that Art. 8 aims to provide. They also require that the customers are sophisticated enough to be able to evaluate the risks involved, a task that easily becomes insurmountable. To a large degree investors will therefore have to rely on the governmental regulatory and insurance systems.

As for the question of the nature of the investor's rights, it has been solved elegantly through the concept of the securities entitlement as a bundle of rights. The issue of identity and property is dealt with by treating the security entitlement as the thing itself. The question of so-called upper-tier attachments, i.e. the possibility to assert claims against intermediaries higher up in the chain or the issuer, is solved in the negative. By providing that the investor can only assert claims against its intermediary, any possibility to trace investment securities is barred.

It can be concluded that the issue of property and identity has not been fully solved. As Kettering puts it:

> [...] The metaphysical issues that underlie the indirect holding system – in particular, the existence and precise nature of the customer's property rights in securities held through an intermediary – seem to be buried too deeply to be disposed of entirely. Like creatures in a horror film, no matter how often they are killed, they just will not stay dead. The deconstruction of repledge unearths them to trouble the world again.[201]

It can be concluded that Arts. 8-9 place great faith in the efficacy of federal regulation of the securities markets. Another conclusion is that investors dealing in the securities markets need to be sophisticated enough to be able to assess the risks that are involved.[202]

---

[201] Kettering (1999–2000), 57.

[202] cf Johnson (1997), 996–997.

Chapter 8
Securities as Property

One of the fascinations of personal property security law is the elusive character of its fundamental concepts.[1]

8.1 Introduction

Securities as assets have been fitted into the traditional property law construct through the makeup of "a thing". The invention of bearer documents facilitate the treatment of these assets as property. The document, which represents the underlying rights in the security, objectifies the rights in the asset and fits them into the property law structure. By giving the document the rights in the underlying asset, it can easily be held and traded with. It can also easily be identified. In relation to the intermediary, however, interests in securities bear a lot of similarity with debt as they are not related to any particular object.[2]

As this book shows, the doctrine of specificity causes severe problems in relation to the developments in the financial markets. This Chapter examines two different questions: Sect. 8.2 analyses the question of securities and fungibility and the thesis developed by Roy Goode that shares are not fungibles as they represent co-ownership of a single identified asset – the share capital. The Chapter ends with a discussion on the doctrine of specificity and its objectives and function as the dividing pillar between rights *in rem* and rights *in personam*.

8.2 Securities and Fungibility

As mentioned in Chap. 5, Goode has advanced a theory that the requirement of identification, whether in relation to tangibles or intangibles, arises only when the subject matter of the transaction is susceptible to division into units capable in law of being separately owned and transferred.[3] In relation to tangibles this depends on

---

[1] R Goode, 'Charges over Book Debts: A Missed Opportunity' (1994) LQR 110 592.

[2] cf Chap. 3.

[3] Goode 63. See also Goode (2003) and Goode (2002).

© Springer-Verlag Berlin Heidelberg 2009

whether they are capable of physical segregation. Goode uses the example of a racehorse to illustrate that since a share of the racehorse is not physically segreable, a charge over a share in the horse is a charge over a single identified asset that cannot be divided. This means that an acquirer of an interest of a particular share in the horse acquires either a co-ownership right or a co-security right. In relation to intangibles the test is not whether they are capable of physical division but whether they are legally divisible into units capable of separate ownership, as opposed to ownership in common.[4] The same considerations that apply to shares apply to bonds, debts (including bank deposits), interests in a fund of assets and other intangibles.[5] As for securities held in bulk, this implies that since the interests are not legally divisible, they are held on a joint basis, i.e. either extending a co-ownership or a co-security right.

> Much of the criticism of the decision of the Court of Appeal in Hunter v Moss stems from a failure to appreciate that shares of the same issue are no more than fractions of a single asset, namely the share capital of the issuing company, and that on a sale or trust of the shares it is not possible to segregate the shares of the subject of the sale or trust from an interest in the remainder of the issuer. In short, such shares are not fungibles at all, they represent co-ownership of a single identified asset.[6]

Goode argues that co-ownership of a single, indivisible asset is incompatible with the concept of fungible units, for the subject matter of any disposition is a share in the single asset itself by way of co-ownership.[7] This applies to all types of indivisible assets that are held on an unallocated basis in bulk, regardless of whether they are tangibles or intangibles. A transfer of proprietary rights in such assets is not void for lack of certainty of the subject matter. The amendment of the Sale of Goods Act 1979 through provisions 20A-B is therefore unnecessary. Another consequence is that the retransfer of securities under a repurchase agreement is a retransfer of the same asset as was transferred in the first place, i.e. not the equivalent asset, as it is a share in the bulk that is transferred.[8]

Goode summarises his thesis as follows:

> "Since fungibility is the antithesis of identification, and since identification is essential for the transfer of ownership, to describe the subject matter of a transfer obligation as a fungible implies that an act of segregation is necessary before ownership can pass. This in turn implies that segregation is possible. In the case of shares it is impossible to segregate part of an issue of shares, or part of a shareholding, from the remainder. If, therefore, shares of a particular issue are to be regarded as fungible, no one can own or transfer shares!"[9]

Although Goode's thesis is intellectually elegant, several factors show that it is flawed. First of all, fungibility is not the antithesisof identification – unidentifiability

---

[4] Goode 64.

[5] Goode (2003), 99.

[6] Goode 64.

[7] cf Lawson and Rudden, 25 who state that goods are fungible if they are treated as such.

[8] Goode 211.

[9] Goode (2003), 384.

is. Fungible units are identifiable as long as they are kept separate. Hence, just because securities held in bulk are unidentifiable it does not mean that they are not fungible.[10]

Furthermore, if Goode's argument is correct, i.e. that securities are not void for certainty of subject matter and only constitute co-ownership rights, it can be questioned how priority between competing interests is to be solved. According to Goode, the fact that unallocated securities held in bulk are not void for lack of identity and constitute co-ownership rights does not affect the allocation of the rights and the determination of how the priority between competing claims should be solved.

> "[...] in the days when shares were numbered, if a fund manager, F, holding shares 1–39 of a particular issue for customer A and shares 40–80 for customer B, were fraudulently to execute a transfer of shares 40–80 to secure a loan made to him by the transferee, that would manifest a clear intention to transfer the shares held for B, not the shares held for A. This allocation does not, however imply that the shares are capable of separate ownership or that if the transfer had omitted the numbers of the shares the transfer would have been void for uncertainty of subject matter; it simply represents a means for determining whether the transferee becomes a co-owner with A or a co-owner with B- in other words, to determine which of A or B loses his co-ownership rights as the result of the fraud."[11]

This analysis can be questioned from several different perspectives. Even if Goode is trying to break away from the doctrine of specificity, Goode's line of reasoning nevertheless involves a certain degree of identification, namely the separation of customer A's shares from customer B's shares.[12] If it makes no sense to resolve disputes among claimants by asking whose shares are whose, why should a dispute between the owner and the transferee be resolved by asking whether the transferred shares belonged to A or B?[13]

The analysis also ignores that numbering of securities traditionally represents ownership in specific shares.[14] Shares in companies represent rights to dividends, voting rights, etc. which can differ significantly from one another.[15]

The creation of shares as the carrier of the rights was an adjustment to fit the invention of limited liability corporations into the existing property law system. The idea that the rights in companies are represented by shares as the bearer of these rights is a very practical concept.[16] It has contributed to the transferability of rights in corporations and the triumph of limited liability companies as separate legal entities.[17] The share certificate resembles the underlying rights and obligations

[10] cf K Pullen, 'Fungible Securities and Insolvency' (1999) 14 JIBFL 287, who points out that any share can be fungible with any other share of the same class of shares.

[11] Goode (2003), 382.

[12] cf Chap. 7.

[13] cf Rogers (1990–1991), 486.

[14] cf Austen-Peters 37–38.

[15] cf Sect. 3.

[16] Undén 19.

[17] Undén 20.

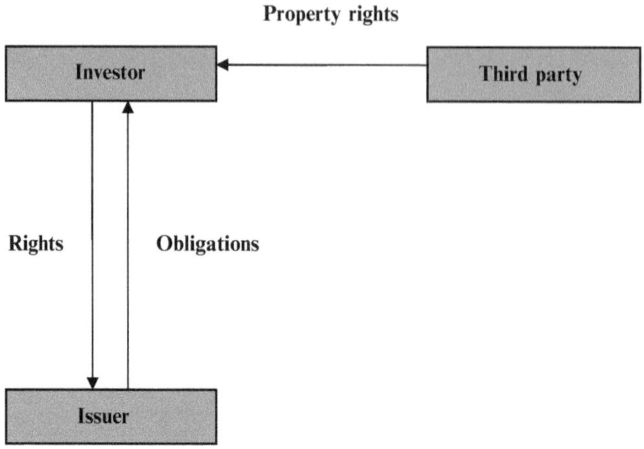

Fig. 8.1 Illustration B: Two-dimensional structure

in relation to the issuer.[18] These rights and obligations are transferred via delivery of possession of the document.

When considering the issues outlined above, the two-dimensional structure in which the legal rules exist should be recognised (see Fig. 8.1). The rules relating to the transfer, holding and settlement of securities that establish the investor's property rights in relation to third parties should be distinguished from the rules defining the investor's rights and obligations in relation to the issuer.[19] The former set of rules is based on the traditional property law system which has its roots in the Roman merchant society where trade took place in assets such as real property, slaves and cattle.[20] In relation to third parties this means that all choses in action – regardless of whether they are shares, bonds, negotiable instruments, promissory notes or simple claims – under the traditional property law structure, are treated as property. The second tier, i.e. the rules establishing the investor's rights and obligations against the issuer is not defined by property law rules but rather through the relevant statutory and contractual aspects of the specific security. The contents of these rights and obligations do, naturally, vary significantly depending on the type of asset. In relation to shares this means that the investor's rights and obligations are defined by the relevant company and contract laws, including the company's memorandum and articles of association.[21]

---

[18] Benjamin 32.

[19] cf J Dalhuisen, *Dalhuisen on International Commercial, Financial and Trade Law* (2nd edn Hart Publishing 2004) 493, 606–607.

[20] D Tamm, *Romersk rätt och europeisk rättsutveckling* (2nd edn Nerenius & Santérus Förlag 1996) 78 ff; cf WW Buckland, *The Main Institutions of Roman Private Law* (Cambridge University Press 1931) 91–92. Only real estate in Italy could, with some exceptions, be the subject of ownership, JA Crook, *Law and Life of Rome* (Thames and Hudson 1967) 140.

[21] cf Ooi 43 ff. The equivalent analyses apply to other choses in action.

As a consequence the legislator is not only faced with the challenge that existing securities laws need to be adjusted to accommodate the developments of the financial markets but also that any new legislation needs to be adjusted to the traditional property law system and the two-dimensional structure.

It is important to recognise that Goode's analysis is based on a look-through approach where the fundament of the share as an asset is revealed. Goode thus looks through the various layers of rules that apply, including the rules that regulate the transfer and holding of securities as between third parties, to the second tier.

Goode's thesis shows that the laws relating to the transfer of securities held in bulk are outdated. Hence, Goode's theory does not prove that shares are not fungible, only that the markets have moved ahead of the law and that intermediated securities do not fit the traditional property law structures. [22] It also supports the argument in this book that securities evidenced in book-entry form have outgrown the traditional property law structure.[23]

8.3 The Doctrine of Specificity

As this book shows the doctrine of specificity causes severe problems in relation to the developments on the financial markets. To a large degree this is due to that securities evidenced in book-entry form on securities accounts are fungible intangibles and as such impossible to identify.[24]

The primary aim of the doctrine of specificity can be said to be to limit the number of proprietary claims in insolvency, i.e. to distinguish rights *in rem* from rights *in personam*. A person who owns an asset in the possession of a debtor who becomes bankrupt can withdraw it from the bankruptcy estate. Similarly, a person who is a secured creditor has a protected property or priority right. Other privileges with ownership are that the owner has a right to possess the asset, a right to claim damages due to negligence should the asset be damaged and does not have to comply with any limitation period to claim the property back from the wrongful possessor. On the other hand, the owner bears the risk of loss or destruction of the asset.[25]

> This is not the place for a detailed account of the history of rights *in rem* and rights *in personam*. A few words should, however, be said about the division between property and obligation, which has its origin in Roman law. Property was in the Roman society deemed to be absolute; the owner had the right to possess the thing in every possible way and a right

---

[22] In *Hunter v Moss* and *Re Pacific* it was the fungibility of shares that made segregation or appropriation unnecessary, *Hunter v Moss* [1994] 1 WLR 452; [1993] 1 WLR 934; *Re CA Pacific Finance Ltd (in Liquidation) and another* [2000] BCLC 494. cf Worthington, who argues that an equitable interest only can arise if the identified bulk is comprised of fungibles. See also Wood 65, 78 ff; K Pullen, 'Fungible Securities and Insolvency' (1999) 14 JIBFL 286 ff; and Lawson and Rudden, 27 who classify shares as fungibles.

[23] cf Goode 63. See also Goode (2003) and Goode (2002).

[24] cf Sects. 3.2 and 8.4.

[25] cf Håstad 152.

to claim it from everyone who in a wrongful way had it in their possession.[26] The nature of a right in rem under Roman law has been described as a person's immediate power over a thing, a *res*. Property was, accordingly, classified as the immediate right over the thing, which is the direct object of that right, whereas a personal right has the action by the debtor as the immediate object, even if the action could consist of a right to deliver a certain thing.[27] Personal rights were often described as limited to the debtor's action whereas property rights depended not on the action of only the debtor but of any other person who had such relationship to the thing that he could deliver it.[28]
Obligation was the creditor's power over the debtor's person and as such the right could only be brought into force through an action *in personam*.Property on the other hand had to be created through an action *in rem* for the right consisted of a mysterious bond between the thing and the person, either in total or in a limited way, for instance through a servitude. From this followed that an action *in rem* had to be effective independently from the counterparty's creditors in the insolvency of the counterparty.[29] Property thus meant that the creditor's right to the thing was not dependant on the debtor's action in order to realize it.[30] Lundstedt notes that modern legal theory does not view property and obligation in this way. Roman law can therefore not be applied to modern legal analysis. He suggests that what should be kept is the distinction made between rights *in personam* and rights *in rem*. The classification of property and obligation should, however, be viewed and determined independently from the outcome in the debtor's insolvency and the question of priority.[31] He also points out that the legal system, without losing in social efficiency, should be constructed as clearly and straightforwardly as possible.[32]

The doctrine of specificity provides a technical method that, in a clear and straightforward way, draws up the boundary between property and obligation.[33] To illustrate, presume that X lends 1,000 tons of grain to Y that shall be returned one week later. Y does not have to return the same grain and is only obliged to return the same quantity of the same sort of grain which can be acquired at a later stage. If the grain is destroyed, Y, who bears the risk for the grain, must acquire new grain and return it to X. The risk is placed on Y who also, in the capacity of being the owner of the grain, can profit by selling it should the price go up. Now, use the same set of facts in relation to a deposit. X deposits 1,000 tons of grain in a silo that is managed by Y. As part of the deposit arrangement X continues to be the owner of it. Since the grain belongs to X, Y lacks a right to dispose of or otherwise to use it. Should the grain be destroyed, for instance in a fire, X, who is the owner of it, bears the risk for it (possible damages are here not relevant). The right of disposal in the first example means that the identification of the grain is broken. It also means that X's rights are classified as a claim. In relation to the deposit, as long as the grain is properly separated from Y's and other depositors' assets and Y lacks a right to

---

[26] D Tamm, *Romersk rätt och europeisk rättsutveckling* (2nd edn Nerenius & Santérus Förlag 1996) 78.

[27] See Lundstedt 334 with references to German prepatory works from 1888.

[28] Lundstedt 337.

[29] Lundstedt 352.

[30] Lundstedt 338.

[31] Lundstedt 352.

[32] cf Lundstedt 343.

[33] That rules are clear and easily accessible benefit commerce in general and thereby society, cf NJA 1910 p 216 and the opinion by Justice Sjögren.

dispose of the grain, X should have a protected property right in the bankruptcy of Y. One major difference between the two cases is that in the case of the advance, X accepts the risk that Y might become insolvent and unable to discharge its obligation in full, whereas in the case of the deposit, X never accepts this risk.[34]

A right of separation would be pointless should all claimants have a protected property right. In the bankruptcy of the debtor some creditors will have to bear a loss as there are not enough assets to cover all claims.[35] One of the objectives can therefore be said to be to protect the principle of equal distribution (*pari passu*).[36]

Another argument is that the requirement for identification counteracts difficult questions in relation to the level of proof: the collateral needs to be individualised for the collateral agreement to be effective. As already indicated, the perfection requirement often facilitates this need. In certain cases where the collateral-provider has not been sufficiently cut off from the collateral or where the collateral is too vaguely specified, problems can however arise.[37] For instance, where X has deposited 1,000 tons of grain in a silo managed by Y and uses grain with a value of GBP100,000 as collateral to secure a loan of the same amount provided by Bank AB, should X have a right to withdraw excess grain it can be questioned whether Bank AB has an enforceable security interest as the collateral is not sufficiently specified and X is not adequately cut off from controlling the collateral.

A strict application of the doctrine of specificity also prevents disputes; once it is departed from, it is difficult to find an alternative rule that is as clear and straightforward.[38] As Håstad points out, the boundaries easily become arbitrary.[39]

An ancillary argument is that it is a practical necessity that claims related to individually specified assets are protected, whereas claims that concern generically specified assets are unprotected. Rogers notes that, 'If we are going to have rules of mine and thine, then we must acknowledge that there will be plenty of cases where outcomes turn on rules or conventions of physics rather than ethics'.[40] Simply, it is difficult to have a protected property right in something to which one cannot point. One clear example is that in the cases where perfection is not required and the security interest is perfected automatically, the identification of the asset becomes the decisive factor that determines when a property right arises.[41] A lower degree of identification requires a stricter perfection requirement and vice versa.

---

[34] cf Goode (1987), 443.

[35] Goode (1987), 433 ff.

[36] The *pari passu* principle can be said to fill the function of preventing a race for the debtor's assets when the bankruptcy is imminent, to facilitate the bankruptcy procedure and to keep the creditors cooperative and willing to accept the outcome of the bankruptcy, cf L Welamson, *Konkursrätt* (Norstedts Förlag 1961) 2 ff.

[37] Myrdal 484; cf Art. 3 Financial Collateral Directive.

[38] Håstad 152.

[39] Håstad 165; cf Chap. 4.

[40] Rogers (1990–1991), 490–491.

[41] cf Sect. 5.4; and §49 of the Swedish Consumer Sales of Goods Act (1990:932); and SOU 1995:11 p 176.

Other objectives are that identification prevents shams and fraudulent transactions as well as undue favouring of certain creditors where the debtor's assets are withheld from other creditors. This could for instance be done if the debtor, who has deposited fungibles assets with a third party and uses them as collateral in a secured transaction with a creditor, when realising that the bankruptcy is imminent, acquires more assets of the same type. If the collateral is not sufficiently identified, this involves a risk that assets that otherwise would be distributed amongst the general creditors are included in the collateral arrangement.[42] Myrdal points out that these objectives are closely connected to the objective related to the level of proof; if the identity of the collateral is uncertain the possibilities for fraudulent or undue transactions increase.[43]

In relation to unallocated and intermediated securities, the difficulties of locating or otherwise identifying these assets means that the custody arrangement becomes increasingly important in evidencing but also establishing what kind of rights the account holder has.[44] The account arrangement is usually documented in the account agreement between the account holder and the intermediary maintaining the account to record book-entry securities deposited with the intermediary.[45] The lack of identification shifts the focus to the account agreement and the perfection requirement as the main factors when determining whether the claimant has entered into a custody arrangement or has extended a securities loan to the intermediary.[46] By changing the provisions in the agreement, it is possible for the intermediary and the account holder to change the contents of the arrangement and thereby also the nature of the account holder's rights.

At a seminar organised by the Law Commission at Norton Rose, London on 23 June 2006, it was discussed whether segregation requires the intermediary to open separate accounts with the intermediary (or issuer) immediately above it. It would, accordingly, not be sufficient for the intermediary to record the accounts in its own books.[47] Registration at the level higher up in the chain of intermediaries minimises the importance of the account arrangement and thereby prevent shams and fraudulent transactions. By requiring an external manifestation of the segregation the level of protection is increased.

Another argument, which has mainly been used in relation to substitution – which is, it shall be pointed out, an exception to the requirement for specificity – is that it would be unjust not to allow the owner to extend a proprietary right into the substitute and that it correspondingly would be unjust to benefit the general creditors in the

---

[42] T Håstad [Mobilia] in *De Lege* (Iustus Förlag) (forthcoming).

[43] Myrdal 483 ff; see also Walin (1998), 166; and Undén 202.

[44] cf the proposed Hague Securities Convention.

[45] cf FMLC, 'Issue 58 – Hague Convention on the Law Applicable to Certain Rights in Respect of Securities Held with an Intermediary' (November 2005) 11.

[46] cf Chap. 9 and the discussion on the placement of the risks and benefits in the assets as between the parties as important factors when establishing the nature of the parties' rights.

[47] It was pointed out that the suggestions made at the seminar are not the official policy of the Law Commission.

bankruptcy.[48] From an economic perspective, substitution is important as it prevents the destruction of value. It prevents an arbitrary transfer of value from one person to another without compensation and also, unjust enrichment of one person and its creditors at the expense of another person and its creditors.[49] It is also argued that substitution facilitates the need of the parties and promotes business.[50] It should, however, be recognised that it contradicts the *pari passu* principle,[51] involves practical difficulties and may involve arbitrariness.[52]

It has also been argued that generically specified claims can be protected by other means, for instance by providing collateral as security against the claim.[53] This argument should, however, be viewed in the light that additional security involves further costs, i.e. the collateral-provider must have collateral that can be spared. A related argument is that the creditor with an unsecured claim knows about the risks it takes.[54]

When considering the above objectives, it becomes clear that it is difficult to draw any general conclusion as to the applicability of the doctrine of specificity and its boundaries without looking at the specific situation at hand. One circumstance that needs to be taken into account is what is practically feasible. Different types of assets and different situations may require different treatments. It is also questionable whether the requirement should be upheld where it is practically meaningless, as is the case in relation to fungible intangibles or shares in indivisible asset such as a racehorse.

It is also difficult to determine how strictly the doctrine of specificity should be applied.[55] Myrdal, who discusses the doctrine of specificity in relation to securities, points out that the upholding of the principle in a specific case requires acceptable reasons.[56] Such reason could for instance be that it is of value not to make exceptions from a clear rule.[57] The contents of the doctrine of specificity are, however, as Myrdal points out – at least as regards its outer boundaries – rather vague. This argument can therefore not be said to be of particular weight in relation to securities evidenced in book-entry form.[58]

---

[48] cf Goode (1987), 438 ff; NJA II 1921 p 619 ff; Håstad 165; and T Håstad, 'Några problem rörande panträtt i en värdepappersdepå' in *Festskrift till Henrik Hessler* (PA Norstedt & Söners Förlag 1985) 318; Walin 1950, 532 ff. The sharing of shortfalls on a *pro rata* basis has also been based on arguments of fairness, cf Austen-Peters 42 with references to *Spence v Union Marine Insurance Co* (1868) 3 LRCP 427, 439 per Bovill CJ.

[49] Walin (1975), 163.

[50] Håstad (1985), 318; cf Persson 503; cf NJA 1959 p 590 and NJA 1971 p 288.

[51] Walin (1975), 165; Persson 493.

[52] Walin (1975), 165.

[53] Hessler 155–156.

[54] U Göransson, *Traditionsprincipen* (Iustus Förlag 1985) 496.

[55] cf Millqvist 133–134.

[56] cf Myrdal 483 ff.

[57] It could however be questioned who should bear the burden of showing that an exemption from the main rule is applicable.

[58] cf Myrdal 483 ff.

As for the developments in the securities markets, several arguments can be identified that show that there is a need to alter the requirement for specificity.[59] In comparison with legal rules that are based on individualised transactions, the trade on the financial markets involves massive volumes of fungible assets. The rapidity with which trades takes place and the number of transactions involved do not fit with a framework which requires identification of the transferor, the transferee and the transferred assets. It is moreover clear that there is a real need for efficient and liquid markets as well as for investors to have protected property rights.[60]

Another reason for abandoning or lowering the requirement for specificity in relation to securities evidenced in book-entry form, is that it is not practically feasible to uphold it as these assets are fungible intangibles. Like shares in a racehorse, fungible intangibles cannot be separated and therefore cannot be identified. The solution with designated accounts is – even though being very practical – a legal construct and does not mean that the securities are located on the account as such. Moreover, since securities by nature are inherently fungible, it does not matter to the claimant which assets it takes as long as it is of the same type and quantity as the assets that the claim refers to.

Furthermore, as most market participants are subject to financial regulation and supervision, the risk for shams and other wrongful behaviour ought to be smaller than in most other areas.[61] Criminal offences such as fraud and embezzlement are regulated by other legislation such as regulatory, criminal and tort law. Shams and fraudulent transactions are also often covered by the voidable preferences rules under the relevant insolvency laws. Hence, abandoning or limiting the doctrine of specificity does not mean that these misconducts are not regulated; only that their prevention is not included as one of the objectives behind the principle.

When evaluating the above objectives and arguments, the strongest argument for upholding the requirement for specificity appears to be that it provides an adequate and practical method that in a clear and straightforward way distinguishes between claims and property. Physical identification serves as a natural divider between what belongs to someone and what is an obligation to deliver assets of a certain kind. It is the lack of identity that requires fungible and unallocated securities to be distributed *pro rata* and that prevents tracing.[62]

In relation to unallocated and intermediated securities, identification is however only possible in terms of upholding the legal construct that the securities exist on the account. As previously pointed out, even in the case of a designated account the securities are not located on the account as such. The established practice is that the ISIN number allocated to the securities only identifies them in relation to the type and series of the security.[63] To prohibit substitution or commingling of

[59] *ibid.*

[60] cf Chaps. 3–4.

[61] cf Myrdal 485 ff.

[62] L Smith 302–303, 320; Austen-Peters 42–43.

[63] cf Sect. 3.2.

book-entry securities is therefore meaningless as securities registered on accounts are in constant transformation.

Arguably, only if the registration on the securities account of the intermediary with whom the investor has a direct relationship is given constitutive effect, would it be possible to separate these assets and thus to identify them. This solution is not desirable, however, as mismatches of credits and debits on accounts regularly occur and a faulty registration or omission to register occurring higher up in the chain of intermediaries (for instance due to an error or fraud) could have significant implications in relation to lower tier intermediaries leading to losses for investors. This solution also involves systemic risk; should an intermediary higher up the chain become insolvent and not be able to indemnify its account holders, it could potentially lead to a fall of all the intermediaries further down the chain. Simply, until the faulty registration or omission to register securities has been restored, the securities cease to exist for the account holders further down the chain. In relation to foreign securities the chain of intermediaries can be very long involving numerous intermediaries located in different jurisdictions, which would increase the risk further.

Another alternative is to give the registration a similar status to possession of bearer documents. This solution means that the registration on the book-entry account would be more than a mere proof of evidence. At the same time, as bearer documents can be lost or misplaced without the investor losing the possibility to re-establish the rights that the document carries, the investor's rights would not be entirely dependent upon the accuracy of the registration. It could be questioned whether this alternative is desirable, however, as the creation of bearer documents as the carrier of the rights in the security is a construct in itself and the proposal would involve adding a construct to a construct which increasingly is becoming outdated.

A third possible solution is to give the registration on the account evidentiary effect, which thus serves as proof of the entitlements of the investor. The problem in this case is, as pointed out above, that identification of the securities, or for that matter the pool, is impossible.

It cannot be denied though that the construct that the rights in the securities are attached to the book-entry registration is a useful tool. It is therefore argued that even if the perception that securities are held on accounts is a construct, it should nevertheless be kept in order to keep the protection for property rights in securities evidenced in book-entry form. Since errors regularly occur in relation to credits and debits on accounts, it is however inadvisable to give the registration any other effect than an evidentiary one. Mistakes are easier to correct if the registration merely evidences the securities held by the account holder. By giving investors the opportunity to choose between different alternatives of holding securities on designated or omnibus accounts, the level of protection can be adjusted and also priced. The higher the degree of segregation, the more protected the investor is in the insolvency of the intermediary.

In relation to legislative works, the following recommendations are made. The protection for property rights in securities held by an intermediary on behalf of its customers could be increased by providing that the intermediary is obliged to hold a sufficient quantity of securities at all times which corresponds to its customers' claims.[64] By requiring that the intermediary should be able to account for the securities and deliver a quantity to the customers that corresponds to their claims on a continuous basis, the customers would, unless the intermediary acted fraudulently or erroneously or a settlement failure occurred, be protected even if the intermediary substitutes the securities or commingles them with other customers' securities. An explicit provision should also be included prohibiting the intermediary to use, dispose off or commingle the securities with its own securities without its customers' consent. By requiring that the intermediary registers its customers' securities without delay, the intermediary would be required to separate the securities on the customer's account as soon as possible and at the latest in accordance to standard market practise, thereby increasing the protection further.[65]

Another rule that would increase the protection for investors would be to give them rights in the intermediary's proprietary positions should there be a shortfall. To the extent necessary to satisfy all investors' claims, investors should thus be allowed to assert a claim in the intermediary's securities.[66] This provision gives the investors a cushion and forces the intermediary to manage its customers' assets in an accurate and prudent manner, which includes choosing safe and sound intermediaries higher up the chain.

At the seminar organised by the Law Commission at Norton Rose in London on 23 June 2006, it was discussed whether the allocation of losses should depend on whether the intermediary is responsible for the loss or not. It was proposed that where the intermediary has commingled its own securities with those of its account holders, a loss arising from the intermediary's insolvency or breach of duty should first be allocated to reduce those securities held for the intermediary's own account. It was pointed out that if the intermediary is not responsible for the loss (for example, because it originated at a higher tier), it is arguable that the intermediary should only share the loss *pro rata*. It was moreover proposed that where an intermediary has segregated its house securities in a separate account, a loss in its customer account should first be allocated to the intermediary's house account only if the loss arises from the intermediary's own breach of duty. If the intermediary is not responsible, it is difficult to justify the allocation of any of the losses to its house securities.[67]

This book argues that the intermediary should be responsible for any losses to the extent that it has securities of the same kind, i.e. regardless of whether it is responsible for the loss or not and regardless of whether its securities are commingled with its customers' securities. Only if the loss has been caused by the customer should it be allocated to the customer. The reason for this somewhat harsh stand is to force the intermediary to be cautious and to give it an incentive to be selective and prudent in the supervision of the intermediaries higher up in the chain. As previously pointed out, one of the major weaknesses of the indirect holding system is that the investor

---

[64] cf Sect. 7.4.4.

[65] cf the Swedish Accountable Funds Act.

[66] cf UCC 8–503.

[67] Law Commission, 'Project on Intermediated Investment Securities: Second Seminar – Issues Affecting Account Holders and Intermediaries' (23 June 2006) 6.

is dependant on its interest in the underlying securities being properly accounted for at all levels of intermediaries up the chain to the issuer. By giving the investor's intermediary a strong incentive to protect its own interest, the investor's interest is protected to a higher degree, thereby increasing the confidence in the financial markets.

It is important to recognise that the level of protection also can be increased by shortening the chain of intermediaries that stand between the issuer of the security and the ultimate investor. Thereby the risk that error occurs, or that the legal title to securities or the benefits stemming from an investment is misappropriated when passed down the chain, is limited.[68]

It should also be recognised that a lower degree of the requirement of identity for unallocated and intermediated securities already is in place. The developments of the securities markets have, in effect, led to book entry securities being held on a fungible and unallocated basis. As a consequence, the custody arrangement, including the account agreement, is an increasingly important factor in establishing the content and the nature of the account holder's rights.[69] It also means that the financial regulation and supervision of custody services are imperative in protecting the safety and soundness of the financial system.

8.4 Summary and Conclusions

As this book shows, the doctrine of specificity causes severe problems in relation to the developments of the securities markets. Whereas the legal rules are based on transactions involving individualised assets, the trade on the financial markets involves massive volumes of fungible assets.

To a large extent the identified problems are due to the fact that unallocated and intermediated securities are fungible intangibles and as such impossible to identify. Another important factor is the development of indirect holding structures where intermediaries are often interpositioned between the issuer and the investor.

This Chapter evaluates the thesis developed by Goode that the requirement for identity arises only when the subject matter of the transaction is susceptible to division into units capable in law of being separately owned and transferred. According to Goode, shares are not fungibles as they are fractions of a single asset – the share capital. Instead they represent co-ownership of a single identified asset.

The analysis shows that Goode's theory is incorrect. The main point is that it overlooks the two-dimensional structure in which the legal rules exist. The rules relating to the transfer, holding and settlement of securities that establish the investor's proprietary rights in relation to third parties should, accordingly, be distinguished from the rules defining the investor's rights and obligations in relation

[68] cf Austen-Peters 71.

[69] Austen-Peters 40–41. By upholding formal requirements of written account agreements or evidence of the account arrangement in a durable medium, shams and other misconduct can be counteracted, cf Recitals 10 Financial Collateral Directive.

to the issuer. In relation to third parties, all choses in action are treated as property. As a consequence, the requirement for identity applies. The second tier, which establishes the investor's rights against the issuer, is not defined by property law rules but rather through the relevant statutory and contractual aspects of the specific security. The analysis also shows that Goode ignores the fact that the numbering of bearer securities often represent different rights in relation to the issuer. With respect to shares, these rights can vary significantly in relation to rights to dividends, voting rights, etc.

The Chapter ends with an examination of the objectives behind the doctrine of specificity and its function as the dividing pillar between property and claims. It argues that it is difficult to draw any general conclusion in relation its applicability without looking at the specific situation at hand. Different types of assets and different situations may require different treatment.

The strongest argument for upholding the doctrine of specificity appears to be that it is a powerful baseline rule, which in an adequate and practical manner, distinguishes between property and claims. Simply, it is difficult to identify any alternative rule which is as straightforward and which distinguishes between the two devices. On the other hand, it is clear that the doctrine of specificity is ill-suited to the securities markets and the developments that have taken place. The massive volumes of fungible assets traded and the pace with which transactions take place do not fit a framework that requires identification of the seller, the buyer and the traded securities. Considering that securities are fungible intangibles and as such impossible to identify, it can also be questioned whether a strict application of the principle is reasonable.

Arguably the primary aim for the legislator should be to implement clear and consistent rules that are easily accessible. Investors, including the general public, need to know what rights they have and ought to be able to trust the system that is in place; the integrity and safety of the system must be protected. Clear and consistent rules also counteract problems with evidence and thereby prevent disputes and fraudulent transactions. It is therefore argued that even if the perception that securities are held and separated on accounts is a construct, it should be kept. Property rights in these assets could also be protected by providing that the intermediary is obliged to hold a sufficient quantity of securities at all times which corresponds to its customers' claims.[70] By requiring that the intermediary should be able to account for the securities and deliver a quantity to the customers that corresponds to their claims on a continuous basis, the customers would, unless the intermediary acted fraudulently or erroneously or a settlement failure occurred, be protected even if the intermediary substitutes the securities or commingles them with other customers' securities.[71] By giving investors the opportunity to choose between different alternatives of holding securities on designated or omnibus accounts, the level of protection can be adjusted.

[70] cf Sect. 8.3.

[71] cf the Swedish Accountable Funds Act.

It is also important to recognise that by minimising the number of intermediaries between the issuer and the ultimate investor, the intermediary risk is limited. The longer the chain of intermediaries, the greater the risk that errors occur, or that the legal title to the securities or income distributions and voting rights are misappropriated.

Chapter 9
Property Rights in Securities and the Doctrine of Specificity: A Comparative Analysis with an Outlook *De Lege Ferenda*

In the end, then, the problem with the present structure of the law of securities transfers may be that the concept of transferring items of property just does not fit.[1]

9.1 Introduction

This Chapter provides a comparative analysis of English, Swedish and US law in relation to the questions discussed in this book. It summarises the main problems as well as the main conclusions, and provides some recommendations on how to structure a well-balanced and functional property and security law system.

The analysis, which is made with the aim of identifying possible solutions, supports the main argument of the book that due to the developments of the financial markets and the securities holding systems, securities as assets have outgrown the existing property law structures. The examination also shows that the problems are predominantly the same in all jurisdictions covered by the study.

9.2 Reuse of Financial Collateral

Through the implementation of Art. 5 of the Financial Collateral Directive, a right to reuse financial collateral in accordance with the terms of the security financial collateral arrangement has been established through statute in the United Kingdom and Sweden. In the United Kingdom, Art. 5 of the Directive was implemented through Regulation 16 of the Financial Collateral Arrangements (No 2) Regulations 2003 (SI 2003 No 3226) (Financial Collateral Arrangement Regulations), which came into effect on 26 December 2003. In Sweden, amendments were made to Ch. 3 §§ 1 and 3 of the Trade with Financial Instruments Act (1991:980), effective as of 1 May 2005. In the United States, a right to reuse collateral is provided in UCC 9–207(c)(3).

Art. 6(1) of the Financial Collateral Directive requires EU Member States to ensure that title transfer of financial collateral arrangements, including repos, can take effect in accordance with their terms. Recharacterisation risk is thereby limited. In the United Kingdom, recharacterisation risk was not considered to be a

[1] Rogers (1990–1991), 506.

© Springer-Verlag Berlin Heidelberg 2009

major issue. Due to this there is no specific provision that implements Art. 6 of the Financial Collateral Directive in the Financial Collateral Arrangement Regulations. Similarly, no amendments have been made to the Swedish legislation.

9.2.1 Repledge

Under English law, B's right to repledge has its origin in the common law and is described as a "special property" that is capable of being transferred.[2] In Sweden, Ch. 10 §6 of the Commercial Code (1736:1232) provides an independent right for collateral-takers to repledge collateral, i.e. it regulates the cases that are not covered by an agreement. Where the collateral consists of financial instruments the Trade with Financial Instruments Act (1991:980) applies. The most liberal scheme is that under UCC 9–207(c)(3), which gives B an "unlimited right" to repledge.[3] In all three jurisdictions, the true meaning of repledge and its legal effects are most uncertain.

In the United Kingdom, before the implementation of the Financial Collateral Arrangement Regulations, there were doubts whether a right to repledge existed. The uncertainties were mainly due to the equitable principles "once a mortgage, always a mortgage", the "equity of redemption" and the "rule against collateral benefits". Through the implementation these doubts have been removed. The implementation has however, as in Sweden, created other problems. Since the collateral-taker is allowed to use the financial collateral as the owner and can replace it with the equivalent collateral, the tie with the equity of redemption, which represents the collateral-provider's property rights in the asset, is broken.[4]

In Sweden, even though repledge has been discussed to a much broader extent than in the United Kingdom and the United States, it is still subject to vast uncertainties. Unfortunately the implementation of the Financial Collateral Directive, which aims to ensure that agreement permitting the collateral-taker to reuse collateral for its own purposes are effective, has not removed the ambiguities. At present it is unclear whether A has a right to redeem the collateral when B has a right to use the collateral as the owner under the security financial collateral arrangement. Hence, a mere right to reuse the collateral as the owner may transform A's right *in rem* into a right *in personam,* or a so called *pignus irregulare.*[5]

Also under US law the rights and obligations of A, B and C and the legal effects of repledge are uncertain.[6] Unless the parties have agreed otherwise, UCC Art. 9–207(c)(3) is deemed to give a secured party having possession or control of the collateral an unlimited right to create a security interest in the collateral.[7] There is

[2] *Donald v Suckling* (1865–66) LR 1 QB 585.

[3] Kettering (1999–2000), 176 ff.

[4] cf Sect. 5.3.2.

[5] cf Sect. 6.3.2.

[6] cf Sect. 7.3.1.

[7] cf Kettering (1999–2000), 176 ff.

no requirement that the parties include a clause in their security agreement in order to give B such extensive right.

In all three jurisdictions, third parties can make bona fide purchases of the collateral as long as they lack knowledge of A's interest. As a general rule, no adverse claim can be asserted against a person who acquires an interest for value, obtains control, and who lacks notice of the adverse claim. A's ownership right in the collateral is thereby cut off.[8]

As is shown in this book, the question of reuse of financial collateral is closely related to the question of specificity of the collateral. Under traditional property law rules, identification of the collateral is one of the factors that determine whether the transaction should be characterised as an outright transfer or a security interest. A disposal of the financial collateral by the collateral-taker is in conflict with the collateral-provider's equity of redemption – and the requirement for identification of the collateral. At the moment the right of use is exercised, the bond between the asset and its owner is broken and the owner is left with a contractual claim.

This book argues that under the laws of each jurisdiction included in the study, where B exercises a right of use as the owner without replacing the collateral with a substitute, A's right is effectively transformed from a right *in rem* to a right *in personam*.[9] In other words, before the transfer of the equivalent collateral from B to A, the right of A will most likely be reduced to a claim, which, unless it can be set-off, is worthless in the insolvency of B. A closely related question is whether a right to repledge on more stringent conditions have the same effect or if it is limited to outright transfers. As previously pointed out, the characterisation of the transaction may have severe implications in relation to regulatory, tax and accounting treatments and is also important in relation to the allocation of income and administrative rights.

The analysis of A's right to redeem the collateral and the protection of its ownership rights may vary depending on at what stage the rights are analysed. At least four different phases can be identified: (1) before B has reused the collateral; (2) when B reuses the collateral; (3) when B has acquired the equivalent assets; and (4) when B transfers the collateral back to A.[10]

In Sweden, it is unclear whether A has a right to redeem the collateral when B has a right to use the collateral as the owner under the security financial collateral arrangement in relation to stages (1) and (3).[11] In relation to stage (2), i.e. when B has reused the collateral, it is reasonably clear that A's ownership rights are exchanged for a right to set-off the claim against the underlying obligation. Where B has transferred the equivalent collateral to A, i.e. stage (4), as long as the retransfer is normal, A is deemed to have a protected interest. Considering the position of EC law as being superior to national law of the EU Member States and in light of

---

[8] cf Sects. 5.3.1, 6.3.1 and 7.3.1.

[9] cf Sects. 5.3.2, 6.3.2 and 7.3.1.

[10] cf Sect. 2.3.4.

[11] Prop 2004/05:30 p 53, 122.

the aim of the Financial Collateral Directive to facilitate a reuse of financial collateral, the argument that Swedish law should be interpreted as protecting A's rights is rather strong.

In England, Art. 5 of the Financial Collateral Directive has been interpreted so that A's equity of redemption lasts until B disposes of the collateral. It is uncertain whether the property right of A remains after the disposal of the collateral (stage 2) but before the transfer of the equivalent collateral to A in discharge of the underlying obligation (stage 4). Most probably it is transformed into a right to set-off against the underlying claim. A is thus deemed to keep its property rights in relation to stage 1, i.e. before B has reused the collateral, and stage 4, i.e. when B has transferred the collateral back to A.[12]

Under US law, where A has "consented" to an "impairing repledge" either through agreement, statute or otherwise, in the insolvency of B, A is deemed by some to be left with a contractual claim.[13] An "impairing repledge" includes repledges having more stringent conditions, for instance for a larger amount or for a later maturity than under the original loan, and a right to transfer the collateral outright to a third party. The effect is that the debtor's equity of redemption is weakened as it effectively hinders A's ability to redeem the collateral. It should be noted, however, that the courts have traditionally tended to respect the label of a repledge as a secured transaction regardless of how squeezed it is as long as it is traceable.[14] It should also be noted that the question of A's right to redeem the collateral and the different stages referred to above has not been discussed. A qualified guess is that the courts would try to respect the form of the repledge agreement as a security arrangement. A permissive interpretation would foremost cause difficulties in relation to stage 2 (see above).

Different techniques could be used in the interpretation of a security agreement that gives B a right to reuse financial collateral as the owner. One alternative would be to interpret the agreement as including an option for B to acquire the collateral and thereby transform the agreement into a title transfer arrangement.[15] The ownership rights would accordingly remain with A when the security interest arises but pass to B when B exercises the option. Upon acquisition of the equivalent collateral another option would be exercised and the ownership rights would revive in the substitute.

Another technique, which resembles the solution argued for in relation to repos (cf below), would be to let the interpretation be based on the allocation of the benefits and the burdens in the underlying assets, i.e. whichever of the parties that bears the risk for the financial collateral and gains from a possible profit. A right to dispose of the collateral, to collect income payments and exercise voting rights are accordingly clear indications that the transaction is a true sale.

---

[12] cf Austen-Peters 53–54.

[13] cf Johnson (1997), 973 ff; cf Kettering (1999–2000), 193–194; and Schroeder (1996), 1023.

[14] Kettering (1999–2000), 205.

[15] cf Myrdal 496.

A third possible solution would be to allow a disposal as long as B is obliged to hold a quantity of securities corresponding to A's claim on a continuous basis. A's equity of redemption would accordingly continue to exist in the substitute.

Another alternative would be for the security interest to continue to exist in the proceeds received upon sale of the collateral, i.e. money paid into a bank account linked to the securities account. This alternative requires, however, that the parties have included both the securities account and the bank account in the collateral arrangement and that it is effective and enforceable.

Another possibility would be to utilise the theory outlined in the Official Comments to the UCC, which is referred to by Kettering as the Doppelganger Theory. In accordance with this theory, A's property right would continue to exist despite B's disposal of the collateral. The contractual right to redeem the collateral that A has against B, with a corresponding obligation for B to return the equivalent collateral, is accordingly viewed as the *res* used as collateral under the original security arrangement between A and B. The security entitlement is thus perceived to continue in B's redemption obligation. One argument in favour of treating a personal obligation as a property right is that it is already possible for banks to take charge backs over customers' bank accounts, i.e. their own contractual obligation towards the customers.[16] Similarly, when a charge is taken by a financial institution over debt instruments of its customer issued by the same institution, the chargee has a security interest in its own contractual obligation. It should be recognised, however, that in the event of B's insolvency, regardless of whether the Doppelganger Theory applies or not, what A is left with is an unsecured claim that, at best, can be set-off against the underlying obligation.[17]

Another concern with a right of reuse as the owner is the risk of creating multiple obligations between different parties. Where a collateral-taker has the right to dispose of the collateral and effectively does so, unless the intermediary who holds the collateral recognises that the collateral has been disposed of, for instance by blocking the registration on the relevant account, it is possible that the same securities would be registered as belonging to several investors. The effect is that there are too many registrations in relation to securities issued. Arguably, this could potentially distort the property law system and the distinction between property and claims.[18]

In the attempt of designing coherent rules on repledge the indirect holding structures must also be taken into account. Since securities evidenced by book-entries on accounts *de facto* are held on a fungible basis,[19] and, in addition, are often mixed on omnibus accounts, they are impossible to separate or otherwise to distinguish in relation to their entitlement holders. It is therefore difficult to allocate the specific securities that are used in a repledge transaction and, as a consequence, difficult

[16] In relation to English law, see *Re Bank of Credit and Commerce International SA (In Liquidation) (No 8)* [1998] AC 214 (HL); *Re Charge Card Services Ltd (No 2)* [1987] Ch 150; and R Goode 'Charges over Book Debts: A Missed Opportunity' 1994 110 LQR 606.

[17] Kettering (1999–2000), 221.

[18] See further Sect. 5.3.2.

[19] This argument is based on the fact that unallocated and intermediated securities are fungible intangibles and as such impossible to separate.

to know whether the repledge takes place on more stringent conditions or not.[20] In addition, as the collateral is often specified in relation to a certain value and the value of the collateral, the requirement for collateral under the collateral agreement and the extended credit often fluctuate from time to time, a repledge on more stringent condition could easily occur.[21] Due to this it would be wise to distinguish between repledge in the more traditional sense and the cases where B has a right to extend a security interest on more stringent conditions and/or has a right to sell the collateral outright. It should also be recognised that close-out netting in most cases is sufficient as long as it is acknowledged under the applicable insolvency laws. If close-out netting is recognised, the greatest risk which A takes is the risk of overcollateralisation.[22]

9.2.2 The Use of Repos

Repos are often, for economic purposes, equivalent to secured loans, and are therefore referred to as collateral arrangements by market participants. The element of security is the transfer of ownership of the assets from A to B. Effectively, the security consists of the possibility to set-off the value of the collateral against the underlying obligation upon default by A.

The risk that the transaction is characterised as a security arrangement is commonly referred to as recharacterisation risk. As previously mentioned, the characterisation of the transaction may have great legal effects. Should the transaction be interpreted as a security arrangement, any surplus would have to be returned to A upon sale of the collateral. The security interest may be unenforceable if it has not been properly perfected. The characterisation may also have other legal effects under applicable insolvency, regulatory, accounting, tax and securities laws.

Art. 6(1) of the Financial Collateral Directive requires Member States to ensure that a title transfer financial collateral arrangement can take effect in accordance with its terms and thereby eliminates recharacterisation risk. The implementation of the Directive did not cause much concern in Sweden and the United Kingdom. Recharacterisation risk has caused more concern and been debated more in the US even though, as this study shows, it is still relevant in the EU.

Under English law, recharacterisation risk is not perceived to be a major issue. As long as the parties intend that title to the securities shall pass from the collateral-provider to the collateral-taker and the collateral-taker is free to do what it wants with the transferred securities, recharacterisation risk is generally remote. Before the implementation of the Financial Collateral Arrangement Regulations, the use of repos and title transfer structures were, however, the preferred techniques. After

[20] That is unless the registration is given constitutive effect or the same effect as possession of a bearer document, cf Sect. 8.3.

[21] cf Myrdal 462 ff and Chap. 3.

[22] cf Chap. 3.

the implementation, the liberalisation of the rules on reuse of financial collateral is estimated to have increased the use of repledges.

Under Swedish law, a repo may be recharacterised as a financial collateral security arrangement. Even though the interpretation of each agreement should be based on its substance rather than its form, the assumption in the governmental reports Prop 2004/05:30 and Ds 2003:38 is that repos should be characterised as "*säkerhetsöverlåtelse*" (which loosely can be translated into "security transfer"), i.e. contrary to the intention of Art. 6 of the Financial Collateral Directive.[23]

In the US, the characterisation question has prompted numerous cases and also been subject to wide debate. Notwithstanding the spirit and general principle of the UCC that the interpretation of commercial transactions should be based on substance rather than form, the courts have failed to develop consistent principles that distinguish between the two devices.

This book proposes that upon interpretation of repos it is insufficient to look at the economic rationale or the intention of the parties when determining whether the transaction is a secured transaction or an outright transfer. Even if it is confirmed that the intention is to secure the underlying obligation, it is also often intended that B should have the right to use the collateral as the owner. It is therefore proposed that the characterisation, in addition, should be based on the allocation of the benefits and the burdens in the underlying assets, i.e. the placement of the risk for the securities and gains from a possible profit.[24] A right to dispose of the collateral, to collect income payments and exercise voting rights are accordingly indications that the transaction is a true sale.

9.3 The Doctrine of Specificity

As mentioned, a right to reuse financial collateral under the Financial Collateral Directive involves a right for the collateral-taker to use the collateral as its own and to exchange it with the equivalent collateral. In many jurisdictions, under the traditional property law rules, the scope of the right of use transforms the security interest into a claim.[25] This is due to the extensive right to dispose of the collateral. As a disposal effectively breaks the continuing identity of the collateral, it is in conflict with the requirement of identification.

The requirement of identification of the subject matter is a requirement for acquisitions of property rights in most, if not all, jurisdictions. An asset, regardless of whether it is a tangible or an intangible asset, needs to be identified for a person to have an interest in it – a right *in rem*.

[23] See also Recitals 13 of the Financial Collateral Directive.

[24] cf Schroeder who states that property has been described as constituting three aspects in relation to a thing: the power and right of possession, enjoyment and alienation, Schroeder (1996), 1020–1022.

[25] cf Sect. 6.3.1–2.

This study shows that the conditions for meeting the requirement for identification are much stricter under Swedish law than under English and US law. Under English law, the degree of identification varies depending on the circumstances, for instance whether the assets are fungible or specific. As a general rule, a proprietary interest cannot take effect until it is ascertained. The asset in which a security interest is extended must therefore be identified for the interest to attach. Under US law, the purpose of the identification requirement is foremost evidentiary, i.e. to minimise future disputes. A description is sufficient if it reasonably identifies what is described, which includes references made to a certain category or quantity. Under Swedish law, the doctrine of specificity requires that the claim refers to an individually specified asset that is identifiable on a continuous basis.[26] If the asset has been exchanged for another asset or is mixed with other identical assets so it can no longer be identified, the property right is generally lost.[27] The principle provides a technical method that in a clear and straightforward way draws up the boundary between property and claims. It thereby prevents shams and fraudulent transactions.[28]

The requirement for specificity is, however, not without exceptions. Mixtures, substitutions, floating charges and other universal forms of security allow the collateral to be exchanged without loss of the security interest. A general observation is that the common law is much more generous in expanding property rights into mixtures and substitutes. Through the tracing, claiming and mixing techniques, an interest can be established in the proceeds of the original asset. Tracing and claiming do not exist in Swedish law even though they can be said to be represented by "*surrogation*", which is the acknowledgement of a proprietary right in a substitute, and vindication. *Surrogation* is however only allowed in a few limited cases. Under US law, as a general principle the collateral-taker may assert a security interest in any proceed of the collateral that is identifiable.[29]

It should also be pointed out that, at least in relation to English law, tracing, claiming and mixtures are complex features that still require much analysis in order to understand the rules and principles they invoke. It should also be mentioned that even if these techniques are exceptions from the doctrine of specificity, their application nevertheless requires identification of the substitute as being derived from the original property. In relation to mixtures, it is the pool of assets that must be identified. A proprietary interest must also be established for the claimant to have a legitimate interest. This means that the original asset, at some stage, must be identified.[30]

It is difficult to draw any general conclusion as to the applicability of the doctrine of specificity and its boundaries without looking at the specific situation at hand. At least in relation to English law, but probably also in relation to Swedish and US law, a relaxation of the principle has taken place.[31] As for mixtures of fungible assets

[26] Håstad 152.

[27] There are however several exceptions from this rule, see further Sect. 6.4.

[28] cf Sect. 8.3.

[29] cf Sect. 7.4.

[30] cf Goode (1987), 440 ff; and Sect. 5.4.

[31] cf Chaps. 5.4, 6.4 and 7.4.

it is argued that in cases where it is practically meaningless and costly to separate the collateral, property is not wholly destroyed by the commingling as long as the pool or larger total can be identified, it is kept separate from the depository's own assets, the collateral-provider is cut off from withdrawing or otherwise controlling the collateral and the collateral-taker is not allowed to dispose of the assets.

In relation to investment securities, as this study shows, the requirement for identification is in conflict with the developments in the securities markets.[32] Problems arise under English and Swedish law in relation to unallocated and intermediated securities, as these assets are by nature unidentifiable.[33] The main problem is that these assets are fungible intangibles and as such are impossible to separate or identify. Even if they are registered on a designated account, they do not exist on the account as such and can therefore not be located or otherwise identified. The perception that securities are held on the account, regardless of whether the account has an individual designation or the securities are held on an omnibus account where all investors' interest in the same securities are held on a pooled basis, is therefore an illusion, or rather, a fiction.[34] In reality, securities evidenced in book-entry form on a securities account are never held on the account as they do not exist in physical form. The attempt of trying to save the requirement for specificity by identifying the pool as the subject matter is therefore flawed.[35] By pretending that the securities are located on the account, the requirement for specificity and thereby also property rights in these assets are protected.[36]

Due to the failure to recognise the above, the discussion in the Swedish legal literature, and also in the English legal literature, is to a certain degree out of date. In Sweden, the discussion has, *inter alia*, been concerned with whether investors can have protected property rights in fungible assets when the claim concerns a quantity or value of a larger pool of assets. Some academic authorities have come to the conclusion that in cases where it is costly and practically meaningless to separate collateral which comprises a quantity of a larger part, the collateral-taker ought to have a protected property right in the custody arrangement that it has control over, even if the collateral is only established to be of a certain value or quantity of the whole.[37] In England, the discussion has foremost been concerned with whether the requirement of certainty of the subject matter to establish a valid trust is met. The established view is that securities held in a fungible bulk constitute co-ownership rights – or in the case of security, a co-security interest – in a global trust established in all the assets held in the pool and therefore can be ascertained against

---

[32] cf Chap. 3.

[33] The ISIN number that commonly identifies securities does so only in relation to name, type and series of securities.

[34] cf Goode (2002), 104.

[35] Even if the securities are designated to a specific entitlement holder on a separate account, unless the registration has constitutive effect or a similar effect to possession of bearer instruments, the securities do not exist on the account.

[36] cf Sect. 8.3.

[37] cf Sect. 6.4.4; Ds 2003:38 p 54; Håstad 334–338; Walin (1998), 116; and Myrdal 479 ff.

other creditors.[38] The requirement for certainty of subject matter is met as long as the pool of securities is separated from the intermediary's assets.[39] This analysis, as well as the analysis under Swedish law, requires identification of a pool of assets. As is shown in this book, the identification of the pool is, unless the registration of the securities is given constitutive effect or similar effect to possession of bearer documents, impossible (cf below). It should also be emphasised that both in relation to Swedish and English law, a clarification of whether it is possible to have property rights in unallocated securities is desirable.

It is proposed that, where there is a lack of specificity, there are certain elements that could be used when establishing the nature of the investor's interest. As when determining the nature of a repo or when interpreting a repledge agreement, in addition to looking at the economic rationale and the intention of the parties, the characterisation of the investor's rights ought to be based on the allocation of the benefits and the burdens in the underlying securities, i.e. who of the parties that bear the risk for the asset and gain from a possible benefit. A right for the intermediary to dispose of the security is, accordingly, an indication that title vests in the intermediary and that the investor only has an unsecured claim. Another indication of ownership is whether the intermediary has the right to collect income payments and exercise voting rights without any instructions on how to vote. A right to dispose of the asset without an obligation to return any surplus is also an indication that the party bears the risk for the asset and thus is the owner of it.

As previously mentioned, the requirement for specificity protects and upholds the difference between property and claims. As long as this distinction is maintained, the laws relating to securities registered on accounts must be fitted in or adjusted to the property system. One solution would be to replace the requirement for specificity with other rules that protect the entitlement holders' interest as has been done in the United States. However, one cannot escape the fact that the requirement for identification protects the property rights of the entitlement holder and that a departure from it would lower the protection for the entitlement holder under the applicable bankruptcy laws. The reason for this is that the requirement for specificity is not only a theoretical requirement but also a matter of practical necessity.[40]

In the US the difficulties of identifying securities in the indirect holding system were already recognised in the 1970s. Through the revision of UCC 8–9, which was approved in 1994, the difficulties with applying traditional property law rules to the indirect holding system were addressed.[41] Revised Art. 8 recognises that it is impossible to identify specific securities as belonging to different investors and updates the law to reflect the practices in the securities markets.[42]

[38] Benjamin and Yates 27 ff; Goode (1998), 78; Benjamin 323. See also FMLC, 'Issue 3 – Property Interests in Investment Securities' (July 2004) 9.

[39] cf FSA's Handbook, CASS 2.2 and CASS 6.

[40] cf Sect. 8.3.

[41] Rogers (1996), 1432.

[42] ALI Report Art. 8, xi.

One of the secrets behind the success of Art. 8 lies in the invention of security entitlements.[43] A security entitlement can be described as a bundle of rights, including corporate and economic rights, against the intermediary. Since these rights do not convey an interest in specific assets but rather an interest in common with others, it is unsuitable to refer to them as property rights. The security entitlement is instead described as a *sui generis* interest. It consists of a bundle of rights giving the entitlement holder personal and property rights in relation to its intermediary only, rather than an interest in specific assets.

The analysis in Chap. 6 shows that the following features represent the equivalence of property rights in a security entitlement under UCC Art. 8: (1) the securities intermediary is required to obtain and maintain financial assets in a quantity corresponding to the aggregate of all security entitlements it has established in favour of its customers; (2) to the extent necessary to satisfy all customers' claims, interests held for customers are not the property of the intermediary and therefore not subject to the claims of its creditors; (3) should there be a shortfall, the customer will share *pro rata* with other customers with interests in the same type of asset; and (4) in the case of a deficit the customers can assert claims in the intermediary's positions. Another important aspect is that entitlement holders have the right to require that the holdings of their positions are changed from the indirect to the direct holding system, thereby increasing the protection further.

In contrast to Swedish and English law, there is no provision under UCC Art. 8 that requires that the customers' assets are segregated from the intermediary's assets.[44] As the intermediary has an obligation to obtain and maintain financial assets in a quantity corresponding to the aggregate of its customers' entitlements and since customers can assert claims in the intermediary's positions should there be a shortfall, such requirement is not deemed to be necessary.

With regards to *de lege ferenda*, several issues arise. One difficulty is to fit a new set of rules into the property law system that already exists (cf Chap. 8). The problem is that the legal rules exist in a larger context and cannot be isolated. In the bankruptcy of the debtor, the distribution of the assets takes place under one set of rules that together form one property and insolvency law system. New legislation must therefore be adjusted to the existing legal structure, including the requirement for specificity.

Even under revised Arts. 8–9, the rules concerning securities entitlements draw on the traditional ideas of property and identity. The concept of a security entitlement as a *sui generis* interest co-exists with the idea of a security interest in an identified thing.[45] The explanation of this lies in the security entitlement as a bundle of rights. Once it is accepted that the bundle of rights is a *sui generis* interest that carries with it certain property rights, the bundle is treated as the thing itself. This facilitates trade in, and settlement of, assets held in the indirect holding system.[46]

---

[43] Rogers (1996), 1518.

[44] cf Sect. 7.4.4; and FMLC, 'Issue 3 – Property Interests in Investment Securities' (July 2004) 8.

[45] Schroeder (1994), 367.

[46] cf Chap. 7.

The solution under Art. 8–9 can be compared with the two-dimensional structure outlined in Sect. 8.2. The two-dimensional structure distinguishes between the rules relating to transfer, holding and settlement of securities that establish the investor's proprietary rights in relation to third parties from the rules defining the investor's rights and obligations in relation to the issuer. For third parties, this means that all choses in action – regardless if they are shares, bonds, negotiable instruments, promissory notes or simple claims – under the traditional property law structure, are treated as property. The second tier, i.e. the rules establishing the investor's rights and obligations against the issuer, is not defined by property law rules but rather through the relevant statutory and contractual aspects of the specific security.

The position of this work is that if the concept of property rights in unallocated and intermediated securities should be kept, the legal construct that securities are held on accounts must be preserved to the extent that intermediaries cannot be allowed to dispose of the securities that they hold on behalf of their customers without replacing them with the equivalent assets.[47] As previously pointed out, the property law system is based on tangible assets.[48] Even if the securities are not held on the account the system is based on such presumption. This construct is a matter of necessity and makes the system coherent. Arguably, the same legal construct is not needed in relation to credit balances on bank accounts as the account holder only has a claim against the bank.[49] It should, however, be stressed that the formulation that securities are "held" on accounts is a misconception. The real difference between registered securities and the credit balance on bank accounts lies in the legal framework that applies to these assets. As both types of assets are fungible intangibles, their existence is created by the legal framework.

The rules applicable to securities evidenced in book-entry form determine that they are property claims whereas the rules applicable to credit balances on bank accounts determine that they are claims. In other words, whether securities evidenced in book-entry form on accounts convey property rights depends on the legal rules that apply. Due to the legal uncertainty that is present in relation to English and Swedish law, it is difficult to determine what type of assets one is dealing with (cf Chaps. 5–6).

In this regard it is argued that even if the perception is that securities are held on accounts is a construct, it should nevertheless be kept in order to keep the protection for property rights in securities evidenced in book-entry form. This analysis corresponds to the analysis made in Sect. 8.3. It is proposed that the dividing line between property and claims ought to be guided by the distribution of the risks and benefits in the asset. Accordingly, the right to collect income payments and to exercise voting rights are clear indications that title vests in the party that has those rights (provided that these rights are not passed on to the other party). A right to dispose

[47] That is unless it has been agreed in the custody agreement.

[48] cf Chap. 8.

[49] The fact that an amount has been credited to the bank account has no other effect than to serve as evidence that the account holder has a claim corresponding to the credited amount. It does not mean that the credited amount can be separated or that it conveys a protected property right. The bank holding the account has, accordingly, a right to dispose of the amount as if it was its own.

of the asset without an obligation to return any surplus is an indication that the party having such right bears the risk of the asset and therefore is the owner of it.

It is also argued that the lower degree of protection that the indirect holding system inevitably involves, ought to be supplemented with a strict specification of the account, the account holder and the number and types of securities on the account and a requirement for the intermediary to hold sufficient securities, which correspond to its customers' claims.[50] By requiring that the intermediary should be able to account for the securities and deliver a quantity to its customers that corresponds to their claims on a continuous basis, the customers would, unless the intermediary acted fraudulently or erroneously or a settlement failure occurred, be protected even if the intermediary substitutes the securities or commingles them with other customers' securities. Thereby property rights in the securities are protected even if the claim concerns fungible assets and is only specified in relation to a certain quantity and type of assets.[51]

Another technique which would increase the protection for investors is to give them rights in the intermediary's proprietary positions should there be a shortfall, i.e. to the extent necessary to satisfy the investors' claims they should be allowed to assert a claim in the intermediary's securities.[52] This alternative provides a cushion and gives the intermediary an incentive to manage its customers' assets in an accurate and prudent manner, which includes choosing safe and sound intermediaries higher up in the chain.

To the extent that the securities are not kept on designated accounts and a shortfall occurs, they ought to be shared *pro rata*. Investors should also, preferably, have a right to convert their holdings from an indirect to a direct holding system and to place their securities on a designated account in order to increase the level of protection. By providing investors with the opportunity to choose between different ways of holding securities (e.g. direct vs indirect; designated vs omnibus accounts) the level of security can be adjusted. Inexperienced investors in particular, need to be able to opt for a higher level of protection. They should also be informed about the risks that are involved.

9.4 Concluding Remarks

As is shown in this study the traditional property law structures are in conflict with the developments in the securities markets. This book argues that the heart of the problem is not the development of the indirect holding system as such but rather that it is impossible to identify intermediated securities in relation to each investor. The result is that there is a great degree of legal uncertainty.

---

[50] The parties should also be required to evidence these conditions in a written account agreement.

[51] cf Sect. 6.3 and the analysis of the Accountable Funds Act. The equivalent solution could be provided in relation to collateral specified in terms of value, cf Sect. 6.4.4.

[52] cf UCC 8–503.

The increased level of risk that the legal uncertainty inevitably involves is ultimately borne by the investors. In order to protect their rights and the confidence in the financial markets, protective mechanisms need to be built into the legal framework.

Table of Cases

England and Wales

Agnew v Commissioner of Inland Revenue [2001] 2 AC 710 (PC (NZ))
Re Bank of Credit and Commerce International SA (In Liquidation) (No 8) [1998] AC 214 (HL)
Banque Belge pour l'Etranger v Hambrouck [1921] 1 KB 321 (CA)
Barlow Clowes International Ltd (In Liquidation) v Vaughan [1992] 4 All ER 22 (CA)
Bishopsgate Investment Management Ltd (In Liquidation) v Homan [1995] Ch 211 (CA)
Borland's Trustee v Steel Bros & Co Ltd [1901] 1 Ch 279 (Ch D)
Boscawen v Bajwa [1996] 1 WLR 328 (CA)
Re Brightlife Ltd [1987] Ch 200 (Ch D)
Buhr v Barclays Bank Plc [2001] EWCA Civ 1223 (CA)
Burgis v Constantine [1908] 2 KB 484 (CA)
Burrows v Lock (1805) 10 Ves 470
Re CA Pacific Finance Ltd (In Liquidation) and another [2000] 1 BCLC 494 (CFI (HK))
Re Charge Card Services Ltd (No 2) [1987] Ch 150 (Ch D)
Coggs v Bernard [1703] 2 Ld Raym 909
Re Cosslett (Contractors) Ltd [1998] Ch 495 (CA)
Clayton's Case (1816) 1 Mer 572
Dearle v Hall (1828) 3 Russ 1
Re Diplock [1948] Ch 465 (CA)
Donald v Suckling (1865-66) LR 1 QB 585
Re Ellison Son & Vidler Ltd [1995] 1 All ER 192
Foskett v McKeown [2001] 1 AC 102 (HL)
Re Goldcorp Exchange Ltd (In Receivership) [1995] 1 AC 74 (PC (NZ))
Re Hallett's Estate (1879) 13 Ch D 696
Halliday v Holgate (1868) LR 3 Ex 299

Re Harvard Securities Ltd (In Liquidation) [1997] 2 BCLC 369 (Ch D)
Ex p Hubbard (1886) 17 QBD 690
Hunter v Moss [1994] 1 WLR 452 (CA)
IRC v Crossman [1937] AC 26 (HL)
James Roscoe (Bolton) Ltd v Winder [1915] 1 Ch 62 (Ch D)
Jones v Gibbons (1804) 9 Ves 407
Knight v Knight (1840) 3 Beav 148
Langton v Waite (1868) LR 6 Eq 165 (Ct of Chancery)
Re London Wine Co (Shippers) [1986] PCC 121
Lupton v White (1808) 15 Ves 432
MacJordan Construction Ltd v Bookmount Erostin Ltd [1991] BCLC 350
Marquess of Northampton v Pollock (1890) 45 Ch D 190
The Maule [1997] 1 WLR 528 (PC (HK))
The Mecca [1897] AC 286 (HL)
Morley v Morley (1858) 25 Beav 253
Northern Bank Ltd v Ross [1991] BCLC 504 (CA)
Palk v Mortgage Service Funding Plc [1993] Ch 330
Re Permanent Houses (Holdings) Ltd [1988] BCLC 563 (Ch D)
Roscoe v Winder [1915] 1 Ch 62
Sinclair v Brougham [1914] AC 398 (HL)
Space Investments Ltd v CIBC (Bahamas) Ltd [1986] 1 WLR 1072 (PC (Bah))
Re Spectrum Plus Ltd (In Liquidation) [2005] 2 AC 680 (HL)
Spence v Union Marine Insurance Co (1868) 3 LRCP 427
Re Stapylton Fletcher Ltd (in administrative receivership) [1994] 1 WLR 1181 (Ch D)
Taylor v Plumer (1815) 105 ER 721
Re Wait [1927] 1 Ch 606 (CA)
Warde v Aeyre (1614) 2 Bulstrode 323, 80 ER 1157
Welsh Development Agency v Export Finance Co Ltd [1992] BCC 270 (CA)
Re Yorkshire Woolcombers Association Ltd [1903] 2 Ch 284 (CA)

Sweden

NJA 1881 p 515
NJA 1910 p 216
NJA 1910 p 413
NJA 1912 p 122
NJA 1912 p 156
NJA 1925 p 130
NJA 1930 p 134
NJA 1935 p 277
NJA 1941 p 711 I-II
NJA 1944 p 411

NJA 1949 p 164
NJA 1949 p 744
NJA 1950 p 417
NJA 1952 p 256
NJA 1952 p 407
NJA 1956 p 562
NJA 1959 p 590
NJA 1961 p 2
NJA 1963 p 502
NJA 1971 p 288
NJA 1974 p 463
NJA 1976 p 251
NJA 1979 p 451
NJA 1980 p 197
NJA 1985 p 159
NJA 1987 p 4
NJA 1987 p 105
NJA 1988 p 149
NJA 1989 p 781
NJA 1989 p 705 I
NJA 1990 p 562
NJA 1991 p 550
NJA 1993 p 206
NJA 1994 p 506
NJA 1995 p 367 I-II
NJA 1996 p 52
NJA 1996 p 624
NJA 1997 p 660
NJA 1998 p 379
NJA 1998 p 545
NJA 2004 p 52
NJA 2004 p 633
NJA 2005 p 425
NJA 2007 p 413
NJA 2007 p 599
RH 1986:63

United States

Duel v Hollins 241 US 513 (1916)
Re Gibson Products of Arizona 543 F2d 652 (9th CIR 1976)
Gorman v Littlefield 229 US 19 (1913)
Bombardier Capital 639 A2d 1065 (1994)

Table of Statutes

England and Wales

Bills of Exchange Act 1882
Companies Act 1985
Consumer Credit Act 1974
Financial Collateral Arrangements (No 2) Regulations 2003 (SI 2003 No 3226)
Financial Services and Markets Act 2000
Insolvency Act 1986
Law of Property Act 1925
Sale of Goods Act 1979
Sale of Goods (Amendment) Act 1995
Uncertificated Securities Regulations 2001 (SI 2001/3755)
Uncertificated Securities (Amendment) (Eligible Debt Securities) Regulations 2003 (SI 2003/1633)
Financial Services and Markets Act 2000 (Markets in Financial Instruments) Regulations 2007 (SI 2007/126)(as amended)
Financial Services and Markets Act 2000 (Regulated Activities)(Amendment No 3) Order 2006 (SI 2006/3384)

Sweden

Commercial Code (1736:0123)
Bills of Sales Act (1845:50 s 1)
Co-ownership Act (1904:48 p 1)
Commission Agency Act (1914:45)
Contracts Act (1915:218)
Promissory Notes Act (1936:81)
Act (1936:88) on Pledge of Chattels Held by a Third Party

Accountable Funds Act (1944:181)
Inheritance Code (1958:637)
Trademark (1960:644) Act
Penal Code (1962:700)
Patents (1967:837) Act
Preferential Rights Act (1970:979)
Real Estate Code (1970:994)
Companies Act (1975:1385)
Code of Execution (1981:774)
Consumer Services Act (1985:716)
Act on Entrepreneurs' Right to Sell Chattels that are Uncollected (1985:982)
Good Faith Acquisition of Chattels Act (1986:796)
Bankruptcy Act (1987:672)
Sales of Goods Act (1990:931)
Consumer Sales of Goods Act (1990:932)
Commercial Agency Act (1991:351)
Trade with Financial Instruments Act (1991:980)
Ordinance (1991:1007) on Trade and Services in the Securities Markets
Sea Act (1994:1009)
Financial Instruments Accounts Act (1998:1479)(FIAA)
Act (2003:528) on Company Charges
Insurance Agreements Act (2005:104)
Act (2005:105) on Security Rights in Insurance Compensation
Act (2007:528) on the Securities Markets
Regulations by the Financial Supervisory Authority
FFFS 2007:17
FFFS 2007:16

United States

Securities Exchange Act of 1934
Title 11 of the United States Code (Bankruptcy Code)
Uniform Commercial Code (UCC)
New York Uniform Commercial Code (NY UCC)

European Union

Directive 98/26/EU of the European Parliament and of the Council of 19 May 1998 on settlement finality in payment and securities settlement systems (Settlement Finality Directive)

Directive 2000/12/EC of the European Parliament and of the Council of 20 March 2000 relating to the taking-up and pursuit of the business of credit institutions

Council Regulation (EC) No 1346/2000 of 29 May 2000 on insolvency proceedings

Directive 2001/17/EC of the European Parliament and of the Council of 19 March 2001 on the reorganisation and winding-up of insurance undertakings

Directive 2001/24/EC of the European Parliament and of the Council of 4 April 2001 on the reorganisation and winding-up of credit institutions (Banks Winding-up Directive)

Directive 2002/47/EC of the European Parliament and of the Council of 6 June 2002 on financial collateral arrangements (Financial Collateral Directive)

Directive 2004/39/EC of the European Parliament and of the Council of 21 April 2004 on markets in financial instruments amending Council Directives 85/611/EEC and 93/6/EEC and Directive 2000/12/EC of the European Parliament and of the Council and repealing Council Directive 93/22/EEC (MiFID)

Directive 2004/109/EC of the European Parliament and of the Council of 15 December 2004 on the harmonisation of transparency requirements in relation to information about issuers whose securities are admitted to trading on a regulated market and amending Directive 2001/34/EC

Commission Directive 2006/73/EC of 10 August 2006 implementing Directive 2004/39/EC of the European Parliament and of the Council as regards organisational requirements and operating conditions for investment firms and defined terms for the purposes of that Directive (MiFID Implementation Directive)

Commission Regulation (EC) No 1287/2006 of 10 August 2006 implementing Directive 2004/39/EC of the European Parliament and of the Council as regards recordkeeping obligations for investment firms, transaction reporting, market transparency, admission of financial instruments to trading, and defined terms for the purposes of that Directive

Directive 2007/36/EC of the European Parliament and of the Council of 11 July 2007 on the exercise of certain rights of shareholders in listed companies

International Conventions and Treaties

Convention of 5 July 2006 on the Law Applicable to Certain Rights in respect of Securities held with an Intermediary (Hague Securities Convention)

UNIDROIT Preliminary Draft Convention on Substantive Rules regarding Intermediated Securities

Governmental Reports etc.

United Kingdom

HM Treasury, 'Implementation of the Directive on Financial Collateral Arrangements' (July 2003) [HM Treasury Report]
Law Commission, 'Company Security Interests' (Law Com No 176, 2004)
Law Commission, 'Company Security Interests' (Law Com No 296 Cm 6654, 2005)
Law Commission, 'Ninth Programme of Law Reform' (Law Com No 293 HC 353, 2005)
Law Commission, 'Registration of Security Interest: Company Charges and Property Other than Land' (Law Com No 164, 2002)

Sweden

Prop 1944:81
Prop 1987/88:108
Prop 1994/95:130
Prop 1997/98:160
Prop 1997/98:168
Prop 2001/02:134
Prop 2002/03:17
Prop 2002/03:49
Prop 2002/03:107
Prop 2004/05:30
SOU 1940:20
SOU 1965:14
SOU 1995:11
SOU 1995:52

SOU 2000:56
NJA II 1921 p 619
NJA II 1944 p 404
Ds 2003:38

United States

American Law Institute, 'Proposed Final Draft. Uniform Commercial Code. Revised Article 8. Investment Securities (With amendments to Article 9. Secured Transactions)' (5 April 1994) [ALI Report Art. 8]

American Law Institute, 'Proposed Final Draft. Uniform Commercial Code. Revised Article 9: Secured Transactions (With conforming amendments to Articles 1, 2, 5 and 8)' (15 April 1998) [ALI Report Art. 9]

American Law Institute, 'Uniform Commercial Code 2005 Edition (2005 Official Text with Comments)' [Official Comments]

List of Literature

L Afrell and K Wallin-Norman, 'Direct or Indirect Holdings: A Nordic Perspective' Unif L Rev (2005-1/2) 277 [Afrell and Wallin-Norman]

L Afrell and M Bogdan, 'Något om lagvalsregler vid pantsättning av dokumentlösa finansiella instrument' JT [2001/02] 517 [Afrell and Bogdan]

L Afrell, H Klahr and P Samuelsson, *Lärobok i kapitalmarknadsrätt* (2nd edn Norstedts Juridik 1998) [Afrell, Klahr and Samuelsson]

A Agell, 'Skadeståndsansvaret vid obehöriga förfoganden över annans egendom' in *Festskrift till Hellner* (Norstedts Juridik 1984)

H Allen, J Hawkins and S Sato, Research Paper No 7 'Electronic Trading and its Implications for Financial Systems' (November 2001)

AO Austen Peters, *Custody of Investments: Law and Practice* (OUP 2000) [Austen-Peters]

FOB Babafemi, 'The Proprietary Remedies of Tracing: A Comparative Study of English and American Law' (1973) 2 Anglo-Am L Rev 198

M Beckman, G Jansson, K Wallin-Norman and B Wendleby, *Lagarna på värdepappersområdet* (Norstedts Juridik 2002) [Beckman, Jansson, Wallin-Norman and Wendleby]

J Benjamin and M Yates, *The Law of Global Custody* (2nd edn Butterworths 2002)

J Benjamin, 'Overview of Post-trade Infrastructure, Part 1' (2003) 4 JIBFL 127

J Benjamin, 'Ease of Transfer and Security of Transfer in the Securities Markets' (2001) 5 JIBFL 219 [Benjamin (2001)]

J Benjamin, *Interest in Securities* (OUP 2000) [Benjamin]

P Birks (ed), *Laundering and Tracing* (Clarendon Press 1995)

P Birks, 'Establishing a Proprietary Base' [1995] RLR 83

P Birks, 'Mixtures' in N Palmer and E McKendrick (eds), *Interests in Goods* (2nd edn LLP 1998) Ch. 9 [Birks]

P Birks, 'Overview: Tracing, Claiming and Defences' in P Birks (ed), *Laundering and Tracing* (Clarendon Press 1995) [Birks (1995)]

C Blackburn, *The Effect of the Contract of Sale* (1845)

M Bridge, *Personal Property Law* (3rd edn Clarendon 2002) [Bridge]

WW Buckland, *The Main Institutions of Roman Private Law* (Cambridge University Press 1931)

JA Crook, *Law and Life of Rome* (Thames and Hudson 1967)

SS Curley, 'Problems as to the Degree of Specificity of Descriptions under the Uniform Commercial Code' (1976-1977) 22 N Y L Sch L Rev 679

J Dalhuisen, *Dalhuisen on International Commercial, Financial and Trade Law* (2nd edn Hart Publishing 2004)

PL Davies, *Gower and Davies' Principles of Modern Company Law* (7th edn Sweet & Maxwell 2003)

HJ Diamond, 'Tracing Cash Proceeds in Insolvency Proceedings under Revised Article 9' (2001) 9 Am Bankr Inst L Rev 385 [Diamond]

U Drobnig, 'The Law Governing Credit Security' in the European Parliament Directorate General for Research Working Paper 'The Private Law Systems in the EU: Discrimination on Grounds of Nationality and the Need for a European Civil Code' (June 2000) 173

M Evans, 'Opportunities for Collateralisation: Recent and Prospective Developments in Settlement: Part 1' (1998-2000) 9 JIBFL 365

D Fox, 'Overreaching' in P Birks and A Pretto (eds), *Breach of Trust* (Hart Publishing 2002) Ch. 4 [Fox]

HW Flesig, 'Economic Functions of Security in a Market Economy' in Joseph J Norton and Mads Andenas (eds), *Emerging Financial Markets and Secured Transactions* (Kluwer Law International 1998) Ch. 3

G Gilmore, *Security Interests in Personal Property,* Vol II (Little, Brown and Company 1965) [Gilmore]

G Glenn, 'The Pledge as a Security Device' (1937-1938) 24 Va L Rev 355

R Goode, 'Are Intangible Asset Fungible?' in Birks and Pretto *Themes in Comparative Law – In Honour of Bernard Rudden* (OUP 2002) Ch. 7 [Goode (2002)]

R Goode, 'Charges over Book Debts: A Missed Opportunity' (1994) 110 LQR 592

R Goode, 'Ownership and Obligation in Commercial Transactions' (1987) 103 LQR 433 [Goode (1987)]

R Goode, 'Property Rights in Commercial Assets: Rethinking Concepts and Policies' in R Goode, *Commercial Law in the New Millennium* (Sweet & Maxwell 1998) [Goode (1998)]

R Goode, 'Are Intangible Assets Fungible' [2003] LMCLQ 379 [Goode (2003)]

R Goode, 'The Nature and Transfer of Rights in Dematerialised and Immobilised Securities' (1996) 4 JIBFL 167 [Goode (1996)]

R Goode, 'Rule, Practice, and Pragmatism in Transnational Commercial Law' (2005) 54 ICLQ 539

R Goode, *Commercial Law* (3rd edn Penguin Books 2004) [Goode (2004)]

R Goode, *Legal Problems of Credit and Security* (3rd edn Sweet & Maxwell 2003) [Goode]

R Grantham, 'The Doctrinal Basis of the Rights of Company Shareholders' (1998) 3 CLJ 582

AG Guest and others (eds), *Benjamin's Sale of Goods* (6th edn Sweet & Maxwell 2002)

RD Guynn and NJ Marchand, 'Transfer or Pledge of Securities Held through Depositories' in HV Houtte (ed), *The Law of Cross-border Securities Transactions* (Sweet & Maxwell 1998-2000)

RD Guynn, 'Modernizing Securities Ownership Transfer and Pledging Laws: A Discussion Paper on the Need for International Harmonization' (Capital Markets Forum, International Bar Association 1996)

U Göransson, *Traditionsprincipen* (Iustus Förlag 1985)

RA Hakes, *The ABCs of the UCC. (Revised) Article 9. Secured Transactions* (American Bar Association 2000) [Hakes]

PC Harding and CA Johnson, 'Mastering Collateral Management and Documentation: A Practical Guide for Negotiators' (Financial Times Prentice Hall/Pearson Education 2002) [Harding and Johnson]

D Hayton, 'Overview' in P Birks and A Pretto (eds), *Breach of Trust* (Hart Publishing 2002) Ch. 13

D Hayton, 'Uncertainty of Subject-Matter of Trusts' (1994) 110 LQR 335

D Hayton, H Pigott and J Benjamin, 'The Use of Trusts in International Financial Transactions' (2002) 1 JIBFL 23

D Hayton, 'Equity's Identification Rules' in P Birks (ed), *Laundering and Tracing* (Clarendon Press 1995) [Hayton]

B Helander, *Kreditsäkerhet i lös egendom* (Fritzes AB 1984) [Helander]

J Hellner, 'Redovisningsskyldighet i kontraktsrätten' in *Festskrift till Henrik Hessler* (PA Norstedt & Söners Förlag 1985) [Hellner]

J Hellner, *Metodproblem i rättsvetenskapen: Studier i förmögenhetsrätt* (Elanders Gotab 2001)

J Hellner, *Speciell avtalsrätt II: Kontraktsrätt* (3rd edn Norstedts Juridik 1996)

WH Henning, 'Article Nine's Treatment of Commingled Cash Proceeds in Non-Insolvency Cases' (1981-1982) 35 Ark L Rev 191

H Hessler, *Allmän sakrätt: Om det förmögenhetsrättsliga tredjemansskyddets principer* (PA Norstedt & Söners Förlag 1973) [Hessler]
T Håstad, [Mobilia] in *De Lege* (Iustus Förlag) (forthcoming)
T Håstad, 'Property Rights regarding Movables' in M Bogdan *Swedish Law in the New Millennium* (Norstedts Juridik 2000)
T Håstad, 'Några problem rörande panträtt i en värdepappersdepå' in *Festskrift till Henrik Hessler* (PA Norstedt & Söners Förlag 1985) [Håstad (1985)]
T Håstad, *Sakrätt Avseende Lös Egendom* (6 edn Norstedts Juridik 1996) [Håstad]
P Ireland, 'Company Law and the Myth of Shareholder Ownership' (1998-2000) 62 MLR 32
E Johansson 'Property Rights in Securities and the Doctrine of Specificity under Swedish Law' (2006) 17 EBLR 1099
E Johansson, 'The Law Commission's Consultation Paper No 164: Some Reflections Regarding the Exclusion of Securities' (2004) 15 EBLR 835
E Johansson, 'Transfers and Settlement of Securities: The New Order' (2005) 16 EBLR 1093
CA Johnson, 'Derivatives and Rehypothecation Failure: It's 3:00 pm, Do You Know Where Your Collateral Is? (1997) 39 Ariz L Rev 949 [Johnson (1997)]
H Karlgren, 'Säkerhetsöverlåtelse och pantsättning av lös egendom' SvJT [1936] 161 [Karlgren (1936)]
H Karlgren, *Ändamålsbstämmelse och stiftelse* (1951) [Karlgren (1951)]
H Karlgren, *Obehörig vinst och värdeersättning* (Norstedt & Söners Förlag 1982) [Karlgren (1982)]
H Karlgren, *Säkerhetsöverlåtelse* (Norstedt & Söners Förlag 1952, 1958) [Karlgren (1952, 1958)]
T Keijser, *Financial Collateral Arrangements* (Kluwer 2006)
KC Kettering, 'Repledge Deconstructed' (1998-2000) 61 U Pitt L Rev 45 [Kettering (1998-2000)]
KC Kettering, 'Repledge and Pre-Default Sale of Securities Collateral under Revised Article 9' (1998-2000) 74 Chi-Kent L Rev 1109 [Kettering (1998-2000)]
FH Lawson and B Rudden, *The Law of Property* (3rd edn OUP 2002) [Lawson and Rudden]
G Lennander, *Panthavarens skyldigheter vid pantavtal om lös egendom* (1977)
S Lindskog, 'Pant i egen skuld' SvJT [1983] 537
S Lindskog, 'Om sakrättsligt misstroende' JT [1991-92] 275
S Lindskog, *Preskription* (2nd edn Norstedts Juridik 2002)
J Lowry and A Dignam, *Company Law* (2nd edn Lexis Nexis Butterworths 2003)
V Lundstedt, 'Några rättssystematiska reflektioner' in *Festskrift tillägnad Hans Excellens Riksmarskalken Juris Doktor Birger Ekeberg den 10 August 1950* (1950) [Lundstedt]
BA Markell, 'From Property to Contract and Back: An Examination of Deposit Accounts and Revised Article 9' (1998-2000) 74 Chi-Ken L Rev 963
J Martin, 'Certainty of Subject Matter: A defence of Hunter v. Moss' [1996] Conv (May/Jun) 223 [Martin]
P Matthews, 'The Legal and Moral Limits of Common Law Tracing' in P Birks (ed) *Laundering and Tracing* (Clarendon Press 1995)
E McKendrick, 'The Passing of Property in Part of a Bulk' in N Palmer and E McKendrick (eds), *Interests in Goods* (2nd edn LLP 1998) Ch. 16 [McKendrick]
E McKendrick, 'Unascertained Goods: Ownership and Obligation Distinguished' (1994) 110 LQR 509
A McKnight, 'Seminar Sheet 1' LLM Course: The Law of Credit and Security, Queen Mary, University of London
E Micheler, 'Modernising Securities Settlement in the UK' (2002) 23(1) Comp Law 9
MH Miller, *Merton Miller on Derivatives* (John Wiley & Sons 1997)
G Millqvist, 'Recension Staffan Myrdal, Återpantsättning. Om pantsättning av pant och panträtt, Norstedts Juridik, Stockholm 2005, 594 s' JT [2005-06] 453
G Millqvist, 'Swedish Credit Security Law: A Case for Law Reform?' [2004] 15 EBLR 861
G Millqvist, *Sakrättens grunder* (Norstedts juridik 2003) [Millqvist]
RJ Mokal, 'Liquidation Expenses and Floating Charges–the Separate Funds Fallacy' [2004] LMCLQ 387

CW Mooney, 'Beyond Negotiability: A New Model for Transfer and Pledge of Interests in Securities Controlled by Intermediaries' (1990) Cardozo L Rev 305 [Mooney (1990)]

G Morton and R Potok, 'Position Paper on the Taking of Securities as Collateral in the European Union' (13 December 1998-2000)

G Morton, 'Legal Risk and its Impact on Market Efficiency' in 'Legal Risk and Market Efficiency' UNIDROIT Seminar on Harmonised Substantive Rules regarding Securities Held with an Intermediary (February 2004) 4

S Myrdal, *Återpantsättning. Om pantsättning av pant och panträtt* (Norstedts Juridik 2005) [Myrdal]

F Oditah, *Legal Aspects of Receivables Financing* (Sweet & Maxwell 1991)

M Ooi, *Shares and Other Securities in the Conflict of Laws* (OUP 2003) [Ooi]

N Palmer and A Hudson, 'Pledge' in N Palmer and E McKendrick (eds) *Interests in Goods* (2nd edn LLP 1998) Ch. 24 [Palmer and Hudson]

E Parker, *Credit Derivatives: Documenting and Understanding Credit Derivative Products* (Globe Law and Business 2007)

JE Penner, *The Idea of Property in Law* (Clarendon Press 1997) [Penner]

JE Penner, *The Law of Trusts* (3rd edn Lexis Nexis Butterworths 2002)

R Pennington, 'Can Shares in Companies Be Defined?' (1989) 10 Co Law 144

R Pennington, *Pennington's Company Law* (8th edn Butterworths 2001)

AH Persson, *Förbehållsklausuler: En studie om en säkerhetsrätts nuvarande och framtida ställning* (Stiftelsen Skrifter published by the Law Faculty at Stockholm University 1998) [Persson]

A Pretto-Sakmann, *Boundaries of Personal Property: Shares and Sub-shares* (Hart 2005)

K Pullen, 'Fungible Securities and Insolvency' (1998-2000) 14 JIBFL 286

SM Rocks and CS Bjerre, *The ABCs of the UCC. Article 8: Investment Securities* (American Bar Association 1997) [Rocks and Bjerre]

K Rodhe, *Handbok i Sakrätt* (Norstedts juridik 1985) [Rodhe]

JS Rogers, 'Policy Perspectives on Revised UCC Art. 8' (1996) 43 UCLA L Rev 1431 [Rogers (1996)]

JS Rogers 'Negotiability, Property, and Identity' (1990-1991) 12 Cardozo L Rev 471 [Rogers (1990-1991)]

JL Schroeder, 'Is Article 8 Finally Ready this Time? The Radical Reform of Secured Lending on Wall Street' (1994) Colum Bus L Rev 291 [Schroeder (1994)]

JL Schroeder, 'Repo Madness: The Characterization of Repurchase Agreements under the Bankruptcy Code and the UCC' (1996) 46 Syracuse L Rev 999 [Schroeder (1996)]

JL Schroeder, 'A Repo Opera: How Criimi Mae Got Repos Backwards' (2002) 76 Am Bankr LJ 565 [Schroeder (2002)]

SL Schwarcz, 'Indirectly Held Securities and Intermediary Risk' (2002-01) Uniform L Rev (*Revue de droit uniforme*)

LS Sealy, *Cases and Materials in Company Law* (Butterworths 2001)

J Seligman, 'The Internationalization of the Securities Markets: Preface to a Symposium' Michigan Yearbook of International Legal Studies Volume IX (1988)

EE Smith, 'Overview of Revised Article 9' (1998-2000) 73 Am Bankr LJ 1 [Smith]

L Smith, 'Property Transferred in Breach' in P Birks and A Pretto (eds), *Breach of Trust* (Hart Publishing 2002) Ch. 5

L Smith, *The Law of Tracing* (Clarendon Press 1997) [L Smith]

J Story, *Commentaries on the Law of Bailments* (9th edn Boston: Little, Brown, and Company 1878) [Story]

S Strömholm, 'General Features of Swedish Law' in M Bogdan (ed) *Swedish Law in the New Millennium* (Norstedts Juridik 2000)

D Tamm, *Romersk rätt och europeisk rättsutveckling* (2nd edn Nerenius & Santérus Förlag 1996)

K Tyson-Quah, 'Overview of International Securities Finance Markets' in K Tyson-Quah (ed) *Special Report on Cross-Border Securities: Repo, Lending and Collateralisation* (Sweet & Maxwell 1997)

Ö Undén, *Svensk sakrätt I. Lös egendom* (10th edn Fritzes Förlag 1995) [Undén]
A Underhill and D Hayton, *Trusts and Trustees* (16th edn Butterworths LexisNexis 2003)
G Walin, 'Om separationsrätt efter surrogation' in *Festskrift tillägnad Hans Excellens Riksmarskalken Juris Doktor Birger Ekeberg den 10 August 1950* (Norstedt & Söner 1950) 532 [Walin (1950)]
G Walin, *Lagen om skuldebrev* (2nd edn Norstedts Juridik 1997) [Walin (1997)]
G Walin, *Panträtt* (2nd edn Norstedts Juridik 1998) [Walin (1998)]
G Walin, *Separationsrätt* (Norstedts Juridik 1975) [Walin (1975)]
L Welamson, *Konkursrätt* (Norstedts Förlag 1961)
S Wennberg, *Förskingring* (Almqvist & Winsell International 1977) [Wennberg]
JJ White and RS Summers, *Uniform Commercial Code* (5th edn West Group St Paul Minn 2000) [White and Summers]
P Wood, *Comparative Law of Security and Guarantees* (Sweet & Maxwell 1995) [Wood]
S Worthington, 'Shares and Shareholders: Property, Power and Entitlement: Part 1' (2001) 22(9) Comp Law 258
S Worthington, 'Sorting Out Ownership Interests in a Bulk: Gifts, Sales and Trusts' [1998-2000] 01 JBL 1 [Worthington]
K Zweigert and H Kötz, *An Introduction to Comparative Law* (3rd edn OUP 1998)

Other Resources and Materials

Allen & Overy Briefing Note 'New Law on Financial Collateral' (January 2004)
Allen & Overy Bulletin (February 2005)
BIS, 'Delivery Versus Payment in Securities Settlement Systems' (1992)
BIS, 'Monetary and Economic Department: OTC Derivatives Market Activity in the First Half of 2006' (November 2006)
BIS, 'Triennial Central Bank Survey: Foreign exchange and derivatives market activity in 2007' (December 2007)
CGFS, 'A Review of Financial Market Events in Autumn 1998' (GFS Publications No 12) (October 1998-2000)
CGFS, 'Collateral in Wholesale Financial Markets: Recent Trends, Risk Management and Market Dynamics' (March 2001) [CGFS Report]
City of London Law Society Financial Law Sub-Committee's Working Group, 'Directive on Financial Collateral Arrangements: Replies to Questions from HM Treasury Contained in Note of April 2003 Setting Out Initial Policy and Legal Questions' [City of London Law Society Report]
Committee on the Global Financial System Working Group on Collateral, 'Collateral in Wholesale Financial Markets: Recent Trends, Risk Management and Market Dynamics' (March 2001) [GFS Report]
CPSS and the Euro-currency Standing Committee of the Central Banks of the Group of Ten Countries, 'OTC Derivatives: Settlement Procedures and Counter Party Risk Management' (CPSS Publications No 27) (September 1998)
CPSS, 'Payment and Settlement Systems in Selected Countries: International Payment Arrangements' (April 2003)
CPSS, 'Real-Time Gross Settlement Systems' (March 1997)
CPSS/IOSCO, 'Recommendation for Securities Settlement Systems' (November 2001)
CPSS/IOSCO, 'Securities Lending Transactions: Market Developments and Implications' (CPSS Publications No 32) (July 1998-2000)
CREST White Book, 'The Domestic Legal Framework' (March 2002)
CREST White Book, 'The International Legal Framework' (July 2001)
CRESTCo, 'A Guide to Stock Lending and Collateral Transfers in CREST' (October 2000)
ECB, 'Opinion of the European Central Bank of 17 March 2005 at the request of the Council of the European Union on a proposal for a Council decision concerning the signing of the Hague Convention on the Law applicable to certain rights in respect of securities held with an intermediary, (COM(2003) 783 final) (CON/2005/7)
ECB, 'Opinion of the European Central Bank of 26 June 2003 at the request of the Austrian Federal Ministry of Justice on a draft Federal Law implementing Directive 2002/47/EC of the European Parliament and of the Council of 6 June 2002 on financial collateral arrangements' (CON/2003/11)

EFMLG, 'Proposal for an EU Directive on Collateralisation' (June 2000)
EFMLG, 'Statement on Proposal for a Directive on Financial Collateral Arrangements (COM(2001) 168)'
ESCB-CESR, 'Standards for Securities Clearing and Settlement Systems in the European Union' (July 2003)
ESCB-CESR, 'The Scope of Application of the ESCB-CESR in the Field of Safety, Soundness and Efficiency of Securities Clearing and Settlement' (August 2003)
Euroclear, 'Delivering Low-cost Cross-border Settlement' (January 2003)
European Banking Federation, 'Letter addressed to the European Council Committee on Civil Law and the European Commission' (29 June 2004)
European Banking Federation, 'Letter addressed to the European Commission' (18 November 2004)
European Commission, 'Communication on Securities Clearing and Settlements, Communication from the Commission to the Council and the European Parliament - Clearing and Settlement in the European Union - The Way Forward' (COM/2004/0312)
European Commission, 'EU Clearing and Settlement Legal Certainty Group Advice' (11 August 2006) [Legal Certainty Group Advice]
European Commission, 'EU Clearing and Settlement Legal Certainty Group Questionnaire Horizontal Answers' (24 April 2006) [Legal Certainty Group Comparative Survey]
European Commission, 'EU Clearing and Settlement Legal Certainty Group Summary of Action Points' (13 September 2005)
European Commission, 'Evaluation report on the Financial Collateral Arrangements Directive (2002/47/EC)' (20 December 2006) (DM(2006) 833 final
European Commission, 'Legal assessment of certain aspects of the Hague Securities Convention' (3 July 2006)
European Commission, 'Financial services: Commission sets up expert group on legal certainty issues in clearing and settlement' (IP/05/123) (1 February 2005)
European Commission, 'Financial Services: Implementing the Framework for Financial Markets: Action Plan' Com(1998-2000)232 (11 May 1998-2000)
European Commission, 'FSAP Evaluation – Part I: Process and implementation' (October 2005)
European Commission, 'Progress on the Financial Service Action Plan' (Annex to the Tenth Progress Report) (1 June 2004)
European Commission, 'Proposal for a Directive of the European Parliament and of the Council on Financial Collateral Arrangements' (27 March 2001) COM (2001) 168 final 2001/0086 (COD)
European Commission, 'Proposal for a Directive of the European Parliament and of the Council on the exercise of voting rights by shareholders of companies having their registered office in a Member State and whose shares are admitted to trading on a regulated market and amending Directive 2004/109/EC' COM (2005) 685 final 2005/0265 (COD)
European Commission, 'Securities markets: Commission calls upon Member States to sign Hague Securities Convention' (IP/06/930) (5 July 2006)
European Commission, 'Securities markets: Commission calls upon Member States to sign Hague Securities Convention' (IP/06/930) (5 July 2006)
European Commission 'Securities markets: Commission purposes wider scope for Financial Collateral Directive' (IP/07/22) (9 January 2007)
European Commission, EU Clearing and Settlement CESAME Group: 'Report on Definitions' (24 October 2005)
European Commission, FSAP Forum Group on the Cross-border Use of Collateral, 'Issues Paper for the First Meeting of the Group' (October 1998–2000)
European Commission, Tenth Report 'Financial Services: Turning the Corner – Preparing the Challenge of the Next Phase of European Capital Market Integration' (2 June 2004)
European Commission, 'Legal Certainty Group: Subject 1 – book-entry securities' (first working draft, 4 September 2007)
European Securities Forum, 'Submission on the New Basel Capital Accord' (2001)

European Securities Forum, 'Call for Action on Integration of Clearing and Settlement in Europe' (May 2003)

FMLC, 'Issue 3 – Property Interests in Investment Securities' (July 2004)

FMLC, 'Issue 58 – Hague Convention on the Law Applicable to Certain Rights in Respect of Securities Held with an Intermediary' (November 2005)

FMLC, 'Issue 62 – Trustee Exemption Clauses: Analysis of the role of the trustee in the wholesale financial markets and of the proposals contained in the Law Commission's Consultation Paper No 117 "Trustee Exemption Clauses"' (May 2004)

FSA, 'Cross-sector Risk Transfers' (May 2002)

G Tett, 'CDO case settled but not forgotten' http://www.FT.com (13 June 2005)

G30, 'Clearance and Settlement Systems in the World's Securities Markets' (1989)

G30, 'Global Clearing and Settlement – A Plan of Action' (2003)

Giovannini Group, 'Cross Border Clearing and Settlement Arrangements in the European Union' (November 2001)

Giovannini Group, 'EU Repo Markets: Opportunities for Change' No 35 (October 1998-2000) [Giovannini Repo Report]

Giovannini Group, 'Second Report on EU Cross-border Clearing and Settlement Arrangements' (April 2003)

IBA, 'Banking Law Newsletter: Implementation of EU Financial Collateral Directive' Vol 12 No 2 (September 2004)

ISDA Collateral and Financial Law Reform Group, 'Collateral Arrangements in the European Financial Markets: The Need for National Law Reform' (March 2000) [ISDA EU Collateral Report]

ISDA, '2005 ISDA Collateral Guidelines' (16 March 2005) [2005 ISDA Collateral Guidelines]

ISDA, 'Credit Risk and Regulatory Capital' (March 1998)

ISDA, 'Guidelines for Collateral Practitioners' (1998)

ISDA, 'ISDA 1998-2000 Collateral Review' (1998-2000) [ISDA 1998-2000 Collateral Review]

ISDA, 'ISDA Margin Survey 2001' (31 December 2001) [ISDA Margin Survey 2001]

ISDA, 'ISDA Margin Survey 2003' (9 April 2003) [ISDA Margin Survey 2003]

ISDA, 'ISDA Margin Survey 2004' (26 April 2004) [ISDA Margin Survey 2004]

ISDA, 'ISDA Margin Survey 2005' (4 April 2005) [ISDA Margin Survey 2005]

ISDA, 'ISDA Margin Survey 2006' (4 May 2006) [ISDA Margin Survey 2006]

ISDA, 'ISDA Margin Survey 2007' (29 December 2007) [ISDA Margin Survey 2007]

ISDA, Letter addressed to the French Ministry of Finance 'ISDA remarks on implementation debate in France of the Directive on Financial Collateral Arrangements' (3 July 2003)

Joint Forum, 'Credit Risk Transfer' (October 2004)

Law Commission, 'Project on Intermediated Investment Securities: Second Seminar – Issues Affecting Account Holders and Intermediaries' (23 June 2006)

Law Faculty Committee, Stockholm University, 'Statement on the implementation of the Financial Collateral Directive' (9 August 2003)

London Economics in association with Pricewaterhouse Coopers and Oxford Economic Forecasting, 'Quantification of the Macro-Economic Impact of Integration of EU Financial Markets: Executive Summary of the Final Report to the European Commission – Directorate-General for the Internal Market' (November 2002)

Remarks by Chairman Alan Greenspan, Federal Reserve Board, at Lancaster House, London, United Kingdom (25 September 2002)

Remarks by Governor Edward W Kelley Jr, Clearinghouses and Risk Management at the 1996 Payments System Risk Conference, Washington, DC (3 December 1996)

Remarks by Vice Chairman Roger W Ferguson Jr, The Federal Reserve Board, at the Bond Market Association's 1st Annual Credit and Risk Management Conference, New York, New York (16 October 2001)

'Report on a 'Right of Use' for Collateral-takers and Custodians', prepared for the UNIDROIT Study Group on the Preparation of Harmonised Substantive Law Rules regarding Securities Held with an Intermediary (July 2003) [UNIDROIT Report on a Right of Use]

Roy Goode, Hideki Kanda & Karl Kreuzer - with the assistance of Christophe Bernasconi (Permanent Bureau), 'Draft Explanatory Report on the Hague Convention on the Law Applicable to Certain Rights in Respect of Securities Held with an Intermediary' (25 June 2004) [Draft Explanatory Report]

Swedish Securities Dealers Association, General Conditions Governing Custodian Services, Bank (May 2003)

Swedish Securities Dealers Association, General Conditions Governing Custody & Cash Account Services, Securities Company (May 2003)

UNIDROIT, 'Transactions on Transnational and Connected Capital Markets' (June 2002)

UNIDROIT, 'G30 Plan of Action: UNIDROIT Contribution to Recommendations on Legal Certainty' (May 13, 2003) [UNIDROIT Recommendations on Legal Certainty]

UNIDROIT Position Paper, Doc 8 (August 2003) [UNIDROIT Position Paper]

UNIDROIT Summary Report (13-16 November 2003) [UNIDROIT Summary Report]

UNIDROIT Preliminary Draft Convention, Doc 13 (April 2004)

UNIDROIT Preliminary Draft Convention, Doc 18 (November 2004)

UNIDROIT Explanatory Notes to the Preliminary Draft Convention, Doc 19 (December 2004) [UNIDROIT Explanatory Notes]

UNIDROIT Preliminary Draft Convention, Doc 24 (May/June 2005) [Preliminary Draft Convention]

UNIDROIT Final Report, Doc 23 (August 2005)

UNIDROIT, 'Seminar on Intermediated Securities – Bern, Switzerland', Sem 1 (15-17 September 2005)

UNIDROIT Preliminary Draft Convention on Substantive Rules regarding Intermediated Securities (as adopted by the Committee of Experts at its second session, held in Rome) Doc 42 (06-04 March 2006) [UNIDROIT Preliminary Draft Convention, Doc 42]

UNIDROIT, Preliminary Draft Convention on Substantive Rules regarding Intermediated Securities (as adopted by the Committee of Governmental Experts at its third session, held in Rome, 06-15 November 2006) Doc 57 (November 2006) [UNIDROIT Preliminary Draft Convention, Doc 57]

UNIDROIT, Draft Convention on Substantive Rules regarding Intermediated Securities (Diplomatic Conference to Adopt a Convention on Substantive Rules regarding Intermediated Securities, Geneva, 1 to 13 September 2008) Conf 11 – Doc 3 (February 2008) [UNIDROIT Draft Convention, Conf 11 – Doc 3]

VPC Rules 'Account Keeping and Clearing' (14 February 2005)

VPC, 'Disclosure Framework' (December 2004)

Index

FSC
www.fsc.org
MIX
Papier | Fördert
gute Waldnutzung
FSC® C083411

Kolibri 360 GmbH
Ferdinand-Jühlke-Straße 7
99095 Erfurt, Deutschland
produktsicherheit@kolibri360.de